13424528

WITHDRAWN
NDSU

Chinese
Intellectuals
in Crisis

Chinese Intellectuals in Crisis

*Search for Order
and Meaning (1890–1911)*

HAO CHANG

University of California Press
Berkeley, Los Angeles, London

University of California Press
Berkeley and Los Angeles, California

University of California Press, Ltd.
London, England

© 1987 by The Regents of the University of California

Library of Congress Cataloging-in-Publication Data

Chang, Hao, 1937–
CHINESE INTELLECTUALS IN CRISIS.

Bibliography: p.
Includes index.
 1. China—Intellectual life—1644–1912. 2. K'ang, Yu-wei, 1858–1927. 3. T'an, Ssu-t'ung, 1865–1898. 4. Chang, T'ai-yen, 1868–1936. 5. Liu, Shih-p'ei, 1884–1919. I. Title.
DS754.14.C48 1987 951'.03'0922 86-7031
ISBN 0-520-05378-8 (alk. paper)

Printed in the United States of America
1 2 3 4 5 6 7 8 9

To My Father

Contents

Acknowledgments *ix*

1. Introduction *1*
2. K'ang Yu-wei (1858–1927) *21*
3. T'an Ssu-t'ung (1864–1898) *66*
4. Chang Ping-lin (1869–1935) *104*
5. Liu Shih-p'ei (1884–1919) *146*
6. Conclusion *181*

Appendix: An Elegy by T'an Ssu-t'ung *193*

Glossary *197*

Bibliography *207*

Index *217*

Acknowledgments

ABOUT fifteen years ago, I did some work on the intellectual changes of the "transitional generation" in China that spanned from 1895 through 1911. This book revisits that generation, bringing perspectives and viewpoints that led me to discover some intellectual aspects of that generation that I did not see before. Hence, this book is at once an extension of, and a counterpoint to, my previous studies.

In the process of writing this book, I have incurred many intellectual debts. Among my colleagues at Ohio State University, I owe special thanks to David Y. Ch'en, June and Paul Fullmer, and Yan-hsuan Lao for assistance in translating some of the Chinese poems in this book. Yan-hsuan Lao's Sinological erudition has helped me in many invaluable ways. To Chu Pao-liang, Clara R. Goldslayer, George Potter, and T'ang Chih-chün, I want to express my heartfelt gratitude for their assistance in making available many of the research materials I needed. T'ang Chih-chün was particularly generous in providing me with the personal notes he took of an important piece of K'ang Yu-wei's early writings, recently discovered in mainland China, but not yet published.

Many friends and teachers have influenced me at various stages of writing this book. Among them, I should particularly mention Robert E. Bellah, Whalen Lai, Lin Yü-sheng, K. C. Liu, Liu Shu-hsien, Thomas Metzger, Don C. Price, Benjamin Schwartz, Tu Wei-ming, and Yü Ying-shih. Two names deserve special acknowledgments. Thomas Metzger, through the intellectual challenges and stimulations he has provided me for over a quarter of a century, has contributed greatly to my formulation of the issues and ideas on which this book is built. K. C. Liu, through his personal example of intellectual dedication, his high scholarly standards, and the generous advice he has given me over the years, has been an unfailing source of inspiration and support. My indebtedness to both is immeasurable.

To the National Endowment of Humanities, which granted me a senior fellowship to initiate this study, and to the Department of History, the East Asian Studies Center, and the office of Humanities College at Ohio State University, I express my gratitude for their financial and material assistance, so essential to the completion of this volume. Furthermore, this book could not have been finished without the technical assistance of Eugene Chiu, Alice Meng, Sally Serafim, Sarah Simpson, and the secretarial staff of the Department of History at Ohio State University. To them, I want to express deep appreciation. Finally, I can not complete my acknowledgments without mentioning the indispensable help in innumerable ways of my wife, Jung-Jung, in making this publication possible.

1

Introduction

THIS IS a study of four leading figures of the early Chinese intelligentsia: K'ang Yu-wei, T'an Ssu-t'ung, Chang Ping-lin, and Liu Shih-p'ei. This is not a collection of their intellectual biographies; my focus is on the development of their thought in the period from the early 1890s to 1911 as an avenue to exploring intellectual changes in the "transitional era" (1890–1911). I have chosen these four men partly because they all, in different ways, played major intellectual roles in this era. But, more importantly, their world views reflect a crucial intellectual dimension of the period that has been little studied heretofore. Analyzing these four world views in juxtaposition, I believe, enables us to see their thought and the era in a new light. Such an analysis, however, requires us to depart from certain themes and approaches predominant in the existing literature. A discussion of these at the outset will help put my study in perspective.

One persistent theme is the dichotomy of reformism versus revolutionism.[1] The Chinese intelligentsia emerged as a visible group of new social types toward the end of the nineteenth century. Almost as soon as the group appeared, it bifurcated into reformists and revolutionists over the issue of how to deal with China's political crisis. The growing division between reformists and revolutionists and the heated intellectual debates and controversies it occasioned have long held the attention of historians.

Important as this theme is, however, a preoccupation with it has overshadowed other aspects of the era's thought that have little bearing on the issue of reform or revolution but are nonetheless integral to the period's

---

1. The theme of revolution versus reformism has a central place, e.g., in works by the following authors dealing with this period: Chang P'eng-yuan (1964); Ch'i Ping-feng (1964); Rankin (1971); and Gasster (1969).

intellectual transformation. Furthermore, an examination of these aspects reveals both commonalities and divergences of mind among members of the Chinese intelligentsia that crosscut the dichotomy of reformism versus revolutionism.

My book illustrates this point clearly. Two of the protagonists, K'ang Yu-wei and T'an Ssu-t'ung, are chosen from the reformists; the other two, Chang Ping-lin and Liu Shih-p'ei, from the revolutionists. However, certain important aspects of the thought of K'ang and T'an can be as little understood with reference to reformism as those of the thought of Chang and Liu can be with reference to revolutionism. The two sides have almost as much in common intellectually as they have differences. This is why I use reformism and revolutionism in this book largely as convenient labels to identify the two principal groups among the early Chinese intelligentsia rather than as interpretive categories to probe their thought.

Another much-discussed theme is nationalism. This is quite understandable because, during the transitional era, nationalism for the first time spread beyond the minds of a few intellectuals to become a public ideology on the Chinese scene. No sooner had nationalism emerged as such than two conceptions of it began to appear. One was "reactive nationalism" or "state nationalism," which arose largely as a reaction against imperialist aggression in China. The other was what may be called "ethnic nationalism," which was fed by resentment against the domination of China by the Manchu ethnic minority.

Both conceptions of nationalism, useful as they are in probing the concerns and motives of many Chinese intellectuals in the modern era, have their limitations as explanatory categories. Don Price observes that the thought of the transitional generation carries some "universalistic" orientations and perspectives that cannot be explained by nationalism in either sense.[2] To the extent that these orientations existed, we may speak of a polarity between nationalism and "universalism" with regard to the transitional generation. The thought of the four figures studied in this book reveals an intellectual dimension to this era that clearly gravitates toward the pole of "universalism" and hence brings into question the adequacy of nationalism as a theme of interpretation.

As an explanatory device, modernization is no less prominent a concept than nationalism. Hsiao Kung-chuan, for example, calls K'ang Yu-wei a modernizer.[3] Thomas Metzger, too, tends to view such Chinese intellectuals as K'ang Yu-wei and T'an Ssu-t'ung in similar terms.[4] Are they justified in using the concept of modernization to characterize the thought of K'ang and

---

2. 1974: 9–28.
3. 1975. In the chapter, "Political Reform," (pp. 193–261), "modernization" and "political modernization" are also used to characterize K'ang's political writings.
4. 1977: 212, 219.

kindred spirits? It all depends on how we understand the concept. Many people use it so broadly and loosely that it ceases to have any specific meaning and thus becomes useless as an explanatory category. Those who use it meaningfully usually follow one of two usages. One usage identifies modernization largely with economic development and its concomitant phenomena. The other, under the influence of the Weberian conception of rationalization, defines modernization as the drive to achieve control over human environments by rationalizing human personality, technology, and institutions.[5] As many scholars recognize today, rationalization here refers primarily to the rationalization of means rather than ends. Consequently, whatever the difference between the two usages, they both share the view that modernization is a nonmoral process. In other words, current usage considers modernization an objective, impersonal, societal process. Whether moral motives fuel the process or whether moral goals emerge at the end of the process is immaterial to the characteristics of the process. If these usages represent the standard definition of modernization, then neither K'ang Yu-wei nor any of the other three can be characterized as modernizers, precisely because a moral-spiritual concept of man and society lies at the heart of their thought.

Any discussion of modern Chinese thought unavoidably encounters the issue of continuity versus discontinuity. Until recently, scholarly views on this issue were dominated by the theme of discontinuity. Perhaps the epitome of this view is Joseph Levenson's *Confucian China and Its Modern Fate*.[6] Based on a subtle analysis of cultural identity, Levenson paints a picture of intellectual changes in modern China in which there is little continuity with tradition aside from emotional attachments. But, in the past decade, the pendulum has swung in the other direction. Perhaps the most striking expression of the current emphasis on continuity is found in Thomas Metzger's *Escape from Predicament*. According to Metzger, modern Chinese intellectuals by and large inherited the basic moral goals and aspirations of the Confucian tradition; what they accepted from "Western learning" was nothing more than new technologies and institutions to implement these goals and aspirations.[7] Paradoxically, the writings of our four subjects offer support for both these themes. All four were deeply rooted in the Chinese tradition; at the same time, all of them broke with tradition. This combination of continuity and discontinuity emphasizes the need for a reevaluation of the complex roles of tradition and Western learning as forces shaping modern Chinese consciousness.

Thus, all of the commonly used themes are inadequate for understanding the characteristics of our four subjects. The themes of nationalism and

---

5. For a perceptive discussion of the concept of modernization, see Schwartz (1972).
6. 1958: xiii–xix.
7. 1977: 191–235.

modernization cannot do justice to the universalism and moral-spiritual coloration of their thought. Nor can the thought of the four be neatly pigeonholed by either the dichotomy of reformism versus revolutionism or of continuity versus discontinuity. How, then, are we to make sense of their thought? I propose to start by taking a fresh look at the intellectual milieu in which they grew up.

By "intellectual milieu," I am referring partly to the ideas and values circulating in a particular environment, that is, to the so-called climate of thought to which people living in a particular environment are exposed through formal or informal channels of education. In and by themselves, ideas and values can translate into people's motives, goals, and concerns, especially when they are instilled in people's minds during their formative years. But, more often than not, they take on significance in the context of the situations that people face. By "situation," I mean not a person's objective environment, but rather the surrounding life-world as he perceives it. Because human consciousness is usually structured and hence selective or directed in various ways and in different degrees of intensity, "situation" can be understood as focal points in a person's perception of the life-world that surrounds him. Understood in this sense, then, it is what provides felt relevance to an individual's circulating ideas and values and thereby translates them into influences over his or her mind.

Consequently, to place these four intellectuals in their milieu means not only examining the *influences* that stem from the intellectual climate to which they were exposed, but also discerning the *situations* to which they felt they were responding. But we must not conceive these two factors in terms of a simple, neat dichotomy. There are certain circular or "dialectical" relationships between the two factors that must be kept in mind, because it is usually by dint of the ideas and values from these influences that the intellectuals are able to perceive and define the situations in the way they do. Meanwhile, it is also through the medium of situations that influences from the intellectual climate register in their minds. With this proviso in mind, I will look more closely at influences and situations, the two factors that combine to constitute the intellectual milieu for my four subjects.

To see what these intellectuals were responding to, one must distinguish at least two kinds of situations. First is the historical situation during the transitional era. Apart from the historical situation, some Chinese intellectuals were also responding to what might be called "existential" situations—typical situations of human life everywhere, such as death, suffering, and love. Whereas the existential situations Chinese intellectuals faced can be understood only in the context of their different life courses, the historical situations they encountered feature some common characteristics that can be delineated.

As China moved into the last quarter of the nineteenth century, a new intellectual mood began to set in. The hope that the T'ung-chih Restoration would regenerate China was fast dissipating. The optimism that was kindled for a while during the 1860s and 1870s was quickly giving way to mounting self-doubt and self-reappraisal. Consequently, people began to raise questions about the traditional institutional order. To be sure, doubts about aspects of the institutional order had arisen prior to this time.[8] But the difference was that now skepticism was gradually penetrating from the periphery of the institutional order toward its center. This skepticism cast doubt not only on the functional effectiveness of the institutional order, but also on its moral legitimacy. This self-doubt and self-reappraisal at first appeared in isolated cases, but, by the end of the nineteenth century, it was widely discernible among the Chinese educated elite.

The penetration of self-doubt from the periphery toward the center of the traditional political order was demonstrated clearly in the unfolding of reformism in the latter half of the nineteenth century. The critical views of such early reform-minded scholar-officials as Feng Kuei-fen and Hsüeh Fu-ch'eng in the 1860s and 1870s were confined to the periphery of the traditional institutional order.[9] However, when increasing attention was drawn to the Western idea of parliament in the 1880s and 1890s, self-criticism started to undermine the center of the order.[10] True, before 1895 these criticisms rarely attacked the institution of monarchy or the reigning dynasty, but they did reflect a serious erosion and even a gradual dissolution of the legitimacy of cosmological kingship, the institution that stood at the core of the traditional political structure.

To understand the disintegration of this institution in the late nineteenth century, we must recall the mystique that surrounded the title "Son of Heaven." Although it is somewhat difficult for a modern secular mind to construe its significance, this mystique nonetheless was an essential aspect of Chinese emperorship. In the eyes of Chinese people, the Son of Heaven was not just a ruler of an empire; he was preeminently the agent of Heaven on earth to maintain the cosmic harmony. Through the proper performance of his ritual and nonritual duties, he mediated between the human social order and the sacred cosmic order. Thus, the Son of Heaven was seen by his people as a sort of cosmological linchpin functioning at the center of the world and radiating a universal authority on earth.[11]

During the late nineteenth century, this mystique gradually crumbled and vanished. Several developments contributed to its dissolution. First of

---

8. E.g., Feng Kuei-fen and Hsüeh Fu-ch'eng already saw the need for some institutional adjustments. See *Chung-kuo chin-tai ssu-hsiang-shih lun-wen chi* (1958: 30–33, 56–64).
9. Ibid.
10. Chang Hao (1980: 279–81); Eastman (1968: 695–710).
11. For the cosmological symbolism involved in the Chinese concept of kingship, see Wheatley (1971: 52–63; 112–16; 411–51) and Lei Hai-tsung (1968: 97–122).

all, during the closing decades of the century there was a new awareness of an outside world as geographical writings, such as those by Wei Yüan and Hsü Chi-yü finally sank in. This awareness was deepened and exacerbated by the repeated defeats China suffered at the hands of the outside world.

Equally important were other aspects of Western culture that were seeping in. As Sung Yü-jen, a scholar-official from Szechwan, observed in the 1890s, both Western sciences and Western religion brought in ideas and views at odds with traditional values and world views. The Copernican universe of Western science was bound to collide with the traditional Chinese world view, which explained the cosmos in terms of such cosmological symbolism as the ideas of *yin-yang*, the five elements, and heaven and earth. This conflict, Sung emphasized, would inevitably undermine the whole traditional hierarchical order, inasmuch as the latter was bound up with cosmological symbolism. In addition, the ethical universalism of Christianity as embodied in the ideal of Jesus Christ also ran counter to the ethical particularism of the Chinese order.[12]

As a corollary of these developments, the erosion of the idea of cosmological kingship had advanced to the point that, among many reformist champions of the idea of parliament, the mystique of the institution was no longer a prominent element in their ideas of the Manchu throne. In Cheng Kuanying's thought, for instance, cosmological symbolism still had a place, but the mystique of cosmological kingship was hardly present.[13] Other reformist scholar-officials such as Ch'en Chih and Ch'en Ch'iu also moved away from the cosmological mystique and began to justify monarchy in terms of secular images, such as national solidarity between the ruling and the ruled.[14] Perhaps the most telling example was Chang Chih-tung, who, in defending the Ch'ing dynastic order against radical reformism in his famous *Ch'üan-hsüeh p'ien*, chose to justify it by appealing to such traditional sentiments as repaying the good offices of a conscientious ruler, without invoking the traditional mystique of the cosmological kingship.[15]

To the extent that cosmological kingship was losing its ideological hold on the minds of Chinese intellectuals, a new crisis of consciousness dawned among them—a crisis of order. This crisis was nowhere more clearly reflected than in the fact that the idea *ch'ün* was becoming a focus of debates among the Chinese intellectuals in the 1890s. This debate over *ch'ün* bespoke a growing need on the part of Chinese intellectuals to do something they probably had not done since the Axial Age of the late Chou, namely, to reexamine the institutional foundation of the Chinese sociopolitical order.[16]

12. Sung Yü-jen (1897: pt. 3, pp. 8b–9b; pt. 4, pp. 27b–28a).
13. 1896, chüan 1: 34a–b, 36a–b.
14. Ch'en Chih (1970, 7: 1a–b).
15. 1973, Nei-p'ien [Inner chapters], pp. 5a–12a.
16. Chang Hao (1971: 95–112).

For many Chinese intellectuals, however, the crisis of order was not just a political crisis; it had a deeper, more significant intellectual dimension. We have seen that the institution of cosmological kingship was based on a complex of cosmological symbolisms, which not only functioned to define the political order, but also constituted a part of what can be called "orientational symbolisms." Orientational symbolisms defined life and world in the broadest terms and in the widest contexts. Therefore, the dissolution of the cosmological kingship was bound to have deep, intellectual ramifications and repercussions that went beyond the political order.

The Chinese tradition, like other high traditions, constitutes a universe of meaning for the people who live within it. The function of orientational symbolisms is to maintain coherence and order in the universe of meaning. They perform their function by allowing the Chinese to develop frameworks and perspectives in which self, society, and cosmos may be seen in an overall meaningful order. More specifically, the Chinese depend on these symbolisms to forge world views that serve as a sort of cognitive map of the cosmos. With such a map, they are able not only to structure the cosmos in terms of space and time and to place themselves within it, but also to situate life with an awareness of whence it comes and whither it is headed. Further, these symbolisms serve as the ground of meaning for their social world, because it is within the framework of these symbolisms that social relations are patterned and social values and norms take on more than arbitrary, man-made meanings. In these various ways, orientational symbolisms provide the Chinese mind with a "general order of existence."

We need not assume that these orientational symbolisms were always explicitly conceived and systematically formulated in the mind of every Chinese intellectual. In fact, they are more taken for granted in the background of the mind than clearly spelled out in the foreground of consciousness. Yet whatever the degree of explicitness and deliberateness with which they are conceived, these symbolisms do supply some sort of symbolic order that shields the Chinese mind from cognitive dissonance and value disorientations.

Thus, when the mystique of cosmological kingship was being dissolved and the underlying orientational symbolism was being called into question, the Chinese universe of meaning as a whole was bound to feel the disrupting impact. As new concepts of the cosmos and novel images of the world rushed in, dissonance and incongruity were inevitably felt in the minds of intellectuals. How should they relate these new concepts and images to their long-held world views? How could they reconcile and harmonize them? In short, how could they overcome their mental dissonances and incongruities and restore an overall meaningful order to their perception of life and the world? Toward the end of the nineteenth century, then, Chinese intellectuals had to readjust not only their concept of the sociopolitical order, but also their concept of the order of existence. In other words, what Chinese intellectuals faced was not just a crisis of political order, but a far deeper crisis—a crisis of orientational order. In fact, to many of them the former crisis was a part of the latter.

It was to this crisis of orientational order that Chinese intellectuals, such as the four studied in this book, were partly responding. To be sure, this crisis was not felt to the same degree by all people. Different people had differing sensitivities to it. Some felt it acutely, others only dimly and vaguely. But some Chinese intellectuals certainly felt the need to respond to the crisis by recreating a meaningful cosmos through a comprehensive world view. As Max Weber observes so well in another connection, "the intellectual seeks, in various ways, the casuistry of which extends into infinity, to endow his life with a pervasive meaning and thus to find unity with himself, with his fellow men and with the cosmos. It is the intellectual who transforms the concept of the world into the problem of meaning."[17]

Finally, I must emphasize again that, although the crisis of orientational order was what some Chinese intellectuals found primarily in the historical situation, it was not the only situation they perceived and responded to. They also responded to other situations, especially the existential situations that I mentioned above. In fact, it is part of my main thesis to argue that, to understand the minds of these four subjects, we need at least to see them as speaking both to the historical and the existential situations.

To understand the world views of the four, we need to know not only what kind of situations they faced, but also what sorts of intellectual influences set constraints on and provided "symbolic resources" for their responses to the situations. *Influence*, of course, is vague and difficult to pin down; by this concept I am merely trying to determine the range and configuration of ideas, values, and beliefs that were floating around in the specific backgrounds and environments in which intellectuals such as the four treated here grew up. What were these influences?

One obvious influence came from Western learning. For intellectuals of the transitional generation, the Western influence had a significance that it lacked for those of previous generations. As I note elsewhere, it was during this generation that Western learning began to spread beyond the treaty ports and penetrate into many inland cities on a significant scale.[18] Moreover, it was also during this generation that many Chinese intellectuals went abroad, mostly to Japan. Three of the four figures studied here, for example, had the experience of studying or traveling abroad. Consequently, the exposure of the transitional generation to Western influence was unprecedented both in its breadth and in its depth.

---

17. 1963: 125.
18. 1980: 276–77.

Important as the Western influence was, it is worth remembering that members of this generation generally came under Western influence after they became adults. This does not necesssarily belittle the role of Western influence, as postadolescent learning can still shape minds in important ways; it does mean, however, that Western influences were superimposed on minds already steeped in traditional culture during the formative years of childhood and adolescence.

Even as adults, many intellectuals were still susceptible to the subtle, but nonetheless important, appeal of Chinese tradition. Part of its appeal may have stemmed from what Joseph Levenson calls "cultural identity." True, Levenson's argument in this connection is that Chinese intellectuals turned to tradition not so much out of confidence in its intellectual validity as from an emotional need to get even with the West to assuage the wounds to their cultural pride that they suffered in their encounters with the West.[19] But, to really appreciate the factor of cultural identity as a motivating force drawing people to tradition, one must remember the complex, dialectical relationship between the motives of these early Chinese intelligentsia who studied traditional thought on the one hand and the contents of the thought on the other. A person may have initially become interested in certain traditional texts or strains of thought out of an extraneous motive, such as cultural identity. However, once the person entered into the intellectual world of traditional texts, the ideas and language of these texts may have acted as an autonomous intellectual force that reshaped the motives and interests that initially drew his mind toward them.

One example from late Ch'ing developments helps to illustrate my point. A major indigenous development in this period was the revival of interest in classical Mohism. In certain intellectual circles, the parallel between parts of the *Mo Tzu* and Western logic and physical sciences aroused great interest and even made studying the ancient text a sort of fad.[20] Once the text was being seriously read, however, it is possible that other Mohist ideas, such as universal love and the spirit of the knight-errant, for example, may have appealed to the reader and worked changes on his thinking. As this example shows, the motive behind one's interest in any type of traditional ideas can change over the course of time. The motive that initially arouses one's interest is not necessarily the same motive that sustains it. At least the possibility exists that, just as one's initial interest and motives can condition one's understanding of traditional ideas and beliefs, the latter can also react to alter and reshape the former.

Apart from cultural identity, there was another channel through which

---

19. 1958: xiii–xix.
20. Liang Ch'i-ch'ao, "Mo-ching t'ung-chieh hsü" [Preface to a general interpretation of the classic *Mo-tzu*] (1936, *chuan-chi*, chüan 39: 84–85); also see "Mo-ching chiao-shih, tzu-hsü" [A preface to textual commentaries on two chapters in *Mo-tzu*] (ibid., chüan 38: 1–2).

tradition continued to impinge on the minds of Chinese intellectuals. This is what may be called "internal dialogues." By "internal dialogues," I refer to intellectual discussions of a special nature that went on in the Chinese tradition over the centuries. Like other high traditions, Chinese tradition evolved and accumulated a stock of issues and ideas that have held the enduring interest of every generation of intellectuals. Some of these issues and ideas, such as human nature and the relationship between morality and politics, for example, could be said to be universal, in the sense that in different forms and guises they have been raised and debated in many other cultures, both traditional and modern. Consequently, internal dialogues in some ways have continued among Chinese intellectuals well into the modern era. Certainly this was true of the transitional generation, as the writings of many scholars of that era attest.

In the transitional generation as in the past, such internal dialogues were carried on not only among contemporary intellectuals, but also across the centuries, so to speak. Tradition was perceived not as a dead heritage from the past, but as a community of minds sharing across time the same issues and concerns. By identifying with these issues and concerns, intellectuals could enter into the tradition, listen to minds from the past speaking to them, and speak back to tradition with their own writings. However these internal dialogues were carried on, they must be recognized as important channels through which tradition made its influence felt in the minds of people, such as the four studied here.

In order to understand the influences on the four, I must delineate the indigenous intellectual setting within which their minds first began to take shape and mature. The setting was dominated by three major trends of thought.

One important evolution in the Chinese tradition in the late nineteenth century was the renaissance of interest in the classical noncanonical philosophies, the so-called *chu-tzu hsüeh*.[21] Much of this renaissance was rooted in the internal logic of the development of Han Learning. The principal impetus to Han Learning derived from the dissatisfaction of scholars in the seventeenth and eighteenth centuries with the Sung-Ming neo-Confucian interpretations of Confucian canons and from their attempts to go beyond the neo-Confucian commentaries to recapture the original teachings of Confucius through sources closer in time to the sage. Thus, as Yü Ying-shih observes, there was an inherent impulse in Han Learning to "return to the original text" (*hui-hsiang yüan-tien*) of Confucianism.[22] Out of this impulse grew a revival of the exegetical scholarships of the Ancient Text and the New Text schools of the Han dynasties. Out of this impulse also grew the initial

---

21. Liang Ch'i-ch'ao (1956: 244–47).
22. Yü Ying-shih (1984: 79).

appeal of the classical noncanonical philosophies. For, as one leading scholar of Han Learning in the late Ch'ing remarked, if the exegetical commentaries of the Former Han were already so precious to understanding the Confucian canons, how much better those noncanonical philosophical texts would be that preceded the Former Han.[23] This is why masters of Han Learning, such as Wang Nien-sun and Wang Yin-chih of the eighteenth century, had already delved deeply into the texts of the classical noncanonical philosophies as part of their "evidential research."[24]

To be sure, the bulk of these studies were philological and textual in nature, but the dividing line between these technical studies and those of a philosophical and ideological nature was sometimes rather thin. Even at the height of the development of Han Learning, the philosophical and ideological interest in the classical noncanonical texts was not lacking. This was especially true in the case of Hsün Tzu's thought. Ch'ien Mu and other scholars have called our attention to an undercurrent of interest in Hsün Tzu's philosophical ideas that dated back to the Han Learning of the mid-eighteenth century.[25] This philosophical interest came to the surface of Han Learning in the thought of two important scholars of the late eighteenth and early nineteenth centuries, Wang Chung and Lin T'ing-k'an.[26] Mohism too found a vigorous philosophical advocate in Wang Chung.[27]

What represented the interest of a few in the mid-Ch'ing became the interest of many in the late Ch'ing. In the course of the nineteenth century, the philosophical and textual-philological appeal of the classical noncanonical texts grew. Although in the past Confucian scholars usually emphasized the ideological incompatibility between such texts and Confucianism, scholars now argued for the philosophical affinities between the two. Some maintained that Confucianism contains a synthesis of the noncanonical philosophies. Others held that Confucianism is the original source of Chinese thought from which the noncanonical philosophies branched off.[28] In these ways and others, the *chu-tzu hsüeh* became legitimate and even intellectually faddish in the late nineteenth century. A barometer of the changing intellectual climate is the fact that major scholars of the time, such as Yü Yüeh and Sun I-jang, not only wrote textual commentaries on both Confucian and noncanonical texts; they sometimes also championed the

---

23. See quote in Wang Fan-shen (1985: 26–27). For a perceptive discussion of the study of the development of noncanonical classical philosophies in the School of Han Learning, also see Yü Ying-shih (1984: 77–87).
24. Liang Ch'i-ch'ao (1956: 28); Wang Fan-shen (1985: 27).
25. Liang Ch'i-ch'ao (1956: 228–30); Ch'ien Mu (1964: 357–58, 362–64). Also see Yü Ying-shih (1984: 77–87).
26. See Ch'ien Mu (1964: 491–93); Chang Shun-hui (1962: 90–91); and Yü Ying-shih (1984: 77–87).
27. Chang Shun-hui (1962: 90–91).
28. Wang Fan-shen (1985: 27–28).

heretical ideas of the noncanonical philosophies. Yü Yüeh, for example, beyond doing evidential studies of *Hsün Tzu*, also took a philosophical position that favored Hsün Tzu's negative view of human nature over Mencius' orthodox, optimistic view.[29]

More significantly, as the philosophical interest in the noncanonical ancient texts spread, interest in them tended to become more practical than theoretical, inasmuch as some intellectuals turned to these texts not so much out of intellectual curiosity as out of concern with problems of life and society. In this way, classical texts, such as *Hsün Tzu*, *Mo Tzu*, and those of Legalism, became intellectual resources for the growing moral and political activism of the closing decades of the nineteenth century. However, it must be noted that this interest in the non-Confucian classical philosophies did not lead to the reemergence of any of the classical philosophies as a separate, identifiable school of thought. In most cases, the interest in the *chu-tzu hsüeh* was part of an eclecticism that also drew on ideas from other sources. In whatever form, the *chu-tzu hsüeh* became an important element of the intellectual climate of the time.[30]

Apart from the renaissance of the *chu-tzu hsüeh*, the late nineteenth century also witnessed a revival of Mahayana Buddhism, which took place not so much among Buddhist monks as among lay intellectuals.[31] Among the latter, no one contributed more to this resurgence than Yang Wen-hui (1837–1911).[32] A brief look at Yang's intellectual career helps us to understand the nature of the Mahayana revival. Yang, a scholar from Anhui Province, became converted to Buddhism during his youth. To earn a living, Yang had to enter government service, but this did not prevent him from dedicating himself to studying and spreading Buddhism.[33] For this purpose, he set up schools to train students and also engaged in a sustained, extensive search for Buddhist texts, systematically editing and collating them for publication. This search led him to make contacts abroad, and in these efforts he was aided by his service in the government. Twice during his official career he was sent abroad to work on the staff of the Chinese embassies in Paris and London. These assignments gave him a chance to become acquainted with Buddhist and Sanskrit studies in Europe. More important, while in Europe he also established contacts with visiting Japanese Buddhist scholars. Through these contacts, which he kept up after he returned to China, he was able to find in Japan copies of many Buddhist texts that had been lost in his native country and to bring them to China for

---

29. Chiang Wei-ch'iao (1972: 71–75).
30. Liang Ch'i-ch'ao (1956: 247).
31. Ch'u P'o-shih (1973: 130–33); Liang Ch'i-ch'ao (1963: 73–74).
32. 1919, ts'e 1: 1a-7a. According to a leading Buddhist monk, Tai-hsü, Yang was the motivating force in reviving Buddhism among the lay Buddhists in modern China. See Ch'u P'o-shih (1973: 131–32).
33. Yang Wen-hui (1919, ts'e 1: 1a–4b).

publication.³⁴ In trying to promote Buddhism in these various ways, Yang established himself as the leading Buddhist scholar of his time.

Yang's study of Buddhism was highly eclectic, in the sense that he showed an interest in almost all the major Mahayana teachings.³⁵ Yet, within his broad, eclectic outlook a number of tendencies stood out. In the first place, his Buddhist studies reflected a "practical," soteriological orientation more than a theoretical, intellectual interest. Indeed, his writings on Buddhism as well as his sustained, fervent efforts to collect and publish Buddhist texts were driven throughout by a heightened sense of mission. As he saw it, the world was sinking into an age of spiritual decay, *mo-shih* (the last Buddha-Kalpa), due to the eclipse of Buddhist teachings. Therefore, he set himself the task of reviving the Buddhist Truth to lift the world out of decay.³⁶

This same practical, soteriological orientation can also be seen in his approach to studying Buddhist teachings. One should always start with faith (*hsin*), he said, and further develop it through understanding (*chieh*), which then must be followed by putting faith into practice (*hsing*). Finally, through practice one achieves an experiential confirmation (*cheng*) of the truth of the Buddhist teachings.³⁷ Such an approach clearly bespeaks Yang's embrace of the soteriological and existential intent of Buddhism.

The practical emphasis of Yang's study of Buddhism also explains his clear preference for the Pure Land teachings over those of Zen. In his view, it took a mind gifted with heightened spiritual sensitivities to understand the subtle Zen teachings. Hence, as a vehicle of transmitting the soteriological truth of Mahayana Buddhism, Zen teachings were not as effective as the devotionalism of the Pure Land sect, particularly for beginners.³⁸ There was thus an echo in Yang's thought of a historical tendency apparent in the Buddhist community since Sung: a tendency to synthesize Zen teachings with those of Pure Land.³⁹

In fact, this echo might imply certain direct influences from that tendency. In his writings, Yang often expresses admiration for such precursors of the synthesizing tendency as Yün-ch'i Chu-hung, Han-shan Teh-ch'ing of the late Ming, and P'eng Shao-sheng and Wang Chin of the mid-Ch'ing.⁴⁰ But what made Yang's eclecticism different from the traditional tendency

---

34. Ibid: 4a–5a; ts'e 7, chüan 2 (*Fo-hsüeh shu-mu piao* [A bibliography of Buddhist studies]): 2a–22b; ts'e 10, chüan 7: 1a–25b; chüan 8: 3a–27b; ts'e 8, chüan 3: 4a–b, 9a–b, 14b–19b.
35. Ibid., ts'e 7, chüan 1: 19a–21b; chüan 2: 1a–22b; ts'e 9, chüan 6: 28a.
36. Ibid., ts'e 1: 2b.
37. Ibid., ts'e 4 (*Fo-chiao ch'u-hsüeh k'o-pen* [A primer for the study of Buddhism]): 56a.
38. Ibid., ts'e 4: 23a–30b; 34a–42b ("Shih-tsung lüeh-shuo" [A sketchy discussion of the ten schools of Buddhism]): 5a–5b, 6b–8a; ts'e 8, chüan 3: 22a–23a; ts'e 9, chüan 5: 24a, 27a, 33a–b; chüan 6: 29a–b.
39. Ibid. (*Fo-chiao ch'u-hsüeh k'o-pen*): 30b.
40. Ibid., ts'e 8, chüan 3: 20b, 21a–22a, 24a, 26b–27b; ts'e 9, chüan 6: 10a, 28a.

toward Zen–Pure Land synthesis was his belief that, with Pure Land Buddhism as the foundation, not only Zen teachings but also those of other Mahayana sects would have value as avenues to approach the Buddhist wisdom.[41]

Thus, Yang's preference for Pure Land Buddhism did not inhibit but only served as what he considered a necessary supplement to his appreciation of the teachings of certain other Mahayana sects. Among the latter, however, he did sometimes betray a leaning toward the Yogacara teachings more than toward the rest of them. We can see this from the high priority he always accorded such Yogacara-related texts as *Mahayana-sraddhotpadasastra sutra* and the *Lankavatara sutra* when he advised people on the methods of studying Buddhism.[42] Meanwhile, Yang, through his contacts in Japan, was able to find and bring home some important Yogacara texts long lost in China. Both his personal leaning and his recovery of the lost Yogacara sutras help to explain the pronounced tendency of his disciples to favor Yogacara teachings over other Mahayana teachings. Indeed, Yang has often been credited, although not without some exaggeration, with being the leading motive force for the vogue of Dharma laksana teachings among many lay Buddhist intellectuals in the twentieth century.

Another tendency that marked Yang's study of Buddhism was his effort to synthesize Buddhism either with Taoism or with Confucianism.[43] Coming as it did in the late nineteenth century, especially after 1895, this syncretism should cause no surprise. Confronted with the influx of Western thought, many Chinese intellectuals searched in their own tradition for a response to the West; often, the response they forged turned out to be syncretic in character, involving elements of thought from various indigenous sources. However, the strain of syncretism in Yang's thought seemed to have little to do with the stimulus of the West. Rather, it is strongly reminiscent of the kind of syncretism that had a prominent place in the Chinese intellectual tradition—the "unity of the three teachings" (*san-chiao ho-i*).[44] This syncretism had taken different forms in the past. Some put emphasis on Confucianism or Taoism as the basis for understanding the unity of the three teachings. Others, however, forged the syncretism on the basis of Buddhism; we see this emphasis clearly in the thought of the eighteenth-century scholar P'eng

---

41. Ibid. ("Shih-tsung lüeh-shuo"): 7a–8a.
42. Ibid.: 4a–b; ts'e 9, chüan 6: 5a, 6b–7a, 10b–11a, 11a–12b; ts'e 8, chüan 3: 16b–17a; *Fo-meng jen-wu chih*: 130–33, 145, 148.
43. Ibid., ts'e 5 (*Lun-yü fa-yin* [An exposition of the hidden meanings of *Analects*]): 1a–10b; (*Meng-Tzu fa-yin* [An exposition of the hidden meanings of *Mencius*]): 1a–11a; ts'e 6 (*Yin-fu-ching fa-yin* [An exposition of the hidden meanings of *Yin-fu-ching*]): 1a–17b; *Tao-teh-ching fa-yin* [An exposition of the hidden meanings of *Tao-teh-ching*]: 1a–5a; *Ch'ung-hsü ching fa-yin* [An exposition of the hidden meanings of the *Ch'ung-hsü-ching*]: 1a–55b; *Nan-hua-ching fa-yin* [An exposition of the hidden meanings of the *Nan-hua-ching*]: 1a–20a.
44. For syncretism in the Chinese tradition, see Berling (1980); Yü Chun-fang (1981).

Shao-sheng, whom Yang greatly admired. It was not surprising that Yang basically followed the latter track, interpreting Confucianism and Taoism in terms of the key concepts of Mahayana Buddhism.[45] In this regard, Yang became a channel through which some impulses from the traditional syncretism flowed into the consciousness of modern Chinese intellectuals.

One may see the revival of *chu-tzu hsüeh* and Mahayana Buddhism as a sign that Confucianism's hold on the Chinese mind was weakening. In doing so, however, we must keep in mind the scope of the revival. Up to the mid-1890s, interest in the two had been confined to restricted circles of scholars. Only after the mid-1890s with the appearance of new media did both gradually become visible intellectual trends. But even then they were trends that primarily affected "high" intellectuals and penetrated little beyond that small social group.[46] Hence, it is safe to say that, up to the end of the nineteenth century, Confucianism was still the indigenous belief of the majority of educated Chinese.

Looked at solely in the context of indigenous Chinese thought, the single overriding characteristic that separated the Confucian thought of the nineteenth century from that of the preceding century was the resurgence of the ideal of "practicality" (*chih-yung*) or the practical orientation. This resurgence has often been interpreted as a growing interest in the utilitarian approach to statecraft in response to the impact of the West. Such an interpretation is not entirely wrong, but it is too narrow. The so-called "Statecraft School" was only a part of a larger trend that predated the onset of the Western impact and began around the turn of the nineteenth century. It represented a reorientation of the Confucian scholarship in reaction against the sociomoral indifference of Han Learning, which had dominated the eighteenth-century intellectual world. At the core of this larger trend was a call to return to the two ideals that lay at the heart of Confucian humanism—self-cultivation (*hsiu-shen*) and practical statesmanship (*ching-shih*).[47] True, in the thought of many nineteenth-century Confucian scholars, such as Pao Shih-ch'en and Feng Kuei-fen, this resurgence of the practical orientation meant putting a premium on a utilitarian approach to statecraft. For many others, however, it may have meant just reemphasizing the moral-political orientation of Confucian scholarship.

The hyphenated word "moral-political" is used deliberately here and needs some clarification. "Political" signifies a concern with the outer,

---

45. For P'eng Shao-sheng's Buddhist-inspired syncretism, see Chiang Wei-ch'iao (1972: 89–92).

46. Although there has never been any statistical estimate of the scope of these intellectual trends, all accounts point to their restriction to small circles of the intellectual elite.

47. Chang Hao (1971: 15–34); Liang Ch'i-ch'ao (1963: 51–52, 79). For a thoughtful discussion of the relationship between the two ideals in the Confucian tradition, see Schwartz (1959: 52–54).

sociopolitical world. "Moral" means that this outward-directed, "political" concern must take on a moral cast in two senses. First of all, whatever else the outward concern with the social world may involve, it involves a key role for the moral cultivation of the individual in the process of sociopolitical action in the outside world. Further, the ideal community envisaged is the supranational moral order as epitomized in the idea of "all-under-heaven" (*t'ien-hsia*).[48]

A typical scholar of this persuasion was K'ang Yu-wei's teacher, Chu Tz'u-ch'i (1807–1881), a distinguished Cantonese scholar. For Chu, the thrust of Confucian scholarship was the *shih-hsüeh* (practical study), which aimed to eliminate the time-honored distinction drawn in the neo-Confucian curriculum between *ching-i* (the study of the canonical principles) and *chih-shih* (the study of managing affairs). The point of "practical study," then, was to integrate Confucian canonical study with moral-political concern so that Confucian scholarship was geared to the purpose of moral perfection of self and society. Chu Tz'u-ch'i's conception in this regard may be seen to represent the general drift of the practical orientation, because Chu was widely esteemed as a model scholar of his time.[49]

Even for those who belonged to the Statecraft School, the ideal of practicality did not necessarily refer in any exclusive sense to a utilitarian concern with bureaucratic statecraft. This utilitarian concern might be only a part of a larger outlook still predicated on the Confucian moral conceptions of self and world. In fact, this was largely true of many figures in the *ching-shih* tradition. Wei Yüan is a revealing case in point. Wei, of course, was a major figure instrumental in reviving the ideal of practicality in the late Ch'ing. He was well-known for his writings on such technical problems of statecraft as maritime defense, taxation, the salt monopoly, and water control. Often overlooked is that Wei was also an avid student of Confucian moral philosophy. For him, as for many other thinkers in the Statecraft School, a utilitarian approach to statecraft, important as it was, was still only a supplement to, rather than a substitute for, the Confucian conception of virtuous self and moral community.[50]

Kuo Sung-t'ao, another important figure in the Statecraft School, also illustrates the varied character of the ideal of practicality as it evolved in the nineteenth-century Confucian tradition. Kuo was a close friend of Tseng Kuo-fan's but went further than anyone of Tseng's generation in championing realism and openness toward the West. Yet Kuo too had a profound commitment to the Confucian moral conception of self and society, a commitment that was planted and forged in his mind during his early years as a

---

48. My views here are a further development of my discussions of the *ching-shih* ideal in an article (1974: 36–58).
49. Chien Ch'ao-liang (1964: 64, 65).
50. 1964, esp. the *Nei-chi* [inner section], chüan 1–3.

result of the cultivation of the ideal of practicality in Tseng Kuo-fan's circles.⁵¹

The foregoing examples should suffice to make clear that the resurgence of the ideal of practicality in the Confucian tradition in the early and middle nineteenth century involved a much broader reorientation than merely an emphasis on a utilitarian approach to statecraft. This broad-gauged reorientation continued into the late nineteenth century. Inevitably, the ideal of practicality, as it spread to affect various schools of thought, was given divergent interpretations, resulting in a number of variant versions of the ideal.

Two broad variations of the practical orientation in the late nineteenth-century Confucian tradition were the "inner-personalist" and the "outer-institutional." The former found expression chiefly in the so-called School of Sung Learning and is nowhere more clearly reflected than in the *Ta-hsüeh* (Great learning), the text that Chu Hsi viewed as the gateway to the sacred wisdom of the *Ssu-shu* (Four books).

The burden of the *Ta-hsüeh* was, as the title suggests, the education of a Confucian gentleman, which is predicated on the Confucian life ideal of sage-statesmanship. Running through the educational philosophy that emerges is a heightened moral idealism. First of all, human life is viewed as a process of pursuit of two concerns: the individual concern with self-realization and the social concern with moral order. The two concerns are conceived as mutually interdependent in the sense that one cannot be fully attained without the other. Finally, the pursuit of both is guided by the idea of a ceaseless drive for moral perfection (*chih-shan*).⁵²

This moral idealism is expressed in the paradigm of Confucian statesmanship that lies at the core of the *Ta-hsüeh*. Characteristically, the paradigm starts with the four moral categories that characterize the process of self-cultivation: the investigation of things, the extension of knowledge, the rectification of mind, and sincerity of intention. Thus, self-cultivation is seen as the essential starting point of a process of sociopolitical action that ideally progresses through the stage of ordering the family to culminate in setting in order the state and the world.⁵³

Central to this paradigm is the belief that society is human character written large and that moral order is a function of the perfection of the individual personality. Moral cultivation of the self is thus viewed as an indispensable means to the end of a moral community. Meanwhile, it is also seen as an end no less intrinsic than the latter. In this way, the twin concerns of Confucianism are unified in a single paradigm, thereby giving its practical orientation a distinctively moral-political cast.

---

51. Lu Pao-ch'ien (1978: 402–6).
52. Chu Hsi (1970, chüan 16: 492–94, 502–14).
53. Ibid., chüan 16: 1a–45a.

18   Introduction

In the neo-Confucian tradition, concern with self-cultivation and moral order was sometimes articulated in a mystical strain. From the beginning, the pursuit of these dual concerns was, for many neo-Confucian scholars, more than a mundane matter of moral endeavor. Couched in terms of the Confucian world view of "unity of Heaven and man," the pursuit of self-cultivation and moral order also acquired a cosmic significance. Seen from the perspective of that world view, self-cultivation was an effort of self-transcendence, with the end of merging into the encompassing whole of the cosmos. By the same token, the moral order was also envisaged as a spiritual oneness of the cosmic whole.[54]

In the late nineteenth century, therefore, the resurgence of the practical ideal in the Confucian tradition involved a reemphasis on the moral concern with the paradigmatic self and society. In the mystical version, these concerns may have had only a limited appeal. In the standard version of the *Ta-hsüeh*, however, their appeal could be assumed to be broad. They were certainly held dear by scholars of the School of Sung Learning that, whether as a separate trend or as a part of that syncretism known as the "confluence of Han and Sung Learning" (*Han-Sung ho-liu*), was still a lively intellectual current at the time.[55] Further, it must be remembered that the *Ta-hsüeh*, as a part of the *Ssu-shu*, and Chu Hsi's commentaries were basic readings for almost all educated people. Even scholars of Han Learning, such as those involved in the Yangchou School, to the extent that the practical orientation revived itself there, can be assumed to have accepted the basic values of the *Ta-hsüeh*.[56]

In the Confucian tradition, apart from the "inner-personalist" interpretation there was an "outer-institutional" interpretation of the practical orientation. Its perspective focused on the issue of institutional arrangements for shaping order in the outer world.[57] This interpretation found expression in two intellectual trends in the late nineteenth century. One was an outgrowth of the *ching-shih* trend that, as we have seen, had already started in the early nineteenth century. The salient characteristic of this outgrowth was a growing tendency for its adherents to conceive political order in terms of the ideal of *fu-ch'iang* (wealth and power). But *fu-ch'iang* as they understood it did not necessarily preclude the moral assumptions that usually underlay the traditional Confucian ideal of *ching-shih*. Nor did the ideal of *fu-ch'iang* signify for them the kind of nationalism of its counterpart, *fukoku kyōhei*, in Meiji Japan.

A revealing example in this regard is a group of literati based in the

---

54. This mystic strain had an important place, especially in the Lu-Wang school.
55. Ch'ien Mu (1964, 2: 478–90, 602, 609, 616).
56. For a discussion of the philosophical and ideological relationship between the Yangchou School and Chu Hsi, see Chang Shun-hui (1962: 1–18).
57. Chang Hao (1971: 26–27).

eastern coastal area of Chekiang Province who actively promoted the ideal of *ching-shih* in the last quarter of the nineteenth century.[58] Led by eminent local scholars, such as Sun I-yen and Sun Ch'iang-ming, this group sought to revive the practical philosophy of the Southern Sung Utilitarian School as well as the *ching-shih* ideal as expounded by such seventeenth-century thinkers as Yen Yüan and Huang Tsung-hsi.[59] Following their traditional predecessors, the group endorsed "wealth and power" as a legitimate Confucian value. But, on the other hand, they also understood the ideal in the context of the moral ideals that usually accompany the Confucian idea of practicality. Ch'en Ch'iu, for example, one of the best known in the group,[60] was strongly influenced by the utilitarian concept of Confucian statesmanship that had long been a hallmark of the intellectual tradition of his native area, and he attached great importance to the ideal of wealth and power in his reformism, which was centered on the ideal of *ching-shih*. But wealth and power represented only the end-in-view of his quest for order; beyond that he also looked forward to the emergence of a universal order in the future. Such an order would embrace the whole of mankind in a single world community organized around the twin institutions of feudalism (*feng-chien*) and extensive patrilineage (*tsung-fa*).[61] This vision bore the clear imprints of the ancient Confucian ideal of moral *gemeinschaft*.

The writings of Sung Shu, another articulate member of the group, also serve to illustrate the place of the ideal of wealth and power in the *ching-shih* tradition. Like Ch'en Ch'iu, he too was willing to accommodate the ideal of wealth and power within the Confucian conception of order.[62] But he was even more emphatic than Ch'en Ch'iu in understanding the ideal from the Confucian moral perspective. In his view, there were important differences between the Confucian and the Legalist conceptions of wealth and power. The Legalists' overriding goal was political aggrandizement, but Confucianism was defined by its moral concern for stopping aggression and protecting the weak.[63] Consequently, Confucians accepted the idea of wealth and power as secondary to their ideal of universal moral order (*chih-p'ing*), whereas Legalists prized wealth and power as a primary value.[64] In short, Sung Shu's more inclusive concept of Confucian practicality, while allowing him to accept the ideal of wealth and power as a legitimate concern, did not lead him to jettison the Confucian moral world vision.

---

  58. The intellectual role of the *ching-shih* trend in the late nineteenth century is still largely unexplored. For a brief characterization of the trend, see Su Yüan-lei (1947: 6) and Chang Hao (1971: 7–120).
  59. Ibid.
  60. 1893; one section bears the title *ching-shih*.
  61. Ibid., chüan 1: 1a; chüan 7: 1a–9b.
  62. 1928, chüan 10: 3a.
  63. Ibid.: 13a.
  64. Ibid.: 3a, 5a. See also Su Yüan-lei (1947: 48–52, 68–70).

In the late nineteenth century, the outer-institutional interpretation of the Confucian practical orientation also found expression in an outgrowth of another development in the Confucian tradition, which, like the *ching-shih* trend, had begun during the intellectual transition from the late eighteenth century to the early nineteenth century. This was the New Text School of Han Learning, which was basically a resurgence of mainstream Confucianism of the early Han. Central to New Text Confucianism was a tendency to articulate the Confucian ideal of practicality in institutional arrangements in the outer world. To begin with, New Text Confucianism evolved primarily around the Confucian classic, *Ch'un-ch'iu* (Annals of Spring and Autumn), a text in which Confucius' moral ideals were propounded through the medium of a political chronicle of his native state of Lu. This medium imparted to the moral teachings of *Ch'un-ch'iu* a predominantly "externalist," political orientation, in striking contrast to the inner, spiritual orientation of most neo-Confucian texts. Further, the New Text interpretations of the *Ch'un-ch'iu* projected an image of Confucius as a sage-king who "founded" new institutions for the future much as the ancient sage-kings from Yao to the Duke of Chou had.[65]

This image of a prophetic, institution-founding sage-king was articulated in a mythical world view in which history was seen as an impersonal process of development from disorder toward universal order through phases of changes in social and ritual institutions. Thus, New Text Confucianism carried a heightened outer-institutional interpretation of the Confucian ideal of moral order. Such an interpretation would have had little intellectual impact in the late Ch'ing were it not for the fact that the New Text version of Confucian scholarship was not only undergoing a revival since the late eighteenth century but was ideologically reenergized by the resurgence of Confucian practical spirit in the course of the nineteenth century.[66]

The effect of the recrudescence of the ideal of practicality in the Confucian tradition, then, was to recharge the Confucian scholarship with moral and social concerns in various forms. It was this "practically" recharged Confucianism that interacted with the revived classical noncanonical Chinese philosophies and Mahayana Buddhism as well as with the influx of Western learning. The complex interactions and the consequent fusion of different cultural horizons constituted the intellectual climate that not only provided the symbolic resources, but also set the constraints for the responses made by intellectuals like the four studied here to both the historical situation and the existential situation with which they were confronted.

---

65. Ch'ien Mu (1958b: 235–83).
66. T'ang Chih-chun (1957: 71–81).

2

K'ang Yu-wei (1858–1927)

IN THE 1890s an intellectual movement began that shook up the world of Chinese official-literati like a "volcanic eruption and hurricane storm," in the words of a contemporary scholar. The leader of this movement was the Cantonese scholar K'ang Yu-wei. K'ang was born and reared in a scholar-official family that was locally renowned for its long-standing, strong tradition of neo-Confucian scholarship. Consequently, his early education was steeped in Confucian moral philosophy, often under the personal tutelage of his grandfather, a dedicated neo-Confucian scholar.[1] K'ang's biographies portray him as an extremely bright child with an imaginative mind and a literary gift. According to some reports, he developed the self-image of a sage early in childhood.[2]

THE BEGINNING OF AN INTELLECTUAL JOURNEY

His early precociousness of mind gave rise to a frenzied intellectual search during his youth, beginning with some unusual life experiences and moral-spiritual developments during his late teens and early twenties. To begin with, at the age of 19 K'ang failed to pass the provincial examination. His autobiography hints that this failure, following as it did several earlier ones during his teens, caused the sensitive and proud young K'ang much disappointment and anguish.[3] The very next year an even greater blow came, when his grandfather was drowned in a flood. K'ang was especially

---

1. Liang Ch'i-ch'ao (1936, *wen-chi*, ts'e 3, chüan 6: 59–60). See also K'ang's chronological autobiography (1976c, 22: 1–7).
2. Liang Ch'i-ch'ao (1936, *wen-chi*, ts'e 3, chüan 6: 60); K'ang (1976c, 22: 3–7).
3. K'ang (1976c, 22: 7).

close to his grandfather, who had taken personal charge of the youth's life and education since his early childhood, and the old man's death was a traumatic loss to him. This trauma took place right after K'ang had entered into a new mental ferment as he began studying with a distinguished Confucian philosopher in Canton, Chu Tz'u-ch'i.[4] This apprenticeship proved to be a milestone in his intellectual life.

Chu Tz'u-ch'i was a leading scholar of the so-called "Kwangtung Learning" (*Yüeh-hsüeh*) that dominated the province's intellectual climate in the nineteenth century.[5] Evolving around the famous academy Hsüeh-hai t'ang in Canton, Kwangtung Learning combined the two salient aspects of contemporary Confucian scholarship: first, the convergence of the "evidential studies" of Han Learning and the moral-metaphysical studies of Sung Learning, and, second, the accommodation within the Han Learning of the exegetical scholarship of both the Ancient Text and the New Text persuasions.[6] In developing his own style of scholarship in the context of these trends of the Kwangtung Learning, Chu emphasized what he found lacking in the intellectual tradition of his home province, namely, the moral praxis of Confucian teachings.[7]

Thus, K'ang's study under Chu Tz'u-ch'i initiated him into the intellectual world of Kwangtung Learning and opened up new horizons of contemporary Confucian scholarship to him. In addition, Chu's emphasis on the moral praxis of studies made K'ang acutely aware of the living, practical significance of Confucian scholarship. This was why he found Chu's teaching so refreshing and inspiring.[8]

Years later, K'ang recalls his teacher's impact on him: "At that time, as I received his instructions, it was like a traveler finding a place of lodging or a blind man seeing light; I emptied my mind and curbed my passions to devote myself wholeheartedly to study." As a result, he began to acquire a new confidence and to see himself in a new image. He says in his autobiography:

> I then believed that it was possible for me to read all the books before I was thirty, that I alone could establish myself in life, and that I could remake the world. From this time on, I gave up the writing of examination-style essays and forsook thoughts of becoming rich and exalted. I stood, towering and lofty, above the common people, associating myself with the great and good men of the past. It is true indeed that a man of great virtue can inspire other men.[9]

Apparently, Chu Tz'u-ch'i's impact on K'ang was not just intellectual; it also deeply affected his personality.

---

4. Ibid.: 3–9.
5. Chien Ch'ao-liang (1964: 24b–32b).
6. Liang Ch'i-ch'ao (1936, *chuan-chi*, ts'e 24, chüan 103: 67); Elman (1978: 6–13).
7. Ch'ien Mu (1964, 2: 639–40); Chien Ch'ao-liang (1964: 25a–25b, 27b, 28b, 29a).
8. 1976c: 7–8.
9. Ibid.: 8.

The emotional anguish and intellectual excitement that K'ang underwent in the last two years of his teens proved to be a prelude to a most unusual period of his mental life. In his chronological autobiography, he relates that at the age of 20 he suddenly found himself plunging into an intensive spiritual quest, a search for something on which to "rest the mind and settle the destiny" (*an-hsin li-ming*). He was soon led to seclude himself from his friends "to practice quiet-sitting and the cultivation of mind." At the height of this spiritual pursuit, he experienced a kind of illumination. "So I engaged in the quiet-sitting, I suddenly came to see the heaven and earth and the myriad things as all parts of myself. A light dawned within me and, believing that I was a sage, I became joyous and laughed. Then, thinking about the sufferings of the people of the world, I became sad and I cried."[10]

Meanwhile, he also engaged in what his schoolmates thought were offbeat and bizarre activities. He grew self-confident to the point of appearing arrogant in their eyes. He argued with his teacher, challenged the reputation of illustrious intellectual figures of the past such as Han Yü and Tai Chen, and questioned the meaning of the studies he had pursued so far, such as reading, literary composition, and textual criticisms. This intellectual rebelliousness was accompanied by a tendency to segregate himself from his friends and schoolmates. Eventually, he even quit his studies with Chu and went into the nearby mountains.[11]

There he lived like a hermit, sometimes roaming in the wilderness and enjoying nature's beauties, sometimes practicing quiet-sitting and various other Buddhist and Taoist meditative activities. His autobiography refers in particular to a Hinayana-Buddhist kind of meditation that led him to feel revulsion toward the ugliness of life on earth. Obviously, he was going through a world-denying, introverted phase of an intellectual search.[12] Years later, looking back on all these activities, he borrows a concept from Ch'an Buddhism and explains them as a case of "demons flying into the mind." In retrospect, he says that the possession of his mind by these demonic forces was a sign of his spiritual thirst and restlessness before he settled on a faith.[13]

K'ang's bizarre activities in the mountains did not last long. He soon was pressured to go home and resume "normal" life. His spiritual restlessness did not stop, however. He recollects later that for several years thereafter he continued to engage in the cultivation of mind (*yang-hsin*) and make frantic efforts to reach out intellectually. This prolonged intellectual search not only led him into new subjects of traditional scholarship; it also launched him into

---

10. Ibid.: 10. For a stimulating, Eriksonian approach to K'ang's mental development during this period, see Lai (1982).
11. 1976c: 9–10.
12. Ibid. See also Lai (1982).
13. 1976c: 10.

a voracious reading of Western learning. Although he had been exposed to it in his teen years, he emphasizes that his serious, comprehensive reading of Western learning really began during this period.[14]

These events should not be seen in isolation from each other but rather together, as different phases of a prolonged period of spiritual ferment stretching from his late teens to his mid-twenties. In his autobiography, he often describes these events in vague terms. Further, because his description is based on recollections written in 1895, ten years after the events, it is possible that K'ang might have read some of his later experiences and thought back into his account of these events. However, it is safe at least to draw one conclusion from his retrospective accounts, namely, that he was then repudiating his own past and coming up with a new self-identity.

K'ang first hints at this self-identity in the passage quoted above on his experience of spiritual illumination.[15] His description of it as a state of becoming one with the universe is reminiscent of similar experiences in the neo-Confucian tradition, and it points to a self-image of the Confucian sage.[16] This Confucian self-image became submerged for a while during his period of hermitage in the mountains. It returned, however, during his ensuing intellectual search. But in the process of this intellectual search, the self-image of sagehood gradually blended with that of the suffering savior of Mahayana Bodhisattva. This blended self-image was clearly reflected in a section in his autobiography under the heading "Age twenty-six," which summed up the spiritual ferment that he had just gone through.[17]

> In my thoughts I began with the origins of living things, the organization of society, the realms of the universes and the realm of the stars, the causes of their creation, their shapes, sizes, and motions, the changes in their spirit and substance; and from these thoughts I endeavored to find my place in society and my purpose in life. Having acquired an understanding of various subjects, I was quite pleased with myself. Avoiding intercourse with other people, I accepted my fate without blame or self-praise; caring not for losses or gains in life, I permitted my mind to wander about freely, without beginning or end. I thought of the countless generations who had been born and who had died, the rich and the highborn, the poor and the humble, enjoying happiness or suffering misery; the emperors and kings, generals and ministers; the beggars and the famine-stricken; and even the oxen, horses, chickens, and pigs.... The purpose of my creation was to save the masses of living things, even if instead of residing in heaven, I would go to purgatory to save them; if instead of going to the Pure Land, I had to come to this unclean world to save them; and if

---

14. Ibid.: 10–11, 11–14, 7, 11.
15. See n. 10 above.
16. K'ang's experience of spiritual illumination in this regard is similar to mystic experiences found in the writings of neo-Confucian philosophers, such as Wang Yang-ming, Wang Ken, and Kao P'an-lung. For a discussion of the mystical experiences of these three, see Ching (1976: 31); de Bary (1970: 158); and Taylor (1978: 64–65).
17. 1976c: 10–11, 14–15.

instead of being an emperor or a king, I became a common scholar in order to save them. Instead of enjoying cleanliness, instead of enjoying pleasure, instead of attaining exalted position, I would rather go among the masses of living beings to be on hand to save them. Thus, every day the salvation of society was uppermost in my thoughts and every moment the salvation of society was my aim in life, and for this aim I would sacrifice myself. Since there are many worlds, some large and some small, I could only sympathize with and try to save the men who lived close to me and whom I should meet. I would appeal to them every day and hope that they would listen to me. I made this my principle, my aim to fulfill.[18]

As reflected clearly both here and elsewhere in K'ang's autobiography regarding this period, his newly acquired self-identity as a sage-Bodhisattva involved a heightened sense of mission, a mission to order and save the world. But what were his philosophy and program for this world mission? At another place in the section quoted above, he claims that he had already evolved some of the basic ideas of the moral-historical world view for which he later became famous, but his claims are probably a projection of later ideas onto his early thought.[19] All indications are that he did not have such a world view at that time. True, his mind was reaching out in many directions and opening up to new horizons. But the ideas, visions, and experiences he had acquired had not yet cohered into a unified, overall world view. Still, driven by his sage-Bodhisattva identity, he pressed on with his intellectual search.

GROPING FOR AN INTELLECTUAL SYNTHESIS

Because K'ang's self-identity was forged by the Confucian ideal of sagehood and the Buddhist ideal of Bodhisattvahood, it was inevitable that his intellectual search was driven largely by a universalistic concern at the core of both the Confucian and Buddhist ideals, that is, a concern that speaks to the human condition as such and takes the whole of humanity as its purview. In his twenties, however, his intellectual search came to be reinforced by another, more "particularistic," and mundane concern that resulted largely from his encounter with the West.[20] His discovery of Western learning during his years of spiritual ferment inevitably drew his attention to the national crisis that lay behind the influx of Western learning. In fact, since he had grown up in the Canton area, he must have been aware of foreign aggression with a keenness felt by few of his compatriots in inland China. For example, when the Sino-French War was brewing in 1884, he was staying at Canton, where he was likely to have personally experienced all the fears and

---

18. Quoted in Lo Jung-pang (1967: 41–42).
19. 1976c: 14.
20. Ibid.: 11, 12. See also K'ang (1960, chüan 4: 24a–b.)

tensions of a foreign invasion.[21] This first-hand experience of Western power and aggressiveness explains why his political consciousness—a consciousness marked by a growing concern for China's survival as a country—also began to stir in his twenties.[22]

Thus, as K'ang emerged from his intellectual ferment in his late twenties, he was not only pursuing the moral-spiritual quest fueled by his sage-Bodhisattva identity, but he was also facing up to the national crisis of China. His studies of indigenous trends of thought and Western learning were driven both by this quest and by his political, patriotic concern. In his late twenties he began to put into writing all these new ideas and experiences. The result was a series of works, which can be dated to the period roughly from 1885 to 1890. The most important of these works were the *Shih-li kung-fa* (Principles of truth and universal laws) and the *K'ang-tzu nei-wai p'ien* (The inner and outer books of the philosopher K'ang), and the *Chiao-hsüeh t'ung-i* (Discourse on education and learning), a piece of work newly discovered in mainland China. All three works were written between 1885 and 1887 and reflected his struggle to lap up a variety of ideas and experiences and his inability, as yet, to integrate them into a coherent, unified world view.[23]

The two concerns that dominated his thinking at this time, namely, his patriotic concern and his moral-spiritual quest, still lay disjointed in his mind. Therefore, in these writings K'ang speaks in two voices. On the one hand, the would-be statesman speaks to the needs of China as a country. Here his tone of voice reminds us strongly of those in the tradition of Confucian statecraft, such as Pao Shih-ch'en and Wei Yüan. Typical of that tradition, K'ang makes the time-honored distinction between the *wang* and *pa*, that is, between the politics of principle and compassion and the politics of expediency and force.[24] But, true to the spirit of the statecraft tradition, he argues that the distinction between the two politics lies not so much in visible courses of action as in the motives behind these courses of action. The

---

21. 1976c: 14.
22. Ibid.: 11–13. See also some of the poems that he composed before he was 30: "Ai-kuo ko" [Paean to patriotism] and "Ai-kuo tuan ko hsing" [A short song for patriotism] in *K'ang Nan-hai hsien-sheng shih-chi* [A collection of K'ang Yu-wei's poems] (1976c, 20, chüan 1: 6–15); see esp. a poem composed in 1879 when he was 21 and visited Hong Kong for the first time. In this poem he expresses admiration for the Western achievements in Hong Kong but also shows anguish over Hong Kong's status as a colony under foreign domination (1976c, 20, chüan 1: 32).
23. For the *Shih-li kung-fa* and the *K'ang-tzu nei-wai p'ien*, I use the microfilm copies made in 1947 by Mary C. Wright in Peking for the Hoover Institution Library. For an English translation and detailed study of the *K'ang-tzu nei-wai p'ien*, see Li San-pao (1975). *Chiao-hsüeh t'ung-i* has not yet been published. My discussion of it is based on a handwritten summary of the text made by T'ang Chih-chün. See T'ang Chih-chün (1985). Apart from these three major writings, there are some minor writings that were composed before 1891. Considering their contents, some of them, such as K'ang's discussion of Chu Hsi's moral philosophy and educational approach, were probably written in the late or mid-1880s (1976a: 1–4, 9–11).
24. 1947, "Ho-p'i p'ien": 1b–3.

implication is clear: One can be flexible in one's course of action as long as one sets one's heart in the right direction. In this way, K'ang is able to extol the *Realpolitik* of some of the dynastic rulers of China's past and to justify the goal of wealth and power and the principle of expediency and force within the Confucian framework. He also conjures up a political vision of a strong ruler at the center dynamically wielding power and authority to bring about what he called "order and strength" (*chih-ch'iang*) in China. Significantly, the Meiji reforms were already among the historical examples he used to illustrate this political vision.[25] Clearly, his political vision already anticipated some of the basic impulses behind the institutional reformism that he developed later in the 1890s.

At the same time, K'ang speaks in another voice—the voice of a would-be sage engaged in moral discourse. K'ang's discourse was marked by two incongruous strains of thought: a conservative and a radical. The conservative strain was predominant in the *Chiao-hsüeh t'ung-i* and bore the clear imprints of Kwangtung Learning (*Yüeh-hsüeh*) which, as pointed out above, was an important part of K'ang's early intellectual environment. One characteristic of Kwangtung Learning was the accommodation within Han Learning of the exegetical scholarship of both the Ancient Text and the New Text persuasions. This eclecticism found a faint but unmistakable echo in K'ang's text. On the one hand, he saw the presence in the distant past of an ideal order, which began with such sage-kings as Huang Ti, Yao, and Shun, but culminated with the early Chou. This ideal order, which was brought to a brilliant completion by the Duke of Chou, was recorded in the classic, the *Rites of Chou* (*Chou Li*).[26] This exaltation of the Duke of Chou and the *Rites of Chou* clearly bespoke the influence of the Ancient Text School, as the exaltation of both was a hallmark of that school.

On the other hand, at one point in the book where he explicitly discussed the differences between the Ancient Text and the New Text schools, he did not state his preference either way.[27] Meanwhile, he sometimes paid so much tribute to Confucius' greatness and spoke of him together with the Duke of Chou as if he put the two on the same pedestal. For, in his eyes, Confucius, though without the Duke of Chou's status of sage-king, nonetheless had the unsurpassed achievement of having the moral teachings of the ancient sage-king preserved and transmitted to posterity after the ideal order of the early Chou crumbled away during the turbulent period of the late Chou.[28] All these point to the possibility that when K'ang wrote the *Chiao-hsüeh t'ung-i* the New Text teachings also had some sway over his mind.

This possibility becomes stronger when we investigate K'ang's view of

---

25. Ibid.: 2a–3b.
26. T'ang Chih-chün (1985: 5–6, 8, 11, 19).
27. Ibid.: 21.
28. Ibid.: 13–14.

Confucius' relationship with the Six Canons. The Ancient Text School's stance in this regard is that the Six Canons sprung from the Duke of Chou. K'ang sometimes followed this view but sometimes argued, inexplicably, in the vein of the New Text School that the Six Canons stemmed from Confucius.[29] Moreover, when he came to discuss the *Ch'un-ch'iu*, he took a view that reflected the unmistakable influence of New Text teaching. He singled out the *Annals* from among the Six Canons as growing solely out of Confucius' authorship. He also accorded it a special importance on the ground that the classic embodied Confucius' "subtle words and great principles" (*wei-yen ta-i*) to "accommodate the *Rites of Chou* . . . and to establish the kingly Way."[30] With this view, K'ang went on to present some distinctly New Text ideas: that *Ch'un-ch'iu* set forth Confucius' ideals of institutional reforms, that these ideals were spelled out mainly in the *Kung-yang* and *Ku-liang* commentaries on *Ch'un-ch'iu* and that Liu Hsin was responsible for derailing and corrupting the later development of Confucianism.[31] In short, in the *Chiao-hsüeh t'ung-i*, we find some of the major New Text teachings at least implicitly, if not explicitly, embraced. K'ang indicated in his chronological autobiography that in his early twenties he was an advocate of the Ancient Text teachings.[32] Now we may surmise that, when he wrote the *Chiao-hsüeh t'ung-i* in his late twenties, he was moving away from his early position and groping toward accepting the New Text teachings.

Equally indicative of K'ang's influence by Kwangtung Learning was the tendency in his *Chiao-hsüeh t'ung-i* to combine Han Learning and Sung-Ming neo-Confucianism. Our examination of K'ang's interpretation of Han Learning has shown that he considered Confucius' role to be the vehicle through which the moral teachings of the ancient sage-kings were transmitted to posterity. In K'ang's view, after Liu Hsin's corruption of Confucianism during the Han dynasty, there was no one who did more than Chu Hsi to perpetuate the Confucian moral heritage.[33] In fact he went so far as to regard Chu Hsi as second only to Confucius in the whole Confucian pantheon. True, K'ang did have some reservations about Chu Hsi's interpretation of Confucius' teachings, especially regarding what he considered as Chu Hsi's failure to articulate the aspect of Confucius' teaching that contained institutional reformism.[34] But, in terms of contributions to the development of the Confucian moral philosophy, Chu Hsi deserved the highest credit. K'ang paid special tribute to the moral teachings Chu Hsi evolved on the basis of the *Analects* and *Mencius* and to Chu Hsi's promotion and

---

29. Ibid.: 14.
30. Ibid.
31. Ibid.: 14–15, 18–19.
32. 1976c: 9–12.
33. T'ang Chih-chün (1985: 18–19).
34. Ibid.: 19.

interpretation of the *Great Learning* and the *Doctrine of the Mean*.³⁵ In his view, Chu Hsi opened up the possibility for everyone who is willing to learn to become a sage. Some of the extant philosophical writings of K'ang's, which can be dated to this period, show that K'ang at that time was involved deeply in his efforts to grapple with the meanings of some of the concepts that lay at the heart of Chu Hsi's distinctive approach to the philosophy of self-realization.³⁶

K'ang's synthesis of Han Learning and Sung-Ming neo-Confucianism resulted in a moral outlook that can be characterized as follows: An ideal order is believed to have existed in the ancient age of sage-kings. This ideal order is blessed with rulers who combine virtue and power and with the wondrous institutions these sage-kings created. But these sage-kings were gone, and the wondrous institutional order was no more. Nevertheless, the moral teachings of the ancient sage-kings were fortunately preserved intact and transmitted to us, thanks to Confucius and his followers. Herein consists the message of *Chiao-hsüeh t'ung-i*: moral learning and education must be geared to setting order on earth, and the order that is created must embody moral learning and education.

In the *K'ang-tzu nei-wai p'ien*, the conservative strain of K'ang's moral thinking was still present, though in a different form. Strangely, there was little trace in this text of the kind of interpretation of Confucianism he pursued in the *Chiao-hsüeh t'ung-i*. Instead, we often find a tone reminiscent of the so-called imperial Confucianism in which he spoke expansively not only of the cultural glories of the Chinese tradition, but also of the irresistible, absolute moral authority of the Chinese emperor.³⁷

Meanwhile, side by side with this moral conservatism existed strains of moral radicalism. Because these radical strains were all more or less related to a tendency to elevate *jen* (humanity) as the overriding value in the *K'ang-tzu nei-wai p'ien*, I will examine this tendency before discussing these radical strains. A major point of departure for the discussion of moral values in the text was the Confucian five cardinal virtues (*wu-ch'ang*)—*jen*, *i* (righteousness), *Li* (propriety), *chih* (intelligence), and *hsin* (faithfulness). Admittedly, in his discussion of these five virtues, his emphasis is not on *jen* alone but also on *chih*. But a close reading shows that, whereas he regarded intelligence as a primary distinguishing characteristic of human beings, he viewed *jen* as the universal virtue for all beings. Thus, its primacy on his scale of values is implied.³⁸ The primacy of *jen* is further confirmed by the prominence in the text of the moral sentiment of commiseration and of the

---

35. Ibid.: 10, 19.
36. Ibid.: 10. Also see "Chung-ho chiu-shuo" [On Chu Hsi's old views of *chung-ho*] in K'ang Yu-wei (1976a: 9–11).
37. K'ang (1947, "Ho-p'i p'ien": 1b–3a; "Li-hsüeh p'ien": 5a).
38. 1947, "Jen-chih p'ien": 17b, 18a.

moral vision of all-under-heaven in one family. Both of these ideas had long been associated with the *jen* ideal in the Confucian tradition.[39] Thus, despite the stress he sometimes gives to the complementarity between *jen* and *chih* in his discussion, in the context of the whole text *jen* doubtless stands out as the leading value.

The prominence given to the relationship between *jen* and *chih* by K'ang puts us in mind of the discussion of the two virtues by the famous Han scholar of the New Text School, Tung Chung-shu, who gave it a similar emphasis.[40] In this connection, it is significant to note the explicit reference K'ang makes to Tung's moral philosophy and the radical twist K'ang gives to it in his elucidation of the relationship of *jen* to another of the five cardinal virtues, *i* (righteousness).[41] In the original context of Tung's moral thought, the thrust of his comments on the two values was to point out the complementarity between *jen* as an other-regarding value and *i* as a self-regarding value.[42] In K'ang's interpretation, however, there is an antithetical relationship between the two values. As a self-regarding value, *i* not only sometimes connotes the spirit of selfishness, it also symbolizes an authoritarian spirit of political domination and social differentiation. Meanwhile, *jen* represents a positive spirit of love, liberality, and openness—just the opposite of the authoritarian and inhibitory spirit of *i*.[43]

The dichotomy posed between *jen* and *i* even gives rise to a certain iconoclastic strain in K'ang's writing. K'ang observes in a tone of disapproval and regret that the Chinese cultural tradition gives primacy to the spirit of *i* over that of *jen*, whereas in other traditions it is often the other way around.[44] But, hopeful about the future, he believed that in a hundred years the authoritarian tradition as represented by *i* would be bound to give way to the Buddhist ideal of equality. In this way, he links the Confucian value of *jen*, loosely but unmistakably, with the egalitarianism of Mahayana Buddhism.[45]

Even more significant is his identification of *jen* with the Mohist ideal of universal, undifferentiated love (*chien-ai*).[46] The latter ideal, it must be remembered, is singled out for rebuttal in both classical Confucianism and neo-Confucianism on the grounds that it runs counter to a basic spirit of the Confucian ideal of *jen*, the graded love. This concept of graded love, with its insistence that love be practiced on a differentiated basis, is marked by a strong strain of particularism that distinguishes the ideal of *jen* from the

39. Ibid., "Chüeh-shih p'ien": 13b; "Pu-jen p'ien": 10b.
40. 1929–36, 4, chüan 8: 49–50.
41. 1947, "Jen-wo p'ien": 15b.
42. 1929–36, 4, chüan 8: 47–49.
43. 1947, "Jen-wo p'ien": 15b.
44. Ibid.
45. Ibid.: 16b–17b.
46. Ibid.: 15b–16a.

radical universalism of the Mohist ideal.[47] Although K'ang does not engage in any explicit criticism of the concept of graded love, he does emphasize that there is nothing wrong with the Mohist ideal. Thus, he clearly implies a departure from the traditional Confucian and neo-Confucian stances in this regard.[48] His unreserved identification of *jen* with the Mohist ideal, plus his proclivity to link up *jen* with Buddhist egalitarianism, points to a tendency toward radicalism in *K'ang-tzu nei-wai p'ien*.

This tendency toward radicalism is even more evident in K'ang's *Shih-li kung-fa*, his other work of the mid-1880s. Whereas in the *K'ang-tzu nei-wai p'ien* universalistic values and egalitarian ideals exist side by side with conservative strains, a critique of the central values of orthodox Confucianism dominates all of *Shih-li kung-fa*. Furthermore, in the former writing, though he questions the traditional hierarchical order based on political authoritarianism and social inequality, he stops short of challenging the cardinal familial value of Confucianism—filial piety. However, in the latter he makes this value (along with the institution of the family) a major target for his across-the-board criticisms of the traditional order.[49] The impetus for these criticisms doubtless was partly the universalism and egalitarianism of Buddhism and Mohism. But they might also have stemmed from his expressed belief that "everyone is entitled to the right of self-determination,"[50] a belief that may have been rooted in the Confucian conception of the moral autonomy of self. In this regard, K'ang's Confucian background probably was reinforced by the influence of Christian missionaries, because exactly the same words with which he expresses his belief in individual independence were also found in the writings of Christian missionaries, such as Alexander Williamson and others, who began to introduce Western liberal values in the 1880s.[51] Seen in this light, K'ang's moral radicalism was the result of a convergence of influences from inside as well as outside the Chinese tradition.

Aside from the moral discourse, K'ang also struggles in his *K'ang-tzu nei-wai p'ien* to articulate an overall view of the cosmos. His efforts in this direction are no more successful than he is in his moral discourse; many of his ideas are vague and disjointed. Some broad tendencies, however, are discernible. One tendency was to turn away from the orthodox neo-Confucian world view—a metaphysical dualism in which the world consists of two basic entities, principles (*li*) and material force (*ch'i*), with an emphasis on the ontological primacy of the former. Although he does not spell out his views in

---

47. Chu Hsi (1970, chüan 55: 2086–8, 2096–9).
48. 1947, "Jen-wo p'ien": 15b.
49. For the radical views expressed in *Shih-li kung-fa*, see Hsiao Kung-chuan (1975: 426–33). See also Howard (1962: 311–15).
50. Howard (1962: 313).
51. Shek (1976: 197–98).

this regard systematically, he is inclined to stress the ontological primacy of material force and to see the cosmos as constituted by the interplay between the two modes of material force, *yin* and *yang*. Because the same stress also characterized New Text Confucianism, K'ang, in this metaphysical world view just as in his moral thought, apparently has already come to be influenced by New Text Confucianism.[52]

K'ang's "materialistic" view of the universe might also be credited partly to his dabbling in Western sciences at the time. In fact, some quasi-scientific explanations of the evolution of man and the universe found their way into his writings.[53] However, the influence of Western sciences on his thinking was largely superficial rather than substantial. At least, he had not yet gone far enough to accept a consistent naturalism that would have compelled him to see the universe devoid of spiritual creations or supernatural forces and to explain the external world entirely in terms of cause and effect. Although his writings here and there bear traces of the scientific outlook, he still largely holds a traditional teleological mentality, which saw moral-spiritual values inherent in the structure of the universe. He is inclined to explain the structure of the universe in terms of the material force alone, but the latter, in his view, is infused with moral and spiritual import.[54]

Two strains stand out in the context of K'ang's *ch'i*-only world view. First, this world view leads him to attack the dichotomy between heavenly principle and human desires so much emphasized by orthodox neo-Confucianism. To him, this dichotomy is an error rooted in neo-Confucianism's metaphysical dualism. What orthodox neo-Confucianism called "heavenly principles," in the final analysis, were nothing more than creations of human intelligence. As for "heaven and earth," he asks, where are the so-called principles of heaven outside "light, electricity, heat, and weight?" Meanwhile, he maintained that human desires are doubtless part and parcel of the natural order of the cosmos. In this way he turns the orthodox neo-Confucian desideratum upside down and speaks of "heaven's desires and human principles."[55] Here he sounds a naturalistic note, a note not always present in other places in his writings.

K'ang's views here are pregnant with radical implications. Because human desires are an integral part of the heavenly order of the cosmos, it is necessary to maintain an open and positive attitude toward them. Further, if established institutions and norms are found to be repressive of human desires, it is a natural corollary to challenge these institutions and norms on the ground of these "heavenly desires." K'ang had not yet drawn these radical implications, but they would soon surface in his thought.

52. 1947, "Ai-wu p'ien": 6b; "Shih-je p'ien": 12b.
53. Ibid., "Li-ch'i p'ien": 21b, 22a, 22b.
54. Ibid., "Ai-wu p'ien": 6b; "Pu-jen p'ien": 10b; "Shih-je p'ien": 12b; "Jen-wo p'ien": 15b; "Li-ch'i p'ien": 21b.
55. Ibid., "Li-ch'i p'ien": 22a.

Another theme standing out in K'ang's *ch'i*-only world view is the image of a cosmos engaged in constant movement, an image he derived from the *I ching* (Book of changes). The process of movement, as he envisages it, could be characterized as dialectical, in the sense that he believed it to be propelled by an interplay of *yin* and *yang*. This concept of dialectical process is akin to that of the *I ching* in two ways. First, the interplay of *yin* and *yang* represented a sort of complementary dualism rather than a conflicting dualism, inasmuch as K'ang considers *yin* and *yang* to be two different forces complementing each other. Thus, in contrast to the later Chinese Communist concept of history as a dialectical process, K'ang values harmony rather than struggle in his picture of an evolving universe.[56] Further, true to the spirit of the *I ching*, he sees no final end to the dialectical process. Clearly, the eschatological view of history that would have such a central place in his later thought has not yet developed.[57]

K'ang's three works, while presenting no systematic synthesis of his ideas, adequately reflect his major ongoing concerns. On the one hand, underlying the traditional language of statecraft is a political concern with problems of power and order. On the other, behind all the discussions of values and world views stands an overriding moral concern. Whereas his moral concern expresses itself in some striking strains of radicalism, conservative views retain an important place in his moral thinking. For the moment, these incongruous concerns and strains of thought result only in a smorgasbord of ideas and values, but some trends stand out as signposts to the future. One is a utopian vision of an ideal order couched in a comprehensive interpretation of Confucianism. Another is the emergence of *jen* as a preeminent ideal, accompanied by certain radical moral visions and values. Still another is the view that moral values are rooted in a cosmos constituted and governed by the interplay between two basic modes of material forces. This view is accompanied by a "naturalistic" tendency to keep values and ideals congruent with, rather than militating against, the "natural" forces of life and cosmos. Besides, this view itself, inasmuch as it carries the monistic tendency to see the cosmos as solely made up of the material force of *ch'i*, stands closer to Western Han Confucianism than to the mainstream of neo-Confucianism. This tendency, plus the relative prominence of references to Tung Chung-shu's teaching in the *K'ang-tzu nei-wai p'ien* and especially the important fact that K'ang had accommodated some of the basic ideas of the New Text Confucianism in his *Chiao-hsüeh t'ung-i* clearly points to the likelihood that K'ang had already come under the influence of New Text teachings at that time, although he had not yet fully embraced them. It seems apparent that K'ang accepted New Text teachings as the result of a slow, protracted process, which probably started in his mid-twenties, rather than (as the

---

56. Ibid., "Shih-je p'ien": 12b.
57. Ibid., "Wei-chi p'ien": 4.

established view goes) as the result of his abrupt conversion by Liao P'ing in 1889.[58] Seen in the context of his writings of 1885–1887, these tendencies represent no more than some striking trends in a picture of crosscurrents. They, however, would develop into major themes in an overall, integrated world view that was soon to emerge.

THE MORAL-METAPHYSICAL WORLD VIEW OF JEN

When this integrated world view did gradually emerge in the 1890s, it did so in the midst of K'ang's involvement in a frantic campaign for political reform.[59] The guiding ideal of his political involvements was what he called "change of institutions" (*kai-chih*) or "alteration of laws" (*pien-fa*).[60] At the heart of these ideals was the concept of a powerful and dynamic political center as the propeller of changes, a concept that already figured in his philosophical writings of 1885–1887. In them, it must be remembered, his conception of the political center was largely couched in the language of traditional statecraft.[61] In his political reformism, however, the goals and modes of action that he envisaged for the center evinced some strong influences from outside the Chinese tradition. During his campaign for reform, he made no secret of his fervent admiration for foreign political models, especially the Petrine Reforms of eighteenth-century Russia and the Meiji reforms of nineteenth-century Japan.[62] These foreign models suggest that the immediate, overriding goal of his reformism was national wealth and power.

However, K'ang Yu-wei could not be characterized as a nationalist, because his political reformism did not stand alone. It was part and parcel of a comprehensive, new interpretation of Confucianism that he sets forth between the early 1890s and the early 1900s. This new interpretation of

---

58. My view here is somewhat closer to K'ang's own account in this regard than the generally accepted view is. K'ang writes in his chronological autobiography (*nien-p'u*) that he had come to accept the New Text interpretation of Confucianism on his own (probably not long after he was 24). Other scholars, such as Ch'ien Mu and T'ang Chih-chün, have long disputed K'ang's account and argue that K'ang was converted to the New Text teachings mainly through contacts he had with Liao P'ing during 1889–1890. I believe that K'ang had been exposed to the influences of the New Text teachings long before he met Liao P'ing. After all, K'ang noted in his *nien-p'u* that he had studied *Huang Ch'ing ching-chieh* [The imperial Ch'ing collection of exegeses of the classics] since his early twenties. The collection was published by the Hsüeh-hai t'ang [Sea of Learning Academy], a major center of "Kwangtung Learning" at Canton, which was known for its eclectic accommodation of both the New Text and the Ancient Text versions of Confucian exegetical scholarship. See K'ang (1976c, 22: 11–12, 14–15, 17, 19, 22–23); Ch'ien Mu (1964, chüan 2: 643–53); Elman (1978: 1–23).

59. This integrated world view is spelled out in a series of works that K'ang published from the early 1890s to the mid-1900s. In treating these writings as being dominated by one overarching world view, I don't mean to overlook the significant shifts of view that took place in this period, but they do not affect the basic pattern of K'ang's thought that I present.

60. Hsiao Kung-chuan (1975: 193–216).
61. See nn. 24 and 25 above.
62. See Hsiao Kung-chuan (1975); Howard (1968: 288–302).

Confucianism was an outgrowth of the view that he first intimated in his *Chiao-hsüeh t'ung-i*, and it was based on the New Text teachings that he accepted in full by the end of the 1880s. In this new interpretation, he was also able to reconcile his two basic concerns, his political concern for the survival of his country and his moral-spiritual concern for meaning, which up to this point had remained separate. He now integrates them into an overarching moral-historical world view, which contains nationalism as an element but in its intentionality as a whole, is governed by an overriding, universalistic concern with the moral perfection of individual and society. It is worth noting in this connection that when Liang Ch'i-ch'ao, K'ang's closest disciple at that time, wrote an intellectual biography of him in 1902, he specifically pointed out that nationalism was missing in K'ang's thought. Liang called his teacher an "individualist" and "universalist."[63]

The earliest clue to K'ang's newly formulated world view is found in *Ch'ang-hsing hsüeh-chi*, a syllabus written for the school he set up at Canton in 1891. In the preamble to his syllabus, he emphasizes the ability to learn as the distinguishing characteristic of human beings. Only with learning, he says, is a human being able both to "expand" (*k'uo*) himself and transcend the constrictions of his narrow egoism and also to "counter" (*ni*) and overcome his instincts and desires as well as ingrained habits and long-standing customs. Significantly, he declares *jen* to be the goal of learning. The ideal of *jen* was prominent in his writings of 1885–1887; now it has moved to center stage in his new philosophical outlook.[64]

What did K'ang mean by *jen*? In his previous writings, *jen* appears largely as a moral ideal. As such, it remains, as we shall see. But, first and foremost, it represents for him a metaphysical world view.

Jen *as a World View*

We have seen that, by 1890 K'ang had already embraced the New Text teachings of Western Han Confucianism. The specific version of the New Text teachings that served as a sort of launching pad for his new world view is Tung Chung-shu's philosophy. Following Tung, he believes that the cosmos is impregnated with the material force *ch'i*, which constitutes the primordial substance of the universe.[65] To be sure, in formulating his world view K'ang still sometimes draws, as he had in his writings of 1885–1887, on terms from the Western sciences like "ether," "electricity," and so forth, as though he sees his world view as akin to the materialistic world view of the nineteenth-century sciences.[66]

63. Liang Ch'i-ch'ao (1936, *wen-chi*, ts'e 3, chüan 6: 66).
64. K'ang (1976c, 9: 1–3, 4–5).
65. K'ang (1969, chüan 6, pt. 1: 6a, 8b–9a).
66. In his *nien-p'u*, he reports in several places his interest in such Western sciences as astronomy and mathematics (1976c, 22: 13, 14, 22). For a discussion of K'ang's interest in Western sciences, see Hsiao Kung-chuan (1968: 375–97). For illustrations of the scientific terms in K'ang's writings, see K'ang (1968: 21a).

Significant differences, however, divided the two, because K'ang inherited from Tung Chung-shu some characteristic notions of *ch'i* that mark off his world view from a materialistic cosmology. For one thing, *ch'i*, in K'ang's view, is not an inert substance, inasmuch as it has such vitalistic qualities as creativity and capacity for organic growth. He also goes so far as to accept Tung Chung-shu's view of *ch'i* as something sentient and noetic, which Tung terms *shen-ch'i*.[67] Obviously, in K'ang's mind the cosmos is not the naturalistic order conceived by the nineteenth-century scientific world view.

In addition to carrying vitalistic qualities, material force was also constantly in motion, as a result of the interplay between its two modes, *yin* and *yang*, and the revolution of its five constituent elements. These movements of polar oscillation and cyclical revolution set a cosmic pattern and rhythm for all existences in the encompassing whole.[68] For K'ang, as for Tung Chung-shu, this encompassing whole is Heaven. Thus, Heaven is not an impersonal order but a vast organism with will, purpose, feeling, and a capacity for procreation. Consequently, it is the ground of all beings in the cosmos, including human beings. True, human beings owe their concrete bodily existence directly to their parents. But, inasmuch as Heaven gives birth to life itself, a human individual is also the "son" of Heaven.[69] Being all born of Heaven, people everywhere are integral participants in the encompassing whole permeated by the material force. K'ang writes: "Heaven and Earth are the source of life. All the ten thousand things are given life by partaking of the material force of Heaven and Earth. As a member of the ten thousand things the human being counts as one share of Heaven and Earth. Therefore, all the ten thousand things between Heaven and Earth are united by the same material force."[70]

Thus, all individual beings have kinship with each other as well as with the whole, but only human beings are conscious of this kinship. Because of this self-consciousness, human beings are the cosmic agents through which the unity and harmony of the all-encompassing whole can be made manifest. This is the Confucian belief in the unity of Heaven and man, and the consciousness of the unity is the Confucian ideal of *jen*. It is against this intellectual backdrop that K'ang quotes Tung Chung-shu as saying: "Heaven is *jen*. Heaven covers and nurtures all the ten thousand things in the world. It not only transforms and gives birth to them; it also cultivates and completes them.... People receive humanity from Heaven and become humanized."[71]

---

67. 1969, chüan 6, pt. 1: 7b, 22b–23b.
68. Ibid.: 6a–8a, 11a–18b.
69. Ibid.: 9a–17a.
70. 1968: 3a. For similar ideas in K'ang's writings, see K'ang (1969, chüan 6, pt. 1: 10a; 1968, chüan 1: 4a, 6b).
71. 1969, chüan 6, pt. 1: 10b–11a, 18b–24b.

Thus, like its Confucian prototype, K'ang's idea of *jen*, first of all, represents a metaphysical world view. As such, it, again like its Confucian prototype, reveals not only what the world essentially is, but also what it should be. In this way, the idea of *jen* projects a moral ideal or a value pattern seen as built into the structure of reality.

Jen *as a Moral Ideal*

Jen as a moral ideal was first spelled out in an educational program that K'ang sets forth in his *Ch'ang-hsing hsüeh-chi*.[72] Outwardly, K'ang's educational program is a linear descendant of the eclectic approach to Confucian scholarship in vogue among scholars of the late Ch'ing, such as Tseng Kuo-fan, Ch'en Li, and K'ang's teacher, Chu Tz'u-ch'i.[73] Following their model, he divides the curriculum into four categories: moral philosophy (*i-li chih hsüeh*), practical statesmanship (*ching-shih chih hsüeh*), textual criticism (*k'ao-chü chih hsüeh*), and composition of poetry and prose (*tz'u-chang chih hsüeh*). But, evincing his commitment to the practical orientation of Confucianism, he emphasizes the primacy of the moral philosophy and practical statesmanship in Confucian education and considers the other two as of only secondary significance.[74] To justify and elaborate his view here, he writes detailed commentaries on Confucius' dictum in the *Analects*: "Set one's heart upon the Way, support oneself by its power, lean upon humanity, seek diversion in the arts."[75]

One striking characteristic of this dictum is that the first three precepts deal with moral cultivation; only the last one deals with intellectual study. In adopting this dictum, K'ang clearly accepts the Confucian view that moral education takes precedence over intellectual study. Further, K'ang's commentaries on the first three precepts drew heavily on the moral philosophy of Sung-Ming neo-Confucianism. We have seen that the Sung-Ming neo-Confucian moral philosophy already had an important place in K'ang's writings of 1885–1887, when he was under the heavy influence of Chu Hsi's moral philosophy. Now in the *Ch'ang-hsing hsüeh-chi*, Chu Hsi's influence no longer predominates. Instead, K'ang's program for moral education reflects diverse influences from neo-Confucianism, which, taken together, point to an overall approach to moral cultivation, which stands closer in spirit to the Lu-Wang School than to the Chu Hsi School. It may be recalled here that, in his recollection of his study under K'ang in the early 1890s, Liang Ch'i-ch'ao notes the moral philosophy of the Lu-Wang School as an important component of K'ang's instructional program.[76]

This leaning toward the moral philosophy of the Lu-Wang School

---

72. 1976c, 9: 4–5.
73. Ch'ien Mu (1966: 81–136).
74. 1976c, 9: 16–18, 21–25.
75. Ibid.: 6.
76. Liang Ch'i-ch'ao (1936, *wen-chi*, ts'e 4, chüan 11: 16–17).

is clearly reflected in K'ang's commentaries on the initial precept of Confucius' dictum referred to above. The purpose of his commentaries was to show the primacy of goal-setting in the Confucian concept of self-cultivation by way of elucidating some major categories of neo-Confucian moral philosophy.

As K'ang observes, the goal of Confucian education is, of course, the Confucian Way, which is nothing other than the idea of *jen* and its cognate, *i* (righteousness).[77] But the problem is: how does one set the moral goal? The first thing he emphasizes is the Confucian idea of *ko-wu* (investigation of things). He was well aware of the controversy surrounding this idea in the neo-Confucian tradition, and significantly, he rejected Chu Hsi's "intellectualistic" interpretation, which defines the idea as meaning patient and extensive "investigation of things," in order to grasp the organizing principles underlying the myriad phenomena of reality and hence to achieve the intellectual enlightenment required for self-cultivation. In K'ang's view, such an extensive "investigation of things" is impossible for a novice in moral education. What is needed above all is an awareness and assertion of the primacy of our human mind over the external world. Only with this awareness and assertion can we have the inner, moral will to resist and prevail over the innumerable temptations and distractions of the outside world—in short, to withstand what he calls "the materialization of man" (*wu-chih erh jen-hua-wu*).[78] K'ang's interpretation of *ko-wu* reminds one of Wang Yang-ming's view, which derives from Mencius' conception of mind as the self-sufficient source of moral spiritual cultivation. Consequently, it is of little surprise that, in his interpretation of the idea *ko-wu*, he reaffirms the Mencian emphasis on the priority of inner, moral mind over anything else as the first step to moral education. To support his argument here, he quotes the Mencian dictum: "First establish the most important. Then, on small things, one will not be conquered by the outside world."[79] This Mencian approach, he added, is not confined to Confucianism but is shared by Taoism and Buddhism, because no one can embark on the arduous task of seeking the spiritual way without nurturing a hardened inner will to begin with.[80]

K'ang's stress on the primacy of the inner mind and will for setting the moral goal of life is illustrated by the accent he puts on another important category of Confucian moral thought, *shen-tu* (self-surveillance in solitude). For K'ang, this is a key Confucian category, which was transmitted by Confucius' grandson Tzu Ssu, enshrined in the two sacred texts *The Doctrine of the Mean* and *The Great Learning*, and further developed especially in the thought of Liu Tsung-chou, the late Ming neo-Confucian philosopher of the

---
77. Ibid.: 6–17.
78. Ibid.: 7–8.
79. Ibid.: 7.
80. Ibid.: 8.

Wang Yang-ming School. It is predicated on a problem of major importance entailed by the neo-Confucian idea of the inner, moral orientation of the human mind. If the human mind has this moral potential, how do we make sure that the potential will issue forth in the right action when our minds are confronted with moral situations in our daily life? For K'ang, the answer lies in the idea of *shen-tu*, which enjoins self-surveillance in solitude before one makes any response to a moral situation in the external world. This kind of self-surveillance would keep our inner will and motive in a constant state of moral alertness and preparedness.[81]

Following the precept of "setting one's heart on the Way" was the precept, "support oneself by its power." These comprise a cluster of ideas aimed at the moral transformation of character, most of which have a clear provenance in the spiritual heritage of Sung-Ming neo-Confucianism. This provenance is certainly shown in the first idea K'ang elaborates under the precept, that is, quiet sitting in meditation to induce mental quiescence (*ching*); in his commentaries he makes it clear that he owes his idea of quiescence to such neo-Confucian philosophers as Chou Tun-i and Ch'en Hsien-chang, the Ming philosopher of K'ang's home province. Ch'en was especially important, because K'ang pays a special tribute to Ch'en's philosophy of quiescence.[82] Understood in the context of this philosophy, quiescence refers to a kind of spiritual equanimity and naturalness, born of a profound faith in the unity of Heaven and man.[83] Consequently, as K'ang observes, the attainment of quiescence involves a cosmic feeling of living in communion with "Heaven and Earth," the encompassing whole. It is a form of moral-spiritual self-sufficiency that would enable one to transcend all the worldly vanities.[84]

The premium K'ang put on the idea of quiescence leads logically to the second idea he elaborated for his conception of moral transformation of character: the cultivation of an unperturbed mind. To explain the latter idea, he not only drew upon the Mencian notion of the cosmic feeling that feeds extraordinary moral courage and spiritual élan (*hao-jan chih ch'i*). He also evoked the Buddhist idea of *samadhi*. What both ideas suggest, he pointed out, is a notion of mind tuned to the supernatural order. Because of this feeling of being supported by the supernatural order, one would be enabled to have "a human face but a heart of Heaven" (*jen-mao erh t'ien-hsin*). The latter is meant to connote a peace of mind invulnerable to any worldly temptations or distractions as well as to any earthly fears or worries. This is what Mencius calls an unperturbed mind and what

---

81. Ibid.: 9–10.
82. Ibid.: 10–11.
83. For an analysis of Ch'en's notion of "quiescence," see Jen Yu-wen in de Bary (1970: 53–92).
84. 1976c, 9: 10–11.

K'ang deems indispensable to any worthy achievement one attempts in this world.[85]

The next category K'ang expounds under the topic of moral transformation of character is what he calls metamorphosis of temperament (*pien-hua ch'i-chih*).[86] This is a central category of the neo-Confucian approach to the moral cultivation of self, predicated on the neo-Confucian view of human nature.[87] According to the latter view, the human self, like any other existence, is made up not only of principle (*li*), but also of material force (*ch'i*). This material force is something not necessarily evil, but it is apt to generate evil, inasmuch as it often exists in a turbid and muddy state, thereby making it difficult for principle to manifest itself properly. In consequence, beyond purifying and calming the inner mind, the neo-Confucian transformation of self also involves purification of material force. In his commentaries, K'ang cites example after example from neo-Confucian philosophers to show that extraordinary, painstaking efforts are usually required to purify one's material force and change one's temperament.[88]

As the final category under the rubric of moral transformation of character, K'ang recommends the behavioral manifestation of the moral inwardness he enunciates under the preceding categories. This is what he called "decorum and restraint in manners and conduct." So far, we have seen moral education presented as a step-by-step process, moving from the inner cultivation of mind-heart to the outer control of behavior. But for K'ang this process is only the self-regarding aspect of moral cultivation. For moral fulfillment, this aspect is only the first half of a process that must be continued and completed by an other-regarding aspect of moral cultivation. K'ang treats it under the third precept of the maxim mentioned above: "lean on humanity." Here again, K'ang's model is the Confucian ideal of gradual extension of one's love and concern to broader and broader circles of people in society. Typically, the process starts with one's family, where it manifests itself in the Confucian virtues of filial and brotherly love (*hsiao t'i*). But the emphasis is typically put on the idea of "extending" the family love to people outside the family. Thus, K'ang extolls such social virtues as trustworthiness, sympathy, and generosity. He gives a special accent to fellow feeling as an indispensable part of humanity. It is this feeling, K'ang emphasizes, that allows us to empathize and commiserate with any human being as such. Obviously, K'ang is here translating the Confucian ideal of all-under-Heaven as one single family. For him this universal *gemeinschaft* is the highest expression of *jen* and consequently the ultimate end of moral education.[89]

---

85. Ibid.: 11.
86. Ibid.
87. For an analysis of the centrality of this category, see Mou Tsung-san (1963: 68–78).
88. 1976c, 9: 11–12.
89. Ibid.: 12–15.

Such, then, were K'ang's commentaries on Confucius' dictum, adapted by him from the *Analects* as the guiding principle of his philosophy of moral education. Implicit in these commentaries is a life ideal with two characteristics. First of all, human life involves the fulfillment of two interdependent commitments: a self-regarding commitment to the moral perfection of the individual and an other-regarding commitment to the moral perfection of society. Each complements the other, and both are essential to the realization of *jen* as a sort of *telos* of human existence. Meanwhile, life is also seen as a dramatic, consummatory process that begins with goal-setting and firming up the commitment to the goal. It then proceeds with mental and behavioral disciplines that aim at the moral transformation of character. It culminates in the fulfillment of *jen*, when the moral energy of self is channeled into building up a moral society. Clearly, it is a life ideal harking back to the Confucian life ideal of inner sageliness and outer kingliness, and it justifies the primacy of the two subjects in his educational program: the moral philosophy of self-realization and the study of practical statesmanship.

K'ang's Concept of Human Nature

Beyond the life ideal of quest for moral perfection of self and society, K'ang's program of moral education also implies a note of moral inwardness that underlies many of the neo-Confucian categories with which he defines self-cultivation. However, this note of moral inwardness is inhibited by a concept of human nature focused on the idea of the outer source of morality, which K'ang formulates not only in *Ch'ang-hsing hsüeh-chi*, but also in some other of his early writings, including *Wan-mu ts'ao-t'ang k'ou-shuo*.[90] In these writings, K'ang, in keeping with his cosmological conception that the whole universe is made up solely of material force, argues that human nature is composed entirely of material substance (*ch'i-chih*). Thus he takes sharp exception to the dualistic view of human nature held by the orthodox Ch'eng-Chu School of neo-Confucianism as well as to the Mencian conception of the original goodness of nature.[91] He invokes the view of the ancient philosopher Kao Tzu that human nature is just something given by the birth of life. K'ang once said: "Concerning views of human nature, Kao Tzu was entirely right while Mencius was entirely mistaken."[92] This notion of human nature as nonmoral in itself is nothing new; it represents a further development of the quasi-naturalism already evident in his pre-1890 writings.

More than ten years after K'ang wrote *Ch'ang-hsing hsüeh-chi*, he published a series of commentaries to show that the interpretation of Confucianism he worked out on the basis of the New Text teaching was also valid when

---

90. Ibid.: 1. For *Wan-mu ts'ao-t'ang k'ou-shuo*, see Li Tse-hou (1958: 74).
91. The most complete statement of K'ang's monistic view of human nature can be found in a lengthy letter he wrote to Chu I-hsin in 1891 (1976b, 20: 827–32).
92. Li Tse-hou (1958: 74).

applied to the core of neo-Confucian scripture—the *Ssu-shu*.[93] Not surprisingly, the moral-metaphysical world view as symbolized by *jen* and its concomitant ideal of moral perfection of individual and society still has a pivotal place in these commentaries. True, *jen* as an ideal of moral cultivation is not as systematically spelled out as it is in *Ch'ang-hsing hsüeh-chi*. But the ideal of "inner sagehood and outer kingliness" remains central to these commentaries.[94] However, there is one important difference separating K'ang's commentaries from *Ch'ang-hsing hsüeh-chi*. K'ang's conception of human nature as formulated in the latter went through some significant changes, resulting in an ambiguity or rather a tension in his concept of man that must be noted.

On the one hand, Kao Tzu's view of human nature as nothing but material substance (*ch'i-chih*) is played down, but it is never completely jettisoned. In fact, inasmuch as K'ang retained his cosmological view that all beings under Heaven are made up of material force, his belief in Kao Tzu's naturalistic notion of human nature more or less remains—if not explicitly, at least implicitly. Besides, in these commentaries K'ang still occasionally engages in denouncing the negative, inhibitory view of human desires that he sees at the heart of the neo-Confucian orthodoxy.[95] Meanwhile, he also at times affirms the ideal of *jen* as fulfilling all that is necessary to the growth of life, including our basic needs and desires.[96] All this points to a latent continuity between his commentaries on the *Ssu-shu* and his positive view of human instinctuality found in both his pre-1890 writing and *Ch'ang-hsing hsüeh-chi*.

On the other hand, there is also a clear shift in K'ang's writings over the years in the direction of merging Kao Tzu's view with Tung Chung-shu's dualistic conception of man. This shift reflected a tension in K'ang's thought. As noted above, his monistic world view inclined him to a "naturalistic" conception of man and a positive view of human instinctuality. But this "naturalistic" conception of man made it difficult for K'ang to articulate a major concern of his thinking: the moral-spiritual development of self. If human beings, like the rest of the "ten thousand things," are all basically made up of *ch'i*, how can one explain the unique capacity of human beings for moral-spiritual development? If this moral-spiritual development involves a process of struggle and effort, as K'ang depicts in his *Ch'ang-hsing*

---

93. K'ang made this clear in the preface he wrote for each of his commentaries on the *Ssu-shu*. According to his chronological autobiography, he had written commentaries on each of the *Ssu-shu*, but the text of his commentary on *Ta-hsüeh* is lost. Only his preface to this commentary is extant. See Lo Jung-pang (1967: 189–92).

94. Although K'ang's commentaries tend to emphasize the outer aspect of the ideal, the ideal of inner sagehood and outer kingliness was taken for granted throughout his commentaries. See K'ang's preface to *Ta-hsüeh chu* in *K'ang Nan-hai hsien-sheng nien-p'u hsü-pien* [A sequel to the chronological biography of K'ang Yu-wei] in K'ang (1976c, 22: 31–32).

95. E.g., see K'ang's remarks (1968b, chüan 2: 11a, 12b–13a; chüan 4: 16a–17a).

96. Ibid., chüan 2: 11a; chüan 4: 16b.

hsüeh-chi, how to justify this process without conceiving a notion of good battling against evil for the possession of the human soul? To answer questions like these, some kind of dualistic conception of man has to be worked out to differentiate the moral-spiritual function of the self from its nonmoral, natural endowment. This is why historically some of the thinkers in the Confucian tradition, such as Wang Fu-chih and Tai Chen, who embraced a *ch'i*-only monistic world view often arrived at a dualistic conception of man in one form or another. This is also more or less the logic behind K'ang's shift from a monistic view of man toward a dualistic view.

K'ang accomplishes this shift by emphasizing the complexity of Kao Tzu's view. Kao Tzu's principal position, he notes, was, of course, the view that human nature is nothing other than the physical endowment with which a human being is born. But he now maintains that this view is tenable only as long as one makes the further distinction between the refined part and the coarse part within the physical endowment.[97] These two parts he calls by various names. Sometimes he terms them *chih-ch'i* and *t'i-p'o chih ch'i* or *teh-hsing* and *chih-hsing*.[98] Sometimes he borrows Buddhist or Christian terms to characterize them.[99] Behind the sometimes confusing terminology, the thrust of K'ang's arguments is clear: if the distinction is not made, then there would be no way to distinguish the human beings who have the moral-spiritual capacity from those non-humans who don't.

But this, in K'ang's view, is exactly what Kao Tzu failed to do in his main position. Nevertheless, he notes, Kao Tzu's thought involved another view, apart from his main position, which can be found in Kao Tzu's assertion: "Human nature is like the willow tree, and righteousness is like a cup or a bowl. To turn human nature into humanity and righteousness is like turning willow into cups and bowls."[100] Implied in this assertion is a belief that human beings have an innate moral potential that can be developed through education into actual good conduct just as a willow tree carries in itself a substance that can be made into a cup or a bowl. But K'ang accents the distinction between moral potential and actual moral conduct, arguing that the implication that education needs to be brought to bear from outside to turn a human being into a moral creature presupposes a belief in the presence of something nonmoral in human nature. For K'ang, this view of Kao Tzu merges into Tung Chung-shu's dualistic conception of human nature.[101]

This was made possible by the presence of a basic ambiguity in Tung's anthropological thought. On the one hand, Tung seemed to agree with Kao

---

97. Ibid., chüan 2: 1b–2a, 8a.
98. Ibid., chüan 1: 16a; chüan 2: 2a.
99. 1968a: 32b.
100. K'ang 1968b, chüan 2: 8b.
101. Ibid.: 8b–9a.

Tzu's concept of human nature and looked on *hsing* as a kind of basic substance (*chih*), which is naturally given and hence nonmoral in itself. On the other hand, Tung attempted to synthesize the views of both Mencius and Hsün Tzu by maintaining that the basic substance that he called "nature" (*hsing*) is of two kinds, one with potential for goodness that he also inexplicably termed "nature," the other with potential for evil that he identified as "feelings" (*ch'ing*). The external manifestation of nature is the virtue of humanity (*jen*), and that of feelings, the desire of covetousness (*t'an*).[102]

Central to Tung's dualistic concept is the idea that the potential for goodness is not goodness itself. Failure to make the distinction, Tung believed, was what led Mencius astray. To drive home the distinction, Tung Chung-shu drew analogies from nature:

> Goodness is like a kernel of grain; the nature is like a growing stalk of the grain. Though the stalk produces the kernel, it cannot itself be called the kernel, and though nature produces goodness, it cannot itself be called good.... Therefore, I say that nature possesses the stuff of goodness, but that it cannot by itself act for goodness. This is no mere rhetoric on my part, for it represents actual truth. What Heaven creates stops at the silk cocoon, the hemp plant, or the stalk of grain. From the hemp plant, cloth is produced; from the cocoon, silk; and from the grain stalk, kernels of grain. (Likewise) from nature is produced goodness. These advances are all achieved by the sages by continuing (the work initiated by) Heaven. They could not be reached by the feelings and nature in their raw state.[103]

K'ang echoes this idea effusively in one of his own writings:

> There is nothing more splendid than Tung Chung-shu's statement that what is born by the Heaven and Earth are called "nature" and "feelings." "Feelings" are also part of human nature. Heaven has its dual manifestations of *yin* and *yang*, and the body also has the dual qualities of covetousness and humanity. The same thing was also said in the *Comprehensive Discussions in the White Tiger Hall*. It really is an insightful and subtle observation.[104]

K'ang's acceptance of Tung Chung-shu's dualistic conception of human nature gave rise to the two different concepts of man that underlie his concern for moral perfection. One was a Manichean image of man, which saw a person as composed of two parts locked in an incessant struggle. K'ang says: "The controller of a mind-heart is the soul (*hun-ling*). The controller of ears and eyes is the physical substance (*p'o-chih*). The soul and physical substance are differently disposed and therefore constantly battling with each other."[105] This battle within the self of every human being is usually won by the side of physical substance, because, according to K'ang, "man

---

102. Feng Yu-lan (1959: 515–18).
103. Ibid.: 517–18.
104. 1969, chüan 6, pt. 1: 29b–30a. For similar ideas, see K'ang (1968b, chüan 2: 8a).
105. 1968b, chüan 2: 2a–b, 8a, 21a.

has within himself more physical substance than soul... and stronger physical substance than soul." In brief, an individual person is liable to what K'ang calls materialization (*jen hua wu*), which his mind-heart is often powerless to resist.[106]

But this grim image of man paled before another, more optimistic image that came to dominate, especially, K'ang's commentaries on the *Mencius* and the *Doctrine of the Mean*. As shown above, K'ang's Manichean image of man postulated a soul-like *hun-ling* as opposed to physical substance. For K'ang, this postulate implies a belief in the innate moral potential of man. Consequently, he holds that both Tung Chung-shu's concept of man and the Mencian theory of human nature share a concept of moral inwardness, as long as Mencius' theory is taken to mean that human nature is potentially, rather than actually, good. Theoretically, K'ang thus sees no problem in accepting the Mencian concept of moral inwardness on the premise of Tung Chung-shu's dualistic conception of man. In fact, in many places in his commentaries the concept of moral inwardness bulks so large that it overshadows Tung Chung-shu's dualistic conception of man.[107]

A clear example of K'ang's preoccupation with moral inwardness is in his commentary on the *Chung yung* (Doctrine of the mean), which features moral inwardness as a main theme. This theme is sounded at the beginning of the text: "That which is bestowed by Heaven is called man's nature; the fulfillment of this nature is called the Way; the cultivation of the Way is called culture."[108] K'ang's commentary on this passage is typical of the view he maintains throughout the text: "Human being is not made by human being. He is born by Heaven. [His] nature is the substance which he is born with. It is an endowment from the Heavenly material force and constitutes the numinous light (*shen-ming*) of one's self. It is not the physical body given to one by one's parents."[109] Elsewhere in his commentary, he calls the "numinous light" in our nature "moral nature" (*teh-hsing*), the "substance of nature" (*hsing-t'i*), the "luminous virtue" (*ming-teh*), and the "soul" (*ling-hun*).[110] Whatever he calls it, it clearly points to the priority in his mind of the moral inwardness of man.

K'ang's preoccupation with moral inwardness is evident in his commentary on *Mencius*, too. True, when he comments in detail on Mencius' concept of the original goodness of human nature, he takes pains to qualify it by fitting it into Tung Chung-shu's dualistic conception of human nature. But, in many other places in the text, he merely follows the thrust of Mencius'

---

106. Ibid.: 20b, 21a.
107. K'ang spells out his endorsement of the Mencian conception of moral inwardness on the premise of Tung Chung-shu's dualistic concept of man, mainly in chüan 2 (1968b).
108. 1968a: 1a.
109. Ibid.
110. Ibid.: 32b.

arguments in articulating the belief in moral inwardness. For example, expanding on Mencius' concept of moral inwardness, he observes at one point: "Nature is the bright soul of a person which is an endowment from Heaven." It is something which "would not change or perish with birth and death [of a life]."[111] To drive home the conception of moral inwardness, he sometimes focuses on Mencius' idea of innate moral mind-heart, thus sidestepping the problem of human nature; sometimes he invokes Ch'eng Hao's identification of moral mind with the Heavenly principle; sometime he presses the idea of inner light by analogy with the Buddhist nature of *Dharmakaya*.[112] In these ways the idea of moral inwardness, which existed only implicitly in *Ch'ang-hsing hsüeh-chi*, finally comes to surface in K'ang's commentaries on the *Ssu-shu*. More importantly, it feeds a belief that came to dominate K'ang's conception of man: the kind of quest for moral perfection as depicted in *Ch'ang-hsing hsüeh-chi* can be fulfilled by anyone who is willing to make the effort to develop his inner moral potential. As a corollary, the idea of moral autonomy of self accompanies the idea of moral inwardness in K'ang's interpretation of neo-Confucian moral thought. As he observes at the beginning of his commentary on *Mencius*:

> The mind of commiseration is *jen*; it is electricity; it is ether. Everyone has it. Therefore, we can say that human nature is all good.... What is the proof of the goodness of human nature? The proof lies in the fact that we all have a mind endowed with the feeling of commiseration, the feeling of shame and dislike, the feeling of respect and reverence and the feeling of right and wrong. It is because human nature carries the roots of these four virtues—humanity, righteousness, propriety, and wisdom—that human beings rise above all the myriad things.... It is because everyone has these four moral roots that all human beings can become equal with each other and self-autonomous. Those who say that they cannot [become morally good] are giving up their Heaven-endowed gift, forfeiting their natural obligations.... Consequently they can be seen as debasing themselves.[113]

Thus, from K'ang's commentaries on the *Ssu-shu* emerges a concept of man somewhat different from that of the *Ch'ang-hsing hsüeh-chi*. The Confucian concern with the moral perfection of self and society is no less central to the former than to the latter. But the concern is now supported by a more optimistic notion of human nature—a conception influenced as much by Sung-Ming neo-Confucians as by the Han Confucianism of Tung Chung-shu.

Radicalization of Jen

As analyzed above, *jen* symbolized for K'ang not only a religiometaphysical world view, but an ideal of quest for moral perfection of self and society.

---

111. 1968b, chüan 1: 1b–9b, 16a.
112. Ibid., chüan 1: 2b–3b, 15a.
113. Ibid.: 2b–3a.

Although this quest doubtless derived its basic impulse from Confucian tradition, his definition of moral perfection departs in some major ways from the Confucian definition, particularly in its emphasis on a radicalism that is more than what Confucian moral values could contain. To bring out this radicalism, I will compare K'ang's concept of Confucian ethics with that of Tung Chung-shu, whose major work, as indicated above, served as a sort of springboard for K'ang's formulation of his world view.

Tung Chung-shu's moral thought was a fusion of two kinds of ethics. On the one side was an ethics of spiritual aspiration focused on the ideal of moral perfection, which he inherited from classical Confucianism. Central to this ethics was of course the *jen* ideal believed to be rooted in Heaven, the higher reality of the cosmos. For Tung, this Heaven-endowed virtue manifested itself in the feelings of love, compassion, and other fellow-feelings.[114] Coupled with the other-regarding ideal of *jen* was a self-regarding ideal that Tung also stressed, namely, *i*, the sense of righteousness. For him righteousness was something that nourishes the mind-heart just as material profit nourishes the body. Because the mind-heart was believed to be the noble part of the self, he saw *i* as something that distinguished the inner, higher self from the outer, lower self.[115] Together, then, *jen* and *i* stood for an ethics believed to be imbedded not only in the higher reality of cosmos, but also in the deeper reaches of self.

In Tung's moral thought, the ethics of spiritual aspiration, however, was closely articulated with an ethics of social constraints—*Li*. Just as the ethics of spiritual aspirations has been seen rooted in the higher reality, the latter was also believed to be imbedded in the cosmic order. Because the cosmic order is organized by the relation of superordination and subordination between the two basic cosmic forces of *yin* and *yang*, human society is ordered in the same pattern. Hence, this ethics of social constraints embodied a hierarchical order. For Tung, this hierarchical order was the essence of the ethics of *Li*.[116]

The linchpin of this hierarchical order was the doctrine of the "three bonds." According to Tung, three relations—ruler-subject, father-son, and husband-wife—are the core of the nexus of all human relations. Underlying this concept of three bonds is Tung's view that kingship and family are basically cosmic institutions, and consequently that they are as unalterable and sacrosanct as the cosmic order of Heaven and Earth.[117]

Whereas Tung Chung-shu's thought was marked by a natural harmony between the ethics of spiritual aspirations and the ethics of social constraints, this natural harmony is significantly lacking in K'ang's writings. When

---

114. 1969, chüan 6, pt. 2: 1a–2b.
115. Ibid.: 6a–b.
116. Ibid.: 8a–9a.
117. Ibid.: 13b–17a, 18a–27a.

K'ang wrote his interpretation of Tung Chung-shu's philosophy, *Ch'un-ch'iu Tung-shih hsüeh* (Tung Chung-shu's study of the Annals of Spring and Autumn) in 1897, he made no effort to articulate the fusion of the two ethics. Instead, near the end of his book he lists all the major moral values discussed in Tung Chung-shu's *Ch'un-ch'iu fan-lu* (Luxuriant dew of the Annals of Spring and Autumn). Significantly, the list first names the values that belong to the ethics of spiritual aspirations, such as humanity, righteousness, and wisdom. These values are followed by values that one would group under the ethics of social constraints, including the doctrine of the three bonds. This order clearly reflects K'ang's priorities and emphasis. Further, whereas K'ang writes commentaries on many of the items in the former group to underline his endorsement of the ethics of spiritual aspiration, for the latter group he writes sparse commentaries that reflect no approval on his part.[118]

K'ang's preference for one kind of ethics over the other grew into a tendency in his commentaries on the *Ssu-shu* to set the ethics of spiritual aspiration apart from the ethics of social constraints and to emphasize the former's centrality in the Confucian ethics. This tendency stands out most strikingly in his commentaries on the *Doctrine of the Mean* and *Mencius*. At one place in his commentaries, for example, he discusses the Confucian notion of five relations.[119] Instead of subordinating the five relations to the doctrine of three bonds, as Tung Chung-shu did in his *Ch'un-ch'iu fan-lu*, he first subsumes the five relations under the so-called three cardinal virtues, namely, intelligence, human-heartedness, and courage. Then he collapses the latter three into the moral-spiritual ideal of *jen* or *ch'eng* (sincerity), the two ideals that lay at the core of the Confucian ethics of spiritual aspiration.[120]

A similar tendency marked his commentary on *Mencius*. To the extent that he refers to the ideal of *Li*, he expounds it largely in the context of the Mencian conception of four innate virtues, namely, *jen*, *i* (righteousness), *Li* (sense of propriety), and *chih* (wisdom). In his view, all four can be summed up by the ideal of *jen*.[121] For K'ang, then, the meaning of *Li* lay more in a moral sense of propriety as an integral part of the Confucian ethics of spiritual aspiration than in the ethics of social constraints centered around the doctrine of three bonds as in the Han Confucian thought of Tung Chung-shu and *Pai-hu t'ung* (Comprehensive discussions of White Tiger Hall).

These views alarmed some of his Confucian colleagues. One of them, the well-known scholar Chu I-hsin, wrote to him to warn of the ideological danger that attended his line of interpretation:

---

118. See ibid.: 1a–29b.
119. 1968a: 22a.
120. Ibid.: 22a–b. See also 1968b, chüan 1: 18b.
121. 1968b, chüan 3: 5a.

When the teachings of *Li* are understood, *jen* is there. This is to speak of the substance of the basic truth. Love is (in its very nature) graded.... This is to speak of the manifestation of the truth. If we understand *jen* outside this context, then (we would mistake it for) the Mohist ideal of savior. It is indeed the case that a little confusion (concerning the basics) would result in making enormous mistakes. Everyone should love his relatives and respect his seniors. This sounds selfish, but in fact it is the most public-minded principle.... If we understand love while disregarding this principle, we would ignore four out of the five human relationships. We would then really hurt the way the relationships between ruler and subject, father and son, brother and brother, and husband and wife should work.[122]

Chu's alarm was totally justified, because K'ang at that time was indeed inclined to blend the Confucian ethics of spiritual aspirations with non-Confucian persuasions of moral thought, reflecting the latter's influence over him. One such persuasion was Buddhism. In his commentary on the *Doctrine of the Mean*, for example, he identifies the three cardinal Confucian virtues—intelligence, human-heartedness, and courage—with the Buddhist ideals of wisdom (*prajna*), compassion (*varuna*), and the undaunting, fearless spirit (*virya*).[123] The equivalence K'ang establishes between the Confucian and Buddhist ideals, especially in the case of *jen* and compassion, is not accidental, because it is a recurring tendency on K'ang's part to interpret such moral ideals as *jen* and *ch'eng* in terms of the Buddhist world view of undifferentiated oneness and universal compassion.[124]

More significant, however, is K'ang's incorporation of Western liberal ideals into the Confucian ethics of spiritual aspiration. We noted above that he inherited the Confucian tendency to see *jen* as more than a moral ideal. To him it also symbolized a world view centered on the belief in the unity of Heaven and man. In the course of formulating his interpretation of Confucianism, over the span of more than a decade, K'ang spells out this world view in several versions. One version is that Heaven and human beings are all pervaded by the material force (*ch'i*), to constitute an undifferentiated whole. For him the view of all human beings belonging to an undifferentiated whole makes social egalitarianism a compelling value. Another version revolves around the idea that every person has a Heaven-endowed, innate capacity for moral cultivation and, therefore, for serving Heaven and fulfilling its mandate. On the basis of this idea, K'ang, following Mencius, calls the individual person a "Heavenly citizen" (*t'ien-min*).[125] Linking up this idea with Tung Chung-shu's belief that every human individual is born by Heaven, K'ang maintains that the "son of Heaven" should not just be the

---

122. Li Tse-hou (1958: 84).
123. 1968a: 22b.
124. Ibid.: 29b–30a, 31a–b; see also 1968b, chüan 1: 15.
125. 1968b, chüan 1: 6b–7a.

emperor's title, but the title of every individual person.[126] He thus sees in the Confucian ideal of self-realization a spirit basically kindred to the Western liberal ideal of an "independent and self-governing person."[127] K'ang says in his commentary on Mencius: "Every person is born by Heaven. Therefore, he should not be regarded as a citizen of state (*kuo-min*) but as a citizen of Heaven (*t'ien-min*). Since everyone is born by Heaven, he should subordinate himself to Heaven. [Consequently] all people are independent and equal."[128] In this way he arrives at the view that Western liberal ideals, such as individual liberty, equality, and democracy, are all natural corollaries of *jen* as a moral vision of cosmos and man. Thus, the moral radicalism that appears in his writings of 1885–1887 takes the form of radicalization of *jen* as the epitome of the Confucian ethics of spiritual aspiration in his post-1890 writings.

Historization of Jen

When radicalism appears in K'ang's pre-1890 writings, it appears in an incongruous form, existing side by side with conservative positions. On the surface, this incongruity continues to exist in his interpretations of Confucianism. Although K'ang in his commentaries on the *Ssu-shu* tends to focus on the Confucian ethics of spiritual aspirations, he does not choose to repudiate totally the ethics of social constraints. In fact, he still endorses certain prominent conservative values, most notably the family values centered around filial piety. For example, he still accepts the view that filial piety constitutes the only root out of which gradually grows a much broader feeling of love for the whole of mankind as enjoined by the ideal of *jen*.[129] However, in actuality there is no incongruity. To understand the dissolution of this incongruity in K'ang's post-1890 writings, I must discuss a central dimension of his interpretation of Confucianism so far not noted. This is the view of history that he developed in the context of his interpretation of the New Text teachings of Western Han Confucianism. We saw earlier how the latter projected a picture of the cosmos as a living organism, an encompassing whole made up of material forces constantly engaged in motion. Consequently, the cosmos exists not in a state of stasis, but in an interminable process of movement, growth, and changes.

This cosmological dynamism has a temporal dimension, as reflected in the two views of history predominant in the principal text of New Text Confucianism—the *Kung-yang* commentaries on the *Annals of Spring and Autumn*. One historical view, expressed in the theory of the five elements, saw history as an endless repetition of five stages dictated by the revolution of five

---

126. 1969, chüan 6, pt. 1: 9b.
127. 1968b, chüan 1: 3a, 15a–b.
128. Ibid.: 6b.
129. Ibid., chüan 3: 5a–12a.

cosmic forces in a fixed order.[130] The other was enunciated in the doctrine of the so-called three sequences, which saw history as repetitions of three stages in accordance with the revolution of three cosmic processes.[131] Despite the different forms in which the two conceptions of history were set forth, both share the cyclical view of historical process as the manifestation of cosmic rhythm.

Within this predominantly cyclical framework, there was, however, a cryptic, inchoately formulated view of historical development based on a periodization of the history of Confucius' native state of Lu. According to this view, the history of Lu comprised three stages, evolving from the distant past, which Confucius had only heard about indirectly from tradition, through the period of the recent past, which he had heard about, to the present age, which he had witnessed with his own eyes.[132] For Confucius, these three ages did not just have chronological significance. They also represented three stages of social development—"decay and chaos" (*chü-luan*), "rising peace" (*sheng-p'ing*), and "universal peace" (*t'ai-p'ing*).[133] But because this three-stage periodization was believed to be Confucius' vision as presented in his compilation of *Ch'un-ch'iu*, it was seen as having a significance beyond the history of the state of Lu. In fact, it became part of the prophetic symbolism of the New Text Confucianism, which saw Confucius as an "uncrowned sage-king" speaking to posterity.[134] Seen in this light, the three-stage schema is clearly meant to have a universal significance.

But this three-stage schema, like the prophetic symbolism as a whole, is ambiguous. Although the schema in isolation views history as a unilinear development from past toward present, it is couched within a larger cyclical framework. It is left unclear in the *Kung-yang* texts whether the schema symbolizes a process unrepeatable or irreversible in the future.[135] However, when New Text Confucianism reemerged in the late Ch'ing, leading scholars of this persuasion, such as Kung Tzu-chen and Wei Yüan, understood the concept of the three stages largely in either the cyclical sense or the devolutionary sense.[136] It is against this background that we must consider how K'ang Yu-wei accepted this schema and incorporated it into his moral-metaphysical world view.

In K'ang's writings, the formulations of the schema often vary, because

---

130. Ku Chieh-kang (1970: 11–14, 25–32).
131. Ku Chieh-kang (1957: 3).
132. Ch'ien Mu (1958b: 243–45).
133. Ibid.
134. Ibid.: 241–45, 245–47. For a concise explanation of the New Text teachings, see Chou Yü-t'ung (1926: 1–53).
135. Ch'ien Mu (1958b: 243–45).
136. Lu Pao-ch'ien (1978: 242–43). Although there were some notions of secular historical development in Wei Yüan's thought, these notions were still contained in an historical consciousness that is basically cyclical; see Wu Tse (1971: 81–108).

he also adapts the historical schema of three stages to the social ideals of another major Confucian text, namely, the chapter entitled "Evolution of Rites" (*Li-yün*) in the *Li chi* (Book of rites).[137] The result is a different formulation of historical development by stages, which K'ang uses interchangeably with the version of three stages in the *Kung-yang* tradition. In this *Li-yün* version, he collapses the three stages into two, with the "age of grand unity" (*ta-t'ung*) corresponding to the "age of universal peace" and with the "age of small peace" (*hsiao-k'ang*) presumably covering both the "age of decay and chaos" and the "age of rising peace."[138] Whatever formulation K'ang gives of the historical stages, he clearly conceives these historical stages as constituting a unilinear, irreversible process of evolutionary development. For such a view of history, he is perhaps less indebted to the *Kung-yang* teachings than to the Western view of history, which is a process of unilinear development in both its secular and religious guises.[139]

Because of this evolutionary view of history, K'ang's notion of *jen* goes through a "historization," so to speak. The full realization of *jen* is projected to a distant but definite point in the future, the "age of grand unity" or the "age of universal peace," which was to take a protracted, stage-by-stage process of development to reach.[140] This final fulfillment of *jen* was to be marked by radicalism, in the sense of transcending and negating such central institutions of the current order as family and kingship. In the meantime, however, these institutions were still given a legitimate place in prior stages of historical development. Thus, although the burden of K'ang's commentary on *Mencius* is to develop the implication of moral radicalism that, he believed, would be entailed by the fulfillment of *jen*, he also acknowledges the legitimacy of the doctrine of three bonds for the "age of chaos" in the

---

137. K'ang, *Li-yün chu* (1976c, 9: 1b).

138. There were some ambiguities in K'ang's thought on how to integrate the two schemes. In some of his writings, the "age of grand unity" (*ta-t'ung*) corresponds to the "age of universal peace," and the "age of small peace" (*hsiao-k'ang*) covers both "the age of decay and chaos" (*chü-lüan shih*) and the "age of rising peace" (*sheng-p'ing shih*). See Liang Ch'i-ch'ao (1936, *wen-chi*, ts'e 3, chüan 6: 68). In other writings, whereas the age of grand unity corresponds to the age of universal peace, the age of small peace corresponds only to the age of rising peace, thus leaving the age of decay and chaos no place in his scheme, which he developed on the basis of "Li-yün." For this scheme, see K'ang Yu-wei, *Li-yün chu* [The evolution of the rites annotated] (1976c, 9: 2–4, 7, 10; 1968b, chüan 1: 15a).

139. K'ang first developed his unilinear evolutionary view of history in the decade of the 1890s. By that time, he must already have been familiar with Western views of history through his intensive study of Western learning since the early 1880s (1976c, 22: 11–23). Chinese scholars, such as Chou Yü-t'ung and T'ang Chih-chün, all emphasize the shaping influence of Yen Fu on K'ang's evolutionary view of history. Yen Fu doubtless contributed to K'ang's view in this regard, but he did not necessarily constitute K'ang's only source, because the notion of history as a unilinear development was also made available in China at that time by Christian missionaries, such as Timothy Richard and Young Allen, especially through the *Globe* magazine and the publications of the Society for the Study of Self-Strengthening (Ch'iang-hsüeh hui). See Ch'en Ch'i-yün (1962, 16: 111–13).

140. *Li-yün chu* (1976c, 9: 7); 1968b, chüan 1: 4a–5a.

past. In his *Li-yün chu*, he writes extensive commentaries to give expression to the view that the code of *Li* was something indispensable for human society prior to the final advent of the universal moral community in the future. This was why he spoke of an "evolution of *Li*" (*Li-yün*) preceding the "evolution of *jen*" (*jen-yün*) in the development of human society.[141] In other words, according to K'ang, the advent of *jen* must be prepared by the practice of *Li*, thereby recognizing the relative legitimacy of the traditional values and institutions covered by *Li*. In this way, the moral radicalism and moral conservatism that existed side by side so incongruously in K'ang's writings of the mid-1880s were now brought together and integrated into a single coherent world view.

K'ang's evolutionary view of history also allowed him to resolve another incongruity that had so far marked his thought. From his early youth on, K'ang's mind was dominated by two independent concerns, namely, his political, patriotic concern with the survival of China and his universal, moral-spiritual concern with the meaning of life and the world. In his philosophical writings of 1885–1887, these two concerns are still disjointed. But in the moral-historical world view that he worked out in the 1890s, the two concerns are now meaningfully linked together. His patriotic concern is expressed as political reformism to be accomplished in the present age, and his moral, spiritual concern is given expression in the vision of history as a programmatic march toward a universal community in the future. Consequently, the articulation of his political aspirations no longer competes with his moral-spiritual yearning but has become a necessary step in the historical process leading up to the ultimate fulfillment of that yearning.[142]

Seen in this light, K'ang's evolutionary view of history is obviously not just an ideological instrument to justify his political reformism, as it is often made out to be in the studies of K'ang by Hsiao Kung-chuan, T'ang Chih-

---

141. *Li-yün chu* (1976c, 9: 7, 14–17).
142. Liang Ch'i-ch'ao (1936, *wen-chi*, 63, 85–87). Here I paint a picture quite different from Hsiao Kung-chuan's, who considers K'ang Yu-wei's social thinking to operate on two levels:

> On one level, he directed his attention to the practical affairs of China in the last decades of the nineteenth century when he endeavored to salvage the sinking empire through reform and, later, in the first decades of the twentieth when he engaged himself in scathing criticisms of the faltering republic. On another level, he disengaged himself from concerns with immediate situations and sallied forth into theorizations and speculations which had little direct contact with reality. Often he moved simultaneously on both these levels; sometimes he shifted back and forth from one level to the other. In this way he assumed a double role: as a practical reformer and as a utopian thinker. (Hsiao, 1975)

Hsiao's unqualified images of "two levels" and "double roles" run the risking of missing the organic character of K'ang's thinking as a whole. K'ang started out in his early life with two separate, independent concerns, but these were integrated into one unified moral-historical world view after 1890. His reformism and utopianism basically belonged to the same world view; they represented different aspects of the same overall picture.

chün, and others.¹⁴³ Rather, it is a conceptual framework that he finally discovered after years of intellectual search, enabling him to weave together and integrate into an overall synthesis all the major elements of his thinking, which up to the late 1880s had remained disparate. It is in the context of this new synthesis that his fresh idea, namely, "timeliness" (*shih*), assumes significance.¹⁴⁴ This idea is integral to the very concept of the gradual realization of the *jen* ideal in the process of history. Moral ideals and human institutions all have their specific "times" for realization. They can not prevail until their time comes. This idea of timeliness clearly presupposes a view of history as a temporal process of evolvement in accordance with a predetermined sequence of stages, a view he owed as much to the New Text Confucian view of history as to the Western conception of history.¹⁴⁵

I am tempted to draw from this view of history the conclusion of moral quietism and human passivity, but such a conclusion is precluded by the fact that a view of history as an objective, impersonal process exists side by side with a heightened moral activism and voluntarism in K'ang's thought. From early on, he exhibited a striking interest in the moral development of the individual. This interest came to a head in his acceptance of the Confucian ideal of moral cultivation, as amply demonstrated in his commentaries on the *Ssu-shu*. Underlying this Confucian ideal was a belief that he enthusiastically embraced, namely, the belief that the ideal of the sage as the paragon of moral perfection is attainable by every human being. For K'ang, this kind of moral voluntarism is implicit in every discussion of moral virtues in the *Ssu-shu*. But nowhere did he see it more cogently expressed than in the Mencian idea of the innate moral potential of human nature. As K'ang repeatedly notes, it is this idea that gave rise to the Mencian belief that everyone can be a Yao or a Shun.¹⁴⁶

Although K'ang believed that every human being has the potential for achieving moral perfection, he also takes the view that not everyone has the same potential. Here again he embraces Mencius' idea that some people are endowed by Heaven with greater moral awareness and insight and that these "moral vanguards" (*hsien-chüeh*), therefore, have the responsibility of "awakening people" (*chüeh-min*) and "saving people" (*chiu-min*).¹⁴⁷ Thus, he inherited from the Confucian tradition the idea that the heightened moral activism is at once the privilege and responsibility of the moral vanguard. His belief in the unique activist role of the moral vanguard was reinforced by his study of Mahayana Buddhism and his identification with the Mahayana ideal of Bodhisattva as a suffering savior on earth.¹⁴⁸ Thus, K'ang's concept

---

143. For T'ang Chih-chün's view on this issue, see T'ang (1957: 106–25).
144. 1968b, "Preface": 1b–2a; chüan 1: 4a–5a, 13b–14a; *Chung-yung chu*: 3b–4a.
145. T'ang Chih-chün (1957: 112–13).
146. 1968b, chüan 1: 1a–b, 2b–3a, 6b–7b, 8a.
147. Ibid.: 6b–7b.
148. 1976c, 20: 10, 189, 190–91, 194–96, 199–201, 211–12, 216–17, 217–18; Liang Ch'i-ch'ao (1936, *wen-chi*, ts'e 3, chüan 6: 61, 70).

of history as a suprapersonal process of development is counterbalanced not only by his confidence in the potential of an ordinary person to become a self-determining moral agent, but, more important, by his view that the voluntarism of the moral vanguard has a unique role to play in the moral advancement of mankind. For K'ang, if the cosmos was believed to generate a supraindividual sociohistorical process of development, it was also believed to impart universal cosmic significance to the active role of some exceptional individuals.

From K'ang's perspective, his belief in moral voluntarism is not inconsistent with his concept of history as an objective, impersonal process. His perspective in this connection is not set by the typical modern Western world view, which sees the relationship between the individual and the world in terms of the dichotomy of subject versus object. According to this world view, if the object moves and changes of its own momentum, the subject's role is then reduced to passivity. K'ang's perspective is, rather, set by a world view that he derived from Confucianism and is premised on a belief in the "unity of Heaven and man." From the perspective of this belief, the relationship between self and the cosmos is not that of the dualism of subject over against an object, but between a part and the whole.

In his interpretative commentaries on Confucianism, K'ang repeatedly emphasizes an idea shared by both Han Confucianism and neo-Confucianism, namely, that an individual partakes of the encompassing whole inasmuch as he owes to the latter his physical and spiritual endowment. Thus, when the whole is perceived to have evolved and changed temporarily, the individual does not feel he is caught in an impersonal process of cause and effect over which he has no control. Instead, he feels a kinship with the whole to resonate and coordinate with the cosmic-historical evolvement by exerting himself morally and spiritually. Indeed, we may speak of a cosmic imperative summoning the individual to cooperate and vibrate with the historical course by evolving himself morally.[149] Because of this perspective, moral activism and voluntarism rather than moral quietism are a natural concomitant of K'ang's view of history as a process of cosmic-social evolvement.

---

149. Joseph Needham's notion of "coordinative thinking" or "intuitive-associative thinking" will help us to get a handle on K'ang's mode of thinking in this regard:

> In coordinative thinking, conceptions are not subsumed under one another, but placed side by side in a pattern, and things influence one another not by acts of mechanical causation, but by a kind of mysterious resonance.... Things behaved in particular ways not necessarily because of prior actions or impulsion or other things, but because their position in the ever-moving cyclical universe was such that they were endowed with intrinsic natures which made that behavior inevitable for them. If they did not behave in those particular ways, they would lose their relational positions in the whole, and turn into something other than themselves. They reacted upon one another not so much by mechanical impulsion or causation as by a kind of mysterious resonance. (Ronan [1978, 1: 161–68])

K'ANG'S FUTURISTIC UTOPIANISM

We have seen that K'ang's notion of *jen* inherits from its Confucian prototype a quest for moral perfection of self and society. Out of this quest grew a vision of an ideal society that he projected into the distant future at the end of a three-stage historical process. This new utopian vision was different from the utopianism which, as indicated above, already figured prominently in his early writings of 1885–1887. Whereas his early utopianism located the ideal society in the distant past, his new utopianism envisioned the ideal society in the distant future. The contents of the two utopian visions were also divergent. The early vision was couched almost solely in terms of the Confucian ideal of the golden age of sage-kings, whereas K'ang's new utopianism resulted from the synthesis of the Confucian as well as the non-Confucian influences which were already present in his writings of the mid-1880s but did not yet cohere into a single, unified framework. Just as this synthesis fed his moral-historical world view of *jen*, it naturally also shaped the utopianism that grew out of that world view. What were the exact contents of his new utopian vision?

In the early 1900s K'ang began to spell it out in a book he entitled *Ta-t'ung shu* (A discourse on the grand unity).[150] On the surface, K'ang's futuristic utopianism was marked by some new ideas not found in his radical interpretation of Confucianism, but, in the last analysis, they prove to be peripheral to the core of his utopianism. To see the place and nature of these new ideas in K'ang's futuristic utopianism, we must start by examining the dichotomy of suffering (*k'u*) and happiness (*lo*) that formed a principal theme of his utopian thinking. As he saw it, life as it is is riddled with suffering; hence, it is a natural goal of life to conquer suffering and achieve happiness.[151] What kind of outlook on life and society does this dichotomy suggest? The answer depends, of course, on how K'ang perceived the sources of suffering and how he conceived ways to acquire happiness.

Without question, his study of Buddhism played a part in shaping his perception of the sources of human suffering inasmuch as he saw human suffering partly rooted in the very structure of human existence. Thus, as he surveys the sufferings in this world, he speaks of "sufferings of human life" (*jen-sheng chih k'u*), "sufferings of human paths" (*jen-tao chih k'u*), and "sufferings of human feelings" (*jen-ch'ing chih k'u*). These categories refer

---

150. It is now generally agreed that K'ang's *Ta-t'ung shu* was conceived and written over many years, possibly from as early as the mid-1880s to as late as 1920. But there is no question that most of his basic ideas were put to paper during 1901–1902. The best way to discern K'ang's utopian thinking as spelled out in the early 1900s is to read K'ang's book, guided by Liang Ch'i-ch'ao's summation of his teacher's ideas in his 1901 biography of K'ang Yu-wei. For a discussion of the dating and evolution of K'ang's thinking on the *ta-t'ung* ideal, see T'ang Chih-chün (1957: 126–45); Li Tse-hou (1958: 126–36); Liang Ch'i-ch'ao (1936, *wen-chi*, ts'e 3, chüan 6: 71–85).

151. Liang Ch'i-ch'ao (1936, *wen-chi*, ts'e 3, chüan 6: 71–72, 74–75); K'ang (1956: 1–8).

to all the sufferings that attend such inherent phenomena of life as birth, illness, loneliness, desires, and emotions.[152] Quite understandably, in his depiction of the future utopian society he envisages the dissolution of these sufferings as contributing to the happiness and bliss that he believes will prevail.[153]

In discussing ways to conquer sufferings, K'ang freely borrows ideas from non-Confucian spiritual traditions. For example, he sometimes draws on the Taoist idea of physical immortality and the Christian notion of the immortality of soul in portraying the utopian society of the future as a place where suffering and death are conquerable.[154] However, according to Liang Ch'i-ch'ao, it was Buddhism that furnished the main source for his idea of conquest of death and suffering, especially the Mahayana idea of the ocean of the *bhutathata* in which all separate selves are dissolved into the primordial and ultimate *Dharmakaya*.[155] Thus, there is a strain in K'ang's utopianism that focused on the idea of the conquest of the finitude of the individual, an idea of "the existential utopia" that tends to depart from the Confucian inner-worldly perspective and to turn toward the transcendentalism and other-worldliness of non-Confucian traditions.[156]

This tendency toward transcendentalism, however, never goes far in K'ang's utopian vision. In fact, it remains largely at the periphery of his utopianism, because, as Liang Ch'i-ch'ao also notes, K'ang at the time was mainly under the hold of the Hua-yen philosophy of Mahayana Buddhism. Central to the Hua-yen world view is a radical vision of undifferentiated oneness that precludes any dualistic mode of thinking, including the dualism of this world versus the other world. As Liang paraphrases K'ang, Hua-yen Buddhism does feature a belief in an ultimate spiritual reality— *Dharmadhatu*. But the latter does not exist outside and beyond this world. By the same token, the highest happiness and the ultimate perfection cannot be sought beyond this world.[157] For K'ang, then, the Hua-yen philosophy points to the same truth as Confucianism does, namely, the attainability of moral-spiritual perfection in this world. In short, Mahayana Buddhism converges with, rather than militates against, the this-worldly perspective of Confucianism. Consequently, K'ang's leaning toward transcendentalism is contained by his overall understanding of Buddhism, which is this-worldly in thrust.[158]

---

152. Liang Ch'i-ch'ao (1936, *wen-chi*, ts'e 3, chüan 6: 74–75); K'ang (1956: 1–52).
153. 1956: 52–53; Liang Ch'i-ch'ao (1936, *wen-chi*, ts'e 3, chüan 6: 71–72, 74–75).
154. Liang Ch'i-ch'ao (1936, *wen-chi*, ts'e 3, chüan 6: 71–72, 84); K'ang (1956: 300–1).
155. Liang Ch'i-ch'ao (1936, *wen-chi*, ts'e 3, chüan 6: 83–84).
156. 1956: 300–1.
157. Liang Ch'i-ch'ao (1936, *wen-chi*, ts'e 3, chüan 6: 83–84).
158. Ibid. The convergence of Confucianism and Mahayana Buddhism in K'ang's utopian vision is also borne out by a poem that he claimed to have composed before age 30, apparently after he had finished an early version of his book on the *ta-t'ung* utopia. See K'ang (1976c, chüan 1: 2).

Thus, despite its Buddhist colorations, K'ang's ideal of "grand unity" emerges more as the social utopia of the Confucian type than as the existential utopia of the Buddhist-Taoist type. The affinity between K'ang's utopianism and the Confucian social utopia is hardly surprising in view of the fact that K'ang derived his vision of "grand unity" from his interpretation of the ideal of *jen*, which inherited the inner-worldly orientation of its Confucian prototype. But this very fact also explains why K'ang's utopianism departs from the Confucian social utopia in some critical aspects, because K'ang's interpretation of the ideal of *jen* is not so much an outgrowth of its Confucian prototype as its metamorphosis, thanks largely to the historization and radicalization of *jen* as a result of non-Confucian influences.

One obvious difference that separates K'ang's utopianism from Confucian notions of social utopia lies in his conception of time. K'ang's social utopia is accompanied by a heightened sense of future, which grew out of his view of time as a unilinear process of development, whereas the Confucian ideals of social utopia are usually framed in a temporal perspective that is largely oriented toward the past and hence, in general, prohibits a heightened sense of future. Apart from this temporal perspective, other substantive differences also distinguish K'ang's ideal of social utopia. To see these differences, we again have to turn to the dichotomy of suffering and happiness and see what kinds of suffering need to be conquered and what paths of happiness need to be pursued for the advent of his social utopia.

K'ang's utopianism was marked by a spiritual, transcendental view of conquering suffering and achieving happiness, but the latter was overshadowed by a more mundane, materialistic, and hedonistic view of happiness, which is central to his ideal of social utopia. This earthly hedonism is rooted in the monistic world view of the unity of Heaven and man, which underlies K'ang's ideal of *jen*. This monistic world view repeatedly led him in earlier works to repudiate the orthodox neo-Confucian dichotomy of human desires and moral order and, thereby, to legitimize the fulfillment of human desires. To K'ang, this legitimation of human desires is also basically in tune with the inner-worldly and life-affirming spirit of *jen*. From his monistic world view, it is thus but a short step to singing praises to the pursuit of earthly desires and mundane happiness. This is exactly what he does in his depiction of utopia.[159] For him, the advent of a future social utopia thus means the spread of earthly happiness, involving continual improvement in every aspect of material life—food, clothing, housing, transportation, and so forth.[160] Underlying this concept of earthly happiness is a euphoric vision that, coupled with an expectation that mechanization would play an essential part in all

---

159. 1956: 294–300.
160. Ibid.: 234–51, 263–66, 269–75, 293–300.

aspects of human progress, projects an image of a future society of material abundance and technological advancement, reflecting clearly the influence of the Promethean ethos of modern, industrial civilization.[161] This picture of economic and technological development is a far cry from the Confucian utopia of moral harmony based on the moderation of earthly desires and the frugality of material life.

But K'ang's social utopia is not just a culmination of economic and technological progress; it is also the pinnacle of moral progress. In fact, in his utopianism, this moral motif stands out more strongly than the motif of material abundance. To see what kind of moral progress his *ta-t'ung* ideal represents, we have to examine again his perception of the world as full of suffering. This perception contains an element of transcendentalism, but, on the whole, his sense of transcendence boils down to a rejection more of the existing social order than of life and the world per se. In developing this negative image of the existing social order, he is merely drawing the logical corollary from his interpretation of the *jen* ideal, evolved in his various commentaries on the Confucian classics. His interpretation in this regard was already affected by various non-Confucian influences from both inside and outside the Chinese tradition. Out of this interpretation thus emerges a world view that preserved the moral perspective and the ideal of universality of the Confucian *jen* but that also incorporated radical universalism and egalitarianism from indigenous as well as Western sources. These two ideals are responsible for his view of the existing hierarchical order as flawed and miserable.[162] Liang Ch'i-ch'ao has given particular weight to the Mahayana Buddhist ideal of undifferentiated organic oneness, precluding any distinction and boundary in human relations, as an impetus to K'ang's negative perception of the current order.[163] But when K'ang envisages the institutional expression of the universalism and egalitarianism in his utopianism, his grand vision of the future also bears the strong imprint of Western cultural models.

In keeping with his radical vision of universalism and egalitarianism, K'ang describes his utopia as a universal moral community free of the particularistic distinctions and boundaries that characterize the existing

---

161. K'ang's fascination with the industrial civilization of the modern West (developed in the 1900s) is discussed in Hsiao Kung-chuan (1975: 515–96.) In Liang Ch'i-ch'ao's biography of K'ang (1936, *wen-chi*, ts'e 3, chüan 6: 57–89), K'ang's euphoric view of modern industrial civilization is not given expression, probably because, when K'ang wrote down his utopian ideal of *ta-t'ung* in 1901–1902, he had not yet fully articulated his views, although they are hinted at in his positive notions of human desires and material wants. But his expansive view of industrial civilization was developing fast in the early 1900s and soon culminated in a full articulation in his *Wu-chih chiu-kuo lun* [Material reconstruction to save China] published in 1905. This expansive view of industrialization was eventually incorporated into his published version of the *ta-t'ung* utopia.
162. Liang Ch'i-ch'ao (1936, *wen-chi*, ts'e 3, chüan 6: 71, 74–75); K'ang (1956: 51–53).
163. Liang, ibid.; K'ang, ibid.

social order. He sees these particularistic distinctions and boundaries as falling under two categories: those that separate existing human societies from one another or pit them against one another, and those that exist within each human society and create cleavages and discord among the people who live therein.[164] The abolition of all these barriers and cleavages constitutes another striking characteristic of his utopian society.

One source of intrasocietal discrimination is class inequality, which, according to K'ang, exists in human society everywhere. This class inequality has developed to the extreme in India. It has also been present in traditional Chinese society even though it existed there in a milder form than in many other societies.[165] Looking at the world as a whole, he sees the victims of social inequality falling under three categories: people of despised statuses and occupations (*chien-min*), slaves, and women.[166] He denounces this form of social discrimination on two grounds. First of all, class inequality is a sign of social backwardness: the more backward the society, the greater its social inequality. Furthermore, class inequality is a violation of the justice required by the universal moral law. In short, it is undesirable from both the standpoint of social utility and that of moral conscience. In K'ang's historical framework, class inequality exists in the "age of decay and chaos," and to a lesser degree in the "age of rising peace," but it will disappear in the final "age of universal peace."[167]

Whereas K'ang sees class inequality as a barrier to the realization of the universal community, he does not so regard the social division of labor.[168] In his depiction of his ideal society, he takes for granted the need for occupational specialization, certainly such rudimentary divisions of labor as those between agriculture, commerce, and industry.[169] However, within the framework of a functionally differentiated society, he advocates the abolishment of private property, which he sees as a breeding ground of social conflict and waste. Such conflict and waste can only be avoided by replacing the institution of private property with the system of public ownership and control in agriculture, industry, and commerce.[170]

As K'ang surveys the social scene, he finds no group of people more victimized by social discrimination than women. For him, this observation is just as true of China as of any other part of the world.[171] Again he deplores it from the standpoint of both social utility and moral principle. From the standpoint of social utility, the social discrimination against women is a great

---

164. Liang Ch'i-ch'ao (1936, *wen-chi*, ts'e 3, chüan 6: 71, 73–75).
165. Ibid.: 77–81; K'ang (1956: 108–16).
166. K'ang (1956: 108–68); Liang Ch'i-ch'ao (1936, *wen-chi*, ts'e 3, chüan 6: 81).
167. 1956: 108–14.
168. Liang Ch'i-ch'ao (1936, *wen-chi*, ts'e 3, chüan 6: 77–83); K'ang (1956: 234–83).
169. 1956: 234–53; Liang Ch'i-ch'ao (1936, *wen-chi*, ts'e 3, chüan 6: 79).
170. 1956: 234–53; Liang Ch'i-ch'ao (1936, *wen-chi*, ts'e 3, chüan 6: 80).
171. Liang Ch'i-ch'ao (1936, *wen-chi*, ts'e 3, chüan 6: 81); K'ang (1956: 126–67).

loss to the development of human society, because, in K'ang's view, women are just as able as men, both intellectually and physically. From the standpoint of universal moral principle, it is a flagrant infraction of human rights and dignity. It is thus no surprise that K'ang sees the elimination of discrimination against women as a major premise for the realization of his utopian society. Surprisingly, his revolt against sexist discrimination even leads him to suggest the idea of abolishing the marriage institution altogether. In his view, discrimination against women is rooted in marriage, an institution designed from the beginning to ensure male domination at the sacrifice of women's interests and dignity. He even toys with the idea of replacing marriage with a kind of arrangement whereby a man and a woman could live together just by signing a renewable, one-year contract that allows both sides the freedom of terminating their cohabitation at their own will and convenience.[172] The overriding purpose is to bring about equality between male and female members of society.

K'ang Yu-wei's idea of abolishing marriage in his ideal society implies a negative attitude toward the family as a social institution. This is indeed the case when we examine his view of family from the standpoint of his utopianism. The radical interpretation of *jen* in his commentaries on Confucian classics results in no simple repudiation of the family. Family is given positive value for the past and the present. Only in the distant future—the "age of the grand unity"—would the family need to be dissolved. However, in his future utopia, he rejects the family institution with considerable ambivalence about its value. On the one hand, he is aware of the essential protection that the family provides to the growth of the individual person. Without emotional and material support from a family, a child can hardly survive the many hazards that attend the life process. Furthermore, the cardinal Chinese family virtue, filial piety, also has strong appeal as a moral value for K'ang.[173]

On the other hand, K'ang also recognizes that family is a mixed blessing. To begin with, internally a family, such as the Chinese extended type, is often fraught with petty jealousy, bitterness, and hostility among its members. More importantly, the family institution tends too easily to become the focus of loyalty of the individual person at the cost of the solidarity of the larger society.[174] Eventually, his consciousness of this fissiparous nature of the family institution leads him to overcome his ambivalence and to see it entirely as an obstacle to the realization of his *ta-t'ung* ideal.[175]

So far, we have seen that K'ang's ideal society is one devoid of almost all of the central institutions of the existing society—class, private property,

---

172. 1956: 126–27, 147–49, 160–62, 164–67.
173. Ibid.: 168–69, 173, 178–79.
174. Ibid.: 179–90.
175. Ibid.: 191–93; Liang Ch'i-ch'ao (1936, *wen-chi*, ts'e 3, chüan 6: 76–77).

male domination, marriage, and family. In conjuring up this vision, he was not just looking at the future of China but was thinking about mankind as a whole. This vision of a universal, egalitarian society leads him to see a further need for removing two intersocietal barriers.[176] One is the institution of the territorial state. As K'ang points out, war has been a constant source of tragedies to human beings everywhere throughout the ages. War is inevitable, in his view, given the institution of the territorial state, which separates peoples from each other and spawns suspicion and hostility among them. Thus, the abolition of the territorial state would be a necessity for preventing wars and preserving harmony and peace on earth.[177]

The territorial state aside, racial differences constitute another source of strain and conflict that, in K'ang's view, sets people against people and society against society. However, it is interesting to note that K'ang's stance in this regard conceals a hard-headed Social Darwinian view that is out of character with the general tenor of his utopian philosophy. K'ang states that the four major races in the world (the white, the yellow, the brown, and the black) are inexorably locked in fierce struggles; to him, the fact that the brown and the black are losing the struggle implies that they are inferior races.[178] Even as he looks to the future, his vision remains tinged by this Social Darwinian outlook. When the "age of the grand unity" dawns, we are told, racial harmony will prevail on earth. To prepare for the advent of this age, K'ang proposes the encouragement of interracial marriages. But he also recommends emigration of the black peoples away from the area of hot weather to the temperate zones, change of food habits on the part of both the black and brown peoples, and even the adoption of certain racial eugenics aimed at eliminating certain "undesirable" elements in the two races. In short, racial harmony in his ideal society would be achieved not so much by establishing equality among different races as by assimilation of the black and brown peoples into the white and yellow peoples.[179]

Thus, in K'ang's vision, the society of "grand unity" is not only an egalitarian society; it is also an all-inclusive universal society, with no place for the territorial state. However, K'ang does not repudiate the institution of political authority altogether. In fact, K'ang's utopia of *ta-t'ung* is different from many other utopias both within and outside the Chinese tradition. Whereas many of these other utopias feature the negation of government and authority as such, K'ang's utopia is a politically organized universal state.[180]

---

176. 1956: 54–107, 117–25; Liang Ch'i-ch'ao (1936, *wen-chi*, ts'e 3, chüan 6: 76, 78).
177. 1956: 54–69.
178. Ibid.: 117–18, 118–21.
179. Ibid.: 121–25; Liang Ch'i-ch'ao (1936, *wen-chi*, ts'e 3, chüan 6: 78).
180. Liang Ch'i-ch'ao (1936, *wen-chi*, ts'e 3, chüan 6: 76, 77–81, 81–83); K'ang (1956: 254–86).

The governmental structure of this universal state has two characteristics. One is federalism. More specifically, the universal state is organized as a federation of many small, autonomous regions. Each autonomous region has its own government, while all of them share an overall, federal government.[181] At both levels, the government is democratic in structure.[182] This democratic government, meanwhile, is "heavy" in terms of the functions it performs, especially at the regional level. In the age of the grand unity, we are told, government will assume responsibility for the welfare of the individual citizen "from cradle to grave." Government's extensive welfare responsibilities will require it to take over many of the social and economic functions that otherwise would be performed by either the private household or the private proprietorship.[183] What K'ang envisages, then, is a future society where there would be no private sector and where public ownership and control of property would be the prevailing order. No wonder when Liang Ch'i-ch'ao outlined K'ang's ideal of utopia in the early 1900s, he emphasized the "interventionist" character of K'ang's utopian society. In fact, in Liang's understanding, a basic principle that governs his teacher's social utopia is what he called "socialism."[184] Consequently, far from withering away, the government is expected to undergo tremendous expansion in the universal state of the future.

K'ang's ideal of grand unity largely embodies the twin values of moral perfection and material abundance. Spelled out in the framework of his historical world view, his ideal was of a futuristic utopianism projecting the vision of moral-social progress combined with technoeconomic advancement, a vision that proved to be a powerful ideological mix that was to move the minds and stir the hearts of the twentieth-century Chinese.

K'ang's *ta-t'ung* utopianism must be understood against the backdrop of the moral-historical world view that he had been evolving since the beginning of the 1890s. Lying behind this moral-historical world view is, of course, the intellectual search he had pursued since his early youth. Seen in this perspective, utopianism is neither a romantic flight of K'ang's imagination nor mere philosophical speculation. Nor is it just an ideological instrument designed to justify his political reformism. Rather, it is part and parcel of a structure of meaning that he developed in response to the historical and existential situations as he perceived them.

This structure of meaning, although largely formulated in the context of K'ang's interpretation of Confucianism, is marked as much by continuity with the Confucian tradition as by discontinuity with it. Doubtless a principal impetus to K'ang's utopianism stemmed from the inner-worldly uni-

---

181. Liang Ch'i-ch'ao (1936, *wen-chi*, ts'e 3, chüan 6: 76, 81–83); K'ang (1956: 255–57).
182. Liang Ch'i-ch'ao (1936, *wen-chi*, ts'e 3, chüan 6: 76, 81–83); K'ang (1956: 258–63).
183. Liang Ch'i-ch'ao (1936, *wen-chi*, ts'e 3, chüan 6: 76, 77–81); K'ang (1956: 263–70).
184. Liang Ch'i-ch'ao (1936, *wen-chi*, ts'e 3, chüan 6: 76, 77–78).

versalistic vision of paradigmatic man and society that lies at the heart of the Confucian ideal of *jen*. Whereas the form and pattern of the Confucian vision often remained, the contents of the vision are drastically altered by K'ang's acceptance of non-Confucian values, most notably those from Western and Buddhist sources.

The resultant syncretism forms the basis of his interpretation of Confucianism. He maintains that his utopian ideal of grand unity and his personality ideal of the sage-king represent the highest spiritual truths of Confucianism promulgated by Confucius himself and handed down primarily through the teachings of his disciples Tzu Yu and Mencius.[185] But, unfortunately for much of the later Confucian tradition, these sublime truths fell into eclipse due to the prevalence of another set of teachings ascribed by K'ang to Hsün Tzu's teachings that put a premium on arid ritualism, jejune scholasticism, and inhibitory authoritarianism.[186] The two kinds of Confucian teachings he again classifies under the rubrics of the "grand unity" and the "small peace," respectively.[187] Thus, in K'ang's view, the ideals of grand unity and small peace represented not only two different stages of historical development, but two different levels of Confucian teachings—the higher and the lower.

K'ang conceives the two levels of Confucian teachings in conscious analogy with the Buddhist and the Christian traditions. Just as the Mahayana school represented the revival of the original teachings of Buddha and Protestant Christianity the recovery of the original message of Jesus Christ, K'ang often hints that his *ta-t'ung* teachings represent the renaissance of the highest visions of Confucius.[188] K'ang took upon himself the mission of undertaking this renaissance. As a result, among his disciples and followers, he was sometimes compared to Martin Luther of Protestant Christianity or Nagarjuna of Mahayana Buddhism.[189]

K'ang's analogies and images in this regard point to a religious dimension of his thought that so far has not been taken seriously enough by historians. For example, with regard to such ideas as the "propagation of faith" and the "preservation of faith" that he put forward during his campaign for reform in the 1890s, historians in general have tended to look on K'ang's thoughts and actions in this connection as only ideological means to promote his political reformism.[190] With regard to his later involvement in the campaign for Confucianism as a state religion, people again have viewed it primarily in

---

185. 1968b, "Tzu-hsü" [preface]: 1a–b. See also Liang Ch'i-ch'ao (1936, *wen-chi*, ts'e 2: chüan 3: 56–57).
186. 1968b, "Tzu-hsü": 1a–b; Liang Ch'i-ch'ao (1936, *wen-chi*, ts'e 2, chüan 3: 56–57).
187. Liang Ch'i-ch'ao (1936, *wen-chi*, ts'e 2, chüan 3: 56–57).
188. *Lun-yü chu*, "Hsü" [preface], 1976c: 3, 16; 1968b: 1a, 2b; chüan 1: 20a.
189. Liang Ch'i-ch'ao (1936, *wen-chi*, ts'e 3, chüan 6: 67; ibid., ts'e 2, chüan 3: 56).
190. This view is found, e.g., in Li Tse-hou's study of K'ang's thought (1958: 152–54).

the context of his conservative politics.[191] One does not need to deny that his public promotion of Confucianism had some political motives. One may also wonder whether K'ang's efforts in this regard had something to do with what Levenson called "cultural identity." Whatever the motives behind his public promotion of Confucianism, the structure of meaning he formulated in his interpretation of Confucianism must first and foremost be understood in the context of his lifelong moral-spiritual quest.

His studies of Confucianism thus contain not only a political ideology, but also an overall interpretation of life and the world that his intellectual quest had led him to develop. The resulting interpretation speaks to the specific historical condition of China and also to the human condition in general. At the time, it was his political ideology that attracted the attention of the people outside his group and hence appeared important. But as far as K'ang himself and the small circle of his close friends and disciples were concerned, K'ang's overall interpretation of life and the world is what dominated their minds and made their studies of Confucianism much more than just a function of their political interest. In fact, this is exactly how Liang Ch'i-ch'ao understood his teacher's thought and role. In a biographical portrait of K'ang in the early 1900s, Liang emphasizes K'ang's role as a religious leader and sometimes calls him the "Martin Luther of Confucianism."[192] Quite naturally, during the late 1890s when Liang was still K'ang's closest disciple, he considered their political reformism secondary to their moral-spiritual mission, which he himself characterizes as religious. In fact, at the height of the reform movement in 1898, Liang wrote to his teacher, reminding him that their preoccupation with a political campaign should not lead them to forget that their ultimate goal is the universalistic ideal of spreading Confucian moral-spiritual teachings and saving the world (*chiu-shih*), rather than the "particularist" political goal of merely protecting China, the nation.[193]

191. Chou Tse-tsung (1960: 289–92).
192. Liang Ch'i-ch'ao (1936, *wen-chi*, ts'e 3, chüan 6: 67).
193. Ting Wen-chiang (1959, 1: 34–35).

3

T'an Ssu-t'ung (1864–1898)

IN THE summer of 1895, at the height of the reform campaign launched by K'ang Yu-wei in the wake of the Sino-Japanese War, a young scholar from Hunan came to Peking to visit him. K'ang was away in Canton at the time, and instead the scholar met with K'ang's student Liang Ch'i-ch'ao. He quickly became close friends with Liang and converted to K'ang's political cause.[1] Thus, T'an Ssu-t'ung joined the ranks of reformists—a person who became as important as K'ang and Liang among the early Chinese intelligentsia.

THE MAN AND THE MARTYR

T'an Ssu-t'ung was born into the family of a Hunanese official at Peking in 1864. Although his native town was Liuyang, in Hunan, he spent a great deal of time living and traveling outside Hunan. Following the traditional path of success, he took the civil service examination several times but earned only the *sheng-yuan*, a prefectural degree.[2] He did not pursue a career in Chinese officialdom until the last three years of his life. In 1896 he received a supernumerary appointment in the local government at Nanking. The next year, however, he returned to Hunan to become involved in the drive for

---

1. Yang T'ing-fu (1957: 70–72); see also T'an Ssu-t'ung (1954: 521).
2. Existing records say little about his efforts to pass the civil service examinations other than that he was generally unsuccessful. T'an himself once said that between 21 and 30 he had made six unsuccessful attempts to pass the examination at the provincial level. However, because he was allowed to take the provincial level examination, he must have acquired a prefectural degree of *sheng-yuan* by age 21, or he would not have qualified to take the examination. See T'an (1954: 156).

reform that was then raging there.³ After the reform drive in Hunan was stalled by the conservative gentry-officials, he left for Peking in the early summer of 1898, just in time to plunge into K'ang Yu-wei's reform movement, which was then gathering momentum. Appointed to an important staff job in the Grand Council, T'an played a key role in the so-called "One Hundred Days Reform." When the reform movement was cut short by the Empress Dowager's coup d'état in the fall of that year, he died a martyr.⁴

T'an's martyrdom was particularly heroic because, though he had chances to escape before his arrest, he refused to do so. Death was something he sought rather than something that circumstances imposed on him. When death finally came, he accepted it with a defiance and courage that became legendary.⁵ Thus, T'an is remembered as the most dramatic figure among the intellectuals of his generation. His heroic death created an aura around him in the memory of modern Chinese intellectuals.

What kind of mind does this martyrdom reflect? On the face of it, T'an seems to have died for his political cause: the effort to bring about reforms that would strengthen China against foreign aggression. Like K'ang Yu-wei, T'an was intensely concerned from his early youth on with the changing relations between China and the outside world caused by foreign aggression. In an early essay, his attention is already focused on Western expansionism, and he expresses anguish over the fate of China in the modern world.⁶ Later, this anguish would evolve into the patriotism that drove him to join K'ang Yu-wei's reform movement after China's defeat by Japan in 1895. The letters he wrote to his teacher and friends after that war reveal that he was already deeply committed to the ideal of building up the wealth and power of China.⁷

Nonetheless, T'an was not a nationalist. When the patriotism of many of T'an's fellow intellectuals was turning into nationalism in the waning years of the nineteenth century, T'an himself was little affected by this trend. In fact, by that time his outlook ran counter to nationalism in many ways. Consequently, his martyrdom was not an act of nationalism but must be understood against the background of a lifelong intellectual quest.

T'AN'S INTELLECTUAL QUEST

T'an was brought up in the conventional family of a scholar-official, yet from early on he pursued an unconventional intellectual career. What could

---

3. Yang T'ing-fu (1957: 104).
4. Ibid.: 117–18.
5. Ibid.; see also T'an (1954: 524–25).
6. T'an (1954: 103–9).
7. See, esp., his letters to his teacher Ou-yang Chung-ku and to his friend Pei Yüan-cheng (1954: 287–300, 389–430).

account for this? For one thing, he was born with an imaginative mind and a romantic personality. His passion, sensitivity, and adventurous spirit can be seen in the poems he wrote during his adolescence.⁸ Adding to his adventurous spirit, T'an's father's frequent moves in Chinese officialdom and T'an's travels to take the civil service examination developed in him a wanderlust that led him to travel far and wide outside his hometown and meet people he would not have met otherwise.⁹ During these travels he became acquainted with Western scholars like John Fryer, who stimulated his interest in Western learning.¹⁰ And, during a visit to his father's official post as the governor of Hupeh at Wuhan, he also got to know several of the enlightened, knowledgeable scholar-advisers who worked for his father's boss Chang Chih-tung, the governor general of Hu-Kwang.¹¹ Meanwhile, back in his hometown, his intellectual circle included teachers and friends whose outlooks were often unconventional.¹²

Thus, T'an's early life accounts for his ability to break out of the confining environment of his family and acquire a broader intellectual horizon than that of most of his fellow literati, and it also helps explain why he emerged from his early youth already engaged in a frenzied intellectual quest. He developed many interests and engaged in many activities in the course of his quest. He read extensively and voraciously, from Western sciences to traditional textual criticism and ancient Chinese philosophy.¹³ But something deeper than his wide-ranging curiosity drove him on and made him intellectually restless.

What was this something deeper? I shall start my probe with his earliest extant piece of writing, an essay titled "Chih-yen" (On order), composed at the age of 21.¹⁴ The burden of this essay is to place China in the world as T'an

---

8. These qualities are amply shown in the two earliest poems he wrote, one at 15 and one at 18 (ibid.: 277, 487).
9. When T'an wrote a summary of his life at age 30, he considered his wide-ranging travels as his proudest achievement. He estimated that the mileage he had traveled was equivalent to circling the earth (ibid.: 204–7).
10. See T'an's letter to his teacher Ou-yang Chung-ku (ibid.: 316–29); see also Shek (1976: 194–203).
11. Yang (1957: 57–58).
12. Ibid.: 28–29, 38, 54–55, 56–57, 59–60.
13. T'an's broad range of intellectual interests can be seen clearly in the two volumes of study notes he wrote when he was about 30 (1954: 213–79); see also Yang (1957: 32–33).
14. T'an tells us in a letter dated 1895 that he wrote the essay ten years earlier in 1885, when he was 21 (see his letter to Pei Yüan-cheng [1954: 427]). However, Chang Teh-chün argues against this dating on the ground that T'an in this essay refers to his teacher Liu Jen-hsi, whom T'an did not get to know until 1889; Chang prefers to date the essay to 1889 or after. In my judgment, Chang's dating is not necessarily better than T'an's own. Chang's dating rests on T'an's reference to his acquaintance with Liu Jen-hsi, made in a letter to his friend Liu Sung-fu (ibid: 376), in which he makes a vague reference to his travel to Peking to study with Liu Jen-hsi. Chang Teh-chün assumes that this could not have happened before 1889, because 1889 was the year that T'an went to Peking to take the civil service examination. However, according to T'an's testimony elsewhere, he had traveled north and south six times for civil service exami-

sees it. Significantly, China is placed at the center of the world as the *Hua-Hsia chih kuo* (the kingdom of cultural flowering), surrounded to the north, east, and west by the *i-ti chih kuo* (the barbarian countries) and to the south by the *ch'in-shou chih kuo* (the beastly countries). He elevates China above the surrounding countries because it possesses an unsurpassed ritual-moral order, as epitomized by the "three bonds and five constancies" (*san-kang wu-ch'ang*).[15]

This image of China as the center of the world is accompanied in T'an's essay by a devolutionary view of history. T'an professes ignorance about the history of China before the time of the sage-king Yao. He divides history after Yao into three periods. The beginning period, dubbed the "period of prevailing *tao*" (*tao tao chih shih*), consisted of the three dynasties of Hsia, Shang, and Chou. These three dynasties were followed by the period from the Ch'in dynasty to recent times, a period when the *tao* was no longer preserved in purity and the moral order was often compromised. This was followed by the final period, the contemporary era in which T'an lived.[16]

The most important fact about the contemporary era, in T'an's view, was that the "barbarian countries," already in control of the "beastly countries," now began to encroach upon the "kingdom of cultural flowering," thereby challenging its superiority and even threatening its survival.[17]

What could be done about this unprecedented historical situation? This, he believed, was the most urgent question facing his era. His solution to it reveals the hold that the Confucian moral heritage still maintained over his mind.

T'an gives three conventional strategies for coping with the situation: to appeal to China's enemies, to go to war with them, or just to concentrate on defense. To him none of them is adequate. The real solution lay in understanding the trend of historical development and drawing a lesson from it. T'an's view of the present situation has as its basis his view of history as a three-phase process. However, in his perception, history is not only devolutionary, but cyclical as well. Like the devolutionary view of history, the cyclical view arises out of Chinese tradition. Of course, there were several versions of the cyclical view of history in the tradition. The version that T'an embraced was rooted in ancient cosmological thought, as incorporated in

---

nations from 1885 to 1895. Thus, we are not sure that he did not go to Peking before 1889. Even granted that T'an went to Peking in 1889 to study with Liu Jen-hsi, it is entirely unclear that this was the first time he became acquainted with Liu as a teacher, because Liu was a native of Liuyang, T'an's hometown, and was apparently already well known there before he went to Peking. In other words, we cannot dismiss the possibility that T'an already knew Liu before he visited him at Peking in 1889. Consequently, there is insufficient evidence to doubt T'an's own dating. See Chang Teh-chün (1974, 5: 110–11); T'an (1954: 205–6).
15. 1954: 104–5.
16. Ibid.: 103–4.
17. Ibid.: 105.

Han Confucianism. According to this version, each of the three phases of an historical cycle is dominated by an emblematic "virtue," (a sort of *zeitgeist*), namely, *chung* (fidelity), *chih* (unadorned substance), and *wen* (culture). In China, the long-term cultural historical trend had gone from the emblematic virtue of *chung* through *chih* to *wen*; now, in T'an's time, the historical cycle was about to complete its course and to start all over again.[18]

Thus, the emblematic spirit of the modern era would again be *chung*. In the West, meanwhile, the historical process was shorter, and the trend ran in the opposite direction, that is, from *wen* to *chung*. To T'an, the import of this view of history is clear. In response to the modern world, the Chinese people should act in tune with the tide of history and in the spirit of the emblematic virtue of *chung*, as against the opposite historical course and the different *zeitgeist* of the "barbarian lands."[19]

Here T'an is evidently trying to make sense of the current world situation from the historical perspective that he inherited from the Chinese tradition. What did the emblematic spirit of *chung* mean in the Chinese tradition? Understood in the context of the historical consciousness of Western Han Confucianism, it was not only a moral concept, but also carried the magico-ritual connotations of being loyal and pious to Heaven. However, T'an, probably influenced by the latter-day neo-Confucian interpretation of *chung*, understood it in the sense of being true to one's moral nature and exerting oneself to the utmost to fulfill one's nature. Due to this moral interpretation, *chung* for him primarily means sincerity of will and intention.[20]

Therefore, at the end of his essay, T'an reaffirms the basic Confucian approach to achieving political order, as spelled out in the Confucian classic, *Ta-hsüeh*. Sincerity of intention, inasmuch as it constitutes the first step in the purification of mind and the realization of self, provides the key to a process of moral and social action that culminates in setting the state and world in order. In short, T'an holds that, to fulfill the ruling spirit of *chung* of the new era, the Chinese people should exercise moral will and make a moral effort.[21]

This then was T'an's picture at 21 of the world and of China's role in it. It reflects a mind still in the grip of traditional influences, but, in the next decade, his ideas underwent a metamorphosis into a world view that, though still dominated by tradition, was nonetheless radically different. His early world view thus provides us with a baseline for the intellectual quest he undertook during the remainder of his life. From my analysis of T'an's writings, it is clear that he looked at the world largely from a moral perspective, not surprising considering his Confucian education. In the ensuing decade, this moral perspective is still integral to his intellectual development. Although T'an left few writings that give a clear and detailed picture of his thought

---

18. Ibid.: 103–5, 105–7.
19. Ibid.: 105–8.
20. Ibid.: 108–9.
21. Ibid.: 109.

during this period, I have obtained, from a collection of study notes, probably written in his late twenties, a picture that unmistakably points to the persistence of his moral concern.[22] These study notes reveal that his mind was still steeped in the moral thought of the Confucian *Ssu-shu*. His intensely practical interest in this regard is evidenced by his fervent study of the methods of moral nurture (*kung-fu*) presented in *Mencius* and *Analects*.[23]

One moral preoccupation that emerges from these study notes is a concern with controlling desires and emotions to achieve the spiritual equanimity necessary for self-realization. In one place, he details the problem posed in *Analects* of how to cope with "worries and fears" in order to achieve moral peace of mind.[24] Another signpost of his moral concern is the particular interest he took in *Mencius*.

The focus of his interest is not the moral values and sociopolitical ideals enunciated in *Mencius* but the Mencian approach to self-realization that is embodied in Mencius' concept of the cultivation of mind. For T'an, Mencius' signal contribution in this connection is the idea of "nourishing the material force" (*yang-ch'i*). T'an explains that the "material force" is more than something naturalistic like the air that a person breathes. It is also a vital force that, if cultivated and disciplined, can lead to the creation of what Mencius called "great spiritual courage" (*hao-jan chih ch'i*). Hence, "nourishing the material force" is not something like the Taoist practice of breath control; rather, it is a morally directed process of mental cultivation. The end result of this process is Mencius' ideal of the "imperturbable mind" (*pu-tung hsin*), which is the basis for moral-spiritual fulfillment.[25]

Even though a continuity with the Confucian moral perspective emerges clearly from his study notes, the notes do not leave us with the impression that T'an gives any specific value content to this perspective, as he did when he wrote "Chih-yen." On the contrary, these notes and other writings of his from the same period are sprinkled with hints that his mind was reaching out in various other directions for moral guidance. T'an's principal sources of inspiration were such ancient non-Confucian philosophies as philosophical Taoism and Mohism. The latter had had a particular intellectual appeal to him ever since he first read the classic *Mo Tzu* at 19.[26]

He was also inspired by Western learning, thanks to certain teachers and friends of his early youth who were fervent admirers of Western culture.[27] Although the principal attractions of Western learning were, of course,

---

22. According to Yang's chronological biography of T'an (1957: 67–68), he wrote these two volumes of study notes at age 30. However, it is probable that they were actually written during his late twenties but went into print when he was 30.
23. 1954: 260–63.
24. Ibid.
25. Ibid.: 260.
26. For T'an's interest in philosophical Taoism, see the second part of his study notes (1954: 254–56). For his interest in Mohism, see Yang (1957: 42).
27. Yang (1957: 28–29, 38).

science and technology, the impact of T'an's discovery of the West went beyond gaining scientific knowledge. It opened his eyes in ways that inevitably had a bearing directly or indirectly on his moral outlook.[28]

The most palpable influence on T'an's writings in this period, however, came from a heterodox Confucian, Wang Fu-chih, a seventeenth-century thinker from T'an's home province.[29] It is not surprising that Wang should have influenced him, because there was a renaissance of interest in Wang's thought among the Hunanese literati in the late nineteenth century and two of T'an's early teachers, along with some of his close friends, were devoted students of Wang's philosophy.[30] Under their influence, T'an began, in his mid-twenties, to study Wang's writings seriously. Thus, it was no accident that T'an's two earliest philosophical writings dealt with the thought of Wang Fu-chih and that of Wang's intellectual forebear in the neo-Confucian tradition—the early Sung philosopher Chang Tsai.[31] We do not know the content of these writings, because they are no longer extant, but clearly the ideas of Wang and Chang helped shape T'an's thinking.

As a result, T'an's moral thought moved in two directions. First of all, he turned his attention to "practical learning" (*shih-hsüeh*).[32] This was nothing unusual: many of his fellow intellectuals were then advocating *shih-hsüeh* as a practical reorientation of Confucian studies in response to the national crisis facing China.[33] However, T'an's thinking in this direction was not just an echo of this trend; it must also be understood against the background of Wang Fu-chih's position on the subject. Wang Fu-chih has often been regarded as a harbinger of the trend toward practical learning in the Confucian tradition that began in the seventeenth century. His concern for practical learning, like that of the other pioneers of *shih-hsüeh*, grew out of an idea inherent in the humanistic perspective of Confucianism—the idea of practicality.[34] The Confucian tradition understood the idea in two senses: it referred to moral practice, as opposed to the cognitive or contemplative orientation of mind; or it referred to a utilitarian orientation of practice, as opposed to an absolute commitment to moral ends.[35] In the neo-Confucian tradition, the idea of practicality in its moral sense was universally accepted. What people differed about was the relationship between practicality in the moral sense and

---

28. Shek (1976).
29. See the second part of T'an's notes on ideas (1954: 247, 256, 258, 261). See also his letters to Ou-yang Chung-ku (ibid.: 292, 294, 320, 321) and his letter to his friend Liu Sung-fu (ibid.: 376–77).
30. Yang (1957: 28–29, 54–57); see also T'an (1954: 261–62).
31. Ibid.: 56–57, 59–60.
32. See T'an's letter to Ou-yang Chung-ku (1954: 291) and his letter to Pei Yüan-cheng (ibid.: 389–91, 414–15).
33. Chang Hao (1980: 326, 331).
34. McMorran (1975: 413–67).
35. Cheng Chung-ying (1979: 37–61).

in the utilitarian. Many emphasized moral practicality to the exclusion of utilitarian practicality, on the ground that the two were incompatible with each other. Others believed that the idea of moral practicality was not necessarily incompatible with that of utilitarian practicality and could accommodate the latter. Wang Fu-chih held the latter view of practicality.[36]

Wang Fu-chih's idea of moral practicality is best seen in his interpretation of a dichotomy that is central to neo-Confucian thought—the dichotomy between *tao* (way) and *ch'i* (vessel). Underlying his interpretation is an ontological monism, namely, the view that nothing exists that is not made up of material force. It follows that *tao* as the essence and the universal principle is not an ontologically independent reality, inasmuch as it is inseparable from and inherent in the "vessel" (*ch'i*) of concrete existence in which it is embodied.[37] Given the centrality of the humanistic perspective and the lack of differentiation between the moral and the actual in the Confucian perspective, Wang Fu-chih's view has a natural corollary: the *tao* can be realized only through moral practice in the concrete realities of the human world. This way of thinking is also espoused by T'an, who understood practical learning and the ideal of practicality according to Wang Fu-chih's interpretation of the *tao-ch'i* dichotomy.[38] Thus, he argues not just for the utilitarian orientation of study; as a follower of Wang Fu-chih, he considers this orientation to be part of a broader orientation to moral *praxis*. Consequently, his emphasis on practical learning broadened, rather than diluted or dissipated, the moral concern taking shape in his writings at this time.

Under the influence of Wang's thought, T'an also shows a tendency to see moral values embedded in a structure of reality, spelled out in metaphysical world views. Therefore, he views moral practice not as something arbitrary, but as resonating with cosmic rhythms. Of course, this tendency in T'an's thought may have other sources in the Confucian tradition, as the same tendency is inherent in the world view of "unity of Heaven and man" widely accepted in the Confucian tradition. But his study notes amply indicate that he developed this tendency mainly in the framework of Wang Fu-chih's specific interpretation of that Confucian world view—a metaphysical monism based on the idea of the material force.[39]

T'an's study notes also show a fascination with the new cosmology revealed by Western science.[40] However, this fascination did not lead him to accept the naturalistic notion of a self-regulating cosmos. In fact, in the notes

---

36. T'an Shuang-ch'üan (1965: 65–86); see also McMorran (1975: 417–67).
37. T'an Shuang-ch'üan (1965); see also Hsiao Chieh-fu (1965: 25–39).
38. See T'an's letters to Ou-yang Chung-ku and Pei Yüan-cheng (1954: 292–93, 294–95, 389–91).
39. See his study notes, the second part (ibid.: 245–49, 251–52).
40. Ibid.: 242, 243–44, 245, 251–52.

he often discusses the Copernican view of the universe in the context of the teleological Confucian world view, trying to synthesize the two. In his view, the Copernican system fit perfectly into the Confucian, *ch'i*-based world view. He argues, for instance, that the atmosphere that Western sciences believe envelopes the earth is only one mode of what the Confucian tradition calls "the material force." According to Western science, this atmosphere only exists for a certain distance around the earth and vanishes altogether above 200 miles. However, T'an points out that the vanishing of atmosphere beyond a certain distance does not mean the nonexistence of material force in the rest of the universe. He distinguishes two modes of material force and says that, though the atmosphere constitutes the "mode of material force that generates biological existences," a more basic mode of material force—the cosmic force or, in his words, the "material force that moves between the Heaven and earth" (*t'ien-ti wang lai chih ch'i*)—fills up the universe.[41]

This cosmic force is what makes possible such natural phenomena as light and sound, because it is the medium through which both are transmitted.[42] But, in addition to this naturalistic function, the cosmic force also has a moral-spiritual function, inasmuch as T'an sees no difference between this cosmic force and what is called *ch'i* in the Confucian cosmology. He argues that, as with *ch'i*, the cosmic force has *yin* and *yang* as its two basic modes of manifestation. The eternal interplay between them explains the structure and functioning of the universe. Thus, the three constituent parts of the universe—Heaven, earth, and man—can all be explained in terms of interactions between *yin* and *yang*. Obviously, the complementary dualism symbolized by the belief in *yin* and *yang* is still integral to T'an's outlook. As he views *yin* and *yang* as nothing more than two modes of manifestation of the material force, he still sees an all-embracing cosmic oneness underlying the operation of the forces of *yin* and *yang*.[43]

Thus, despite his fascination with some of the Copernican images of the universe, T'an remains under the sway of the Confucian belief in the unity of Heaven and man. He still speaks with enthusiasm of the idea of the immanence of the Heaven in the cosmos as a whole, as well as in every existence in it, and he still has no qualms about echoing the neo-Confucian belief that the cosmos is not only a material organism, but also a moral-spiritual whole.[44] It is easy to understand, then, why in his view cultivation of mind has a moral and a cosmic significance.

Two tendencies emerge clearly from T'an's early writings. On the one hand, there is the tendency for him to see his own moral outlook as rooted in the structure of the cosmos. On the other, there is his proclivity to see a

41. Ibid.: 246–47, 248.
42. Ibid.: 251–52.
43. Ibid.: 245–48.
44. Ibid.: 247–48.

cosmos impregnated with moral-spiritual significance. Both tendencies are really two sides of the mental outlook at the heart of his intellectual quest, namely, what Clifford Geertz calls "the struggle for the real" or "the attempt to impose upon the world a particular conception of how things at bottom are and how men are therefore obliged to feel and act."[45]

However, T'an's "struggle for the real" is no mere fusion of metaphysical perspective and moral concern. Another dimension to this struggle must be taken into account before I can do justice to the complexity of his intellectual quest: the existential anguish that stands out in many of his early writings.

T'an had a rather gloomy childhood, growing up as he did in a patriarchal family where his stepmother often discriminated against and ill-treated him.[46] His marriage was reportedly also unhappy. T'an never divulged his family unhappiness in specific detail, though he did hint once that his family troubles had almost led him to attempt suicide on several occasions.[47] But none of these experiences could compare with the traumas he went through as a result of a series of deaths in his family during his adolescence. Within a few days, an epidemic robbed him of his mother, a brother, a sister, and several other family relatives.[48] Later, deaths continued to befall his family, but he was particularly grieved by the death of an elder brother who was very close to him.[49] These tragedies left a permanent scar on his mind, and memories of the deceased continued to haunt him long afterward, as seen, for example, in a lengthy elegy that he wrote at age 25.[50] This elegy contains scene after scene of memories of the road to his brothers' and sisters' grave sites and about the times they had spent together. These scenes are suffused with sadness and bewilderment about the insuperable separation now standing between him and the dead.[51] The elegy ends on a note of desolation and distress, which bespeaks his acute sense of the tragic in life:

> I used to dream that I was crying in my chair
> When the morning wind rushed resoundingly through the forest, I woke and
>   felt joy to know that this had been merely a dream.
> Now, suddenly, my dream has come to be terribly true.

---

45. Geertz (1973: 316).
46. Yang (1957: 24, 26, 31–32); see also Ou-yang Yü-ch'ien in T'an (1954: 519) and T'an, "Tzu hsü" [Preface] (ibid.: 3).
47. Yang (1957: 44); see also T'an (1954: 519) and T'an (ibid.: 3).
48. T'an, "Hsien-p'i Hsü fu-jen i-shih chuang" [An anecdotal account of my mother's life] (1954: 197–200) and "Hsien chung-hsiung hsing-shu" [An account of my brother's life] (ibid.: 201).
49. 1954: 200–4. T'an poignantly described his sorrow over his brother's death in "Yüan i-t'ang chi wai wen ch'u-pien tzu-hsü" [Preface to the first collection of T'an Ssu-tung's essays] (ibid.: 151).
50. T'an, "Hsiang-hen tz'u pa-p'ien" [Eight stanzas of the Hsiang-hen poems] (ibid.: 452–54). A complete translation is given in the appendix.
51. Ibid.

> Now, how do I know that these present tragedies might not also be a bad dream?
> But I can believe this only for a moment, for I know there are differences between life awake and life in a dream.
> If you want to feel the remorse felt by the dead, watch the cuckoo crying blood from its eyes.
> Only listen to the lone swan, then you will know the feelings of one who is still alive.[52]

This tone of desolation and distress reflects a mood that elsewhere in his writings he describes as *ts'ang-jan chih kan* (a feeling of bleakness).[53] This mood, added to his underlying tragic sense, would account for the tendency of his poems to dwell on the dark side of life: the sorrows of parting, the sufferings he saw in his travels, the pain of unrequited and unfulfilled love, and, above all, the mystery of death.[54] Indeed, preoccupation with death is a striking note in his poems. T'an expresses it vividly in a poem called *Ts'an hun ch'ü* (The song of a lingering soul):

> In daytime a white jade lamp lights dimly in the tomb.
> In the hall of the dead the double golden doors are shut for good.
> In the darkness of night the sounds of a ghastly barn owl are like human speech.
> A white poplar tree stands desolately under a bitter yellow moonlight.
> A lingering soul eerily stands there as the cold fog falls.
> The acid winds that touch the face blow down blood and tears.
> The mountain lightning bug lights up a little here and there.
> Near the tomb, the stone statues of men stealthily fall asleep on the grass-covered ground.
> The insects hum beneath the autumn flowers fallen on the grasses.
> The carriage of ghosts rolls darkly on, unaccompanied by men.
> The mist of dream and the fog of sorrow weave down a secluded path.
> Mournful songs and howls of grief sadden the chill night.
> From time immemorial, human sorrows and aspirations have all been in vain.
> All glories and desolations wind up in the old tomb.
> Don't you hear Pao Chao's poems of gloom, sung sadly in the depths of the woods?
> At daybreak the haze of souls still spreads over rivers and trees.[55]

This poem not only tells us something about the dark shadow that T'an's preoccupation with death has cast over his feelings and mood. It also reveals the question that was raised in his mind. If all lives, high and low, rich and poor, inevitably end in the dark tomb, what is the meaning of human life?

---

52. Ibid.: 454.
53. 1954: 151.
54. Ibid.: 459–60, 461–62, 463–64, 482, 492, 494–95, 499–501.
55. "Ts'an hun ch'ü" (ibid.: 458).

T'an's study notes bear some traces of the struggle he underwent to find an answer to this question and to lift the shadow of death. At one place in his notes, for example, he is led to argue with the popular Taoist ideal of seeking physical immortality and writes that, beyond a certain advanced age, life may not be entirely desirable and death may not always be such a bad thing.[56] For T'an, death may sometimes be preferable to a life lived in isolation and loneliness.

But mainly T'an is looking for ways to make sense of life and death as a whole, and he finds some ideas in the philosophical Taoism of the book of *Chuang Tzu* particularly appealing. One is the view of life on earth as a perpetual flux. At any point in this flux, some lives end and others start afresh. From this perspective, there is no point in making a distinction between life and death.[57] Equally appealing is Chuang Tzu's idea of the mystic oneness, which holds that the phenomenal world and all the mundane distinctions, such as the distinction between self and other and the distinction between large and small, are relative and ultimately meaningless. T'an's discussions along these lines are often brief and cryptic, but it is apparent that, with the help of philosophical Taoism, he was reaching for a larger perspective that would enable him to transcend the fears and anxieties that he found inherent in life.[58]

In view of the dark, oppressive feelings and moods that his poems reflect and his struggle in his study notes to make sense of life and world, it seems clear that T'an's intellectual quest was rooted as much in his existential anguish as in his metaphysical anxiety and his moral concern. He was searching for something to show him the "really real" and also to allow him to satisfy his need for moral fulfillment and to overcome his feeling of desolation about life. It is in this sense that the "struggle for the real" constitutes the spiritual thrust of his intellectual quest.

A STUDY OF HUMANITY (*JEN-HSÜEH*)

T'an's spiritual quest was on display when he made a study tour to the north in 1896. At Shanghai he met John Fryer, who introduced him to some new developments in Western sciences. T'an found them intriguing, but he was more impressed by what he learned about Christianity. He was especially captivated by one book that John Fryer recommended to him, a Chinese translation of Henry Wood's writing on mental healing.[59] At the end of his tour, T'an traveled to Nanking, where he met the Buddhist scholar

---

56. Ibid.: 255.
57. Ibid.: 255–56.
58. Ibid.: 254.
59. T'an's letter to Ou-yang Chung-ku (ibid.: 318, 320). See *Chih-hsin mien ping fa* (1896).

Yang Wen-hui. He immediately plunged into studying Buddhist teachings and became a devoted disciple of Yang's.[60]

T'an said at the time that three things occupied his mind during his travels: intellectual knowledge (*hsüeh*), politics (*cheng*), and religious teachings (*chiao*). Afterward, he became convinced that religious teachings had the highest priority on his agenda of study, because any endeavor in the other two areas would not go far without the spiritual guidance of religious teachings.[61] Why did he attach such importance to religion? He once intimated that religion could explain many things that were inexplicable through human reason or scientific knowledge.[62] But his real reason went much deeper than mere intellectual curiosity. It had to do with the new hope and confidence that he found in life and the world because of his study of various spiritual teachings.

This new note of optimism is evident in a long letter that he wrote to one of his teachers not long after he settled down in Nanking. In this letter he talks of the deep distress that he felt when he saw the sufferings and misery among people in the places he visited, but he also leaves the strong impression that he is no longer discouraged by it, because he now believes that all these sufferings and miseries can be overcome.[63]

The source of this new-found optimism is his belief that the human mind-heart (*hsin*), when properly cultivated and developed, has a saving spiritual power. He was influenced in his new belief in the "power of mind-heart" (*hsin-li*) by several sources that stemmed from the religious traditions he had studied. His "struggle for the real" brought him under the influence of neo-Confucian and Taoist spiritual teachings. Both teachings already inclined T'an to see the spiritual unity of self with the cosmos; in both, the vision of spiritual unity is accompanied by a belief in the spiritual capacity of the human mind for transcendence. The influences of neo-Confucianism and Taoism were now reinforced by a new religious teaching that he studied as a result of his recent tour. The very word *hsin-li* suggests that the teachings of Buddhism were beginning to shape T'an's mind, because it is a word often used in the literature of Mahayana Buddhism. Especially important in this connection is a belief basic to Chinese Mahayana Buddhism, namely, that the human mind-heart has an innate potential for both individual and universal salvation. T'an quotes from the literature of Mahayana Buddhism: "The spiritual power of our mind-heart can be drawn upon to stem the catastrophic advent of *kalpa* (*i hsin wan-chieh*)."[64]

---

60. T'an's letter to Ou-yang Chung-ku (1954: 328). See also Liang Ch'i-ch'ao (1936, *wen-chi*, ts'e 45: 11).
61. T'an's letter to Ou-yang Chung-ku (1954: 322, 323–24).
62. Ibid.: 317–18.
63. Ibid.: 316–29.
64. Ibid.: 318–20, 321, 326–27.

But Mahayana Buddhism, however important, was by no means the only source of his belief in the power of the human mind-heart. T'an at that time was also a fervent student of Christianity and fascinated by Henry Wood's writings on the mind-cure. Drawing on the Protestant faith in the power of the human spirit, Wood preached that mind had such power over body that it could even cure physical disease.[65] T'an, very taken with Wood's idea of mental power, compares it to the Confucian concept of "piety" (*ch'eng*).[66] Such a comparison was by no means accidental, for underlying the idea of piety is the Confucian world view that looks on the human mind as partaking in one way or another of the ultimate reality—Heaven—and therefore as the vehicle of transforming power in the universe. To T'an, it was obvious that Christianity was as confident in the spiritual capacity of mind as Buddhism or Confucianism. Thus, the spiritual teachings he studied all seemed to reinforce each other, convincing him that man could save himself through the power of his own mind.

This note of optimism indicates that T'an's intellectual search was finally bearing fruit. In this regard, the letter mentioned above is a prelude to a philosophical tract, *Jen-hsüeh* (A study of humanity), which he wrote soon after he went to Nanking in 1896 at the end of his study tour.[67] This tract was written at a particularly hectic time for T'an. In Nanking, through his acquaintance with Yang Wen-hui, he had just been initiated into the intellectual world of Mahayana Buddhism. There was much to learn and absorb. Meanwhile, K'ang Yu-wei's reform movement was spreading to T'an's home province of Hunan. Consequently, he had little time to write, and this haste may explain why the tract was not entirely of one piece and often marred by undeveloped themes, loose ends, stray statements, and even contradictory ideas. But these problems notwithstanding, a relatively unified vision of reality dominates the core.

The Philosophical Sources

The fact that he calls his tract "A study of humanity" suggests that T'an was trying to recapture the vision of reality that he believed to be embodied in the Confucian ideal of humanity—*jen*. Inevitably, his efforts bear the marks

---

65. For Wood's thought, see Parker (1973: 61–70).
66. T'an's letter to Ou-yang Chung-ku (1954: 320).
67. The title can also be romanized as *Jen hsüeh* and translated as "Humanity and Study," because T'an states obliquely at one place in his preface (1954: 3) that he treats two subjects in his book, namely, both *jen* and *hsüeh*, by which he says he means *ko-chih*, a term often used at that time to signify Western sciences. T'an thus implies that *hsüeh* is used in the title as a subject in parallel with *jen*, rather than as a modifier of *jen*. Although this interpretation is legitimate, I prefer the translation "Study of *jen*" for two reasons: first, an explication of the ideal of *jen* is clearly the main concern of the book; and, second, to the extent that Western sciences are discussed, the discussions are directly or indirectly geared to T'an's explication of the ideal of *jen*.

of influences he was exposed to in his intellectual quest. The result is a metamorphosis of the ideal of *jen*. To understand this metamorphosis, I must return to the original source from which his conception of *jen* evolved: the neo-Confucian world view, as developed in the philosophies of Chang Tsai and Wang Fu-chih. T'an wrote his first philosophical treatises about these two thinkers. Thus, to understand T'an's vision of reality, we must begin by placing Chang and Wang in the context of the neo-Confucian philosophic tradition.

For neo-Confucians, *jen* not only crystallizes a moral ideal, but also symbolizes a world view often characterized as the "unity of Heaven and man" (*t'ien-jen ho-i*). At the heart of this view is an ontological vision of the primordial state of the world as a harmonious spiritual whole. In the actual world, this primordial harmony is broken by the fissiparous and corrupting tendencies that inevitably attend the birth of an individual being. Harmony, however, would return following the dissolution of the ego-self through the moral transformation of individual human beings. In a broad sense, the world view of "unity of Heaven and man" may be seen as a variation on the story of separation and return that underlies many religious traditions. Within this framework, the symbol *jen* and the Confucian ethics of spiritual aspiration that it represents take on the dimensions of a cosmic drama and transcend the merely mundane concern with moral conduct.[68]

Central to this world view is a concept of self as partaking of the ultimate reality of the cosmos. The focus of the neo-Confucian concept of self is the notion of *hsin* (mind-heart). The ultimate reality is conceived as an encompassing whole that informs and also transcends all the individual existences in the universe. Over the centuries, neo-Confucian philosophers have differed among themselves regarding the nature of the *hsin* and the encompassing whole as well as the relationship between the two. Their differences eventually crystallized into three divergent trends in the neo-Confucian tradition.

The orthodox trend, known as the Ch'eng-Chu School, is characterized by a metaphysical dualism in which the encompassing whole is made up of two all-pervading, but ontologically independent, forces: *li* (principle) which is the source of identity, meaning, and value; and *ch'i* (material force), which is the stuff of actual existence. *Hsin*, the vital center of the individual self, is, like everything else, believed to be a fusion of *li* and *ch'i*. In the neo-Confucian tradition, this dualistic world view is opposed by the *hsin*-based monism of the Lu-Wang School. In this "idealistic" view, the objective reality of the encompassing whole is not so much denied as approached from a "subjective" perspective that focuses on the mind-heart as the sole vehicle

---

68. Chan Wing-tsit (1963: esp. the sections on Chang Tsai and Ch'eng Hao, pp. 495–517 and 518–43).

through which the moral-spiritual force of Heaven's principles can be made manifest in an ego-self. The mind-heart, then, has no place for material force and can be completely identified with the cosmic principle. In reaction to both the *hsin*-based monism of the Lu-Wang School and the dualism of the Ch'eng-Chu School, a third trend developed—a *ch'i*-based monism. Although this trend emerged mainly in the sixteenth century and after, it had a precursor in the early development of neo-Confucianism—the philosopher Chang Tsai.[69]

Chang Tsai's philosophy was built around a vision of reality rooted in the unity of Heaven and man. To refute the nihilistic world views of Buddhism and Taoism, Chang saw the world as made up of the all-pervading substance—*ch'i*. But his *ch'i*-based world view cannot be characterized as either materialistic or naturalistic, mainly because, although *ch'i* is something substantial, it has inherent vitalistic and moral-spiritual qualities as its "nature" (*hsing*). Further, harking back to the idea of a dynamic cosmos in *I ching* (The book of changes), Chang does not conceive of *ch'i* in a static image of fundamental particles or elements but in a dynamic image of material force constantly engaged in evolution, transformation, and movement of every kind. Seen in this light, the existence and extinction of individual beings in the universe are nothing more than the concentration and dispersal of the all-pervading *ch'i*. When an individual existence is formed, *ch'i* fills the individual's body, and the moral-spiritual qualities inherent in *ch'i* constitute the vital center that is connected to the controlling power in the universe: Heaven. In this way, every individual existence is part and parcel of the all-encompassing whole. And "death" never occurs to any individual existence, because to Chang death means nothing more than the immersion of one particular form of existence into the primordial whole. True, the particular form of that existence is no more, but the material force that constitutes the particular being and the *hsing* that inheres in the material force remain in existence. Although the microcosmos of each individual self comes and goes, the macrocosmos of the encompassing whole, of which every individual self partakes, lives on forever.[70]

How can one transcend one's attachment to self and identify with the encompassing whole? How can one see oneself as a part of the encompassing whole where self dissolves and moral harmony prevails? These are the central concerns of Chang Tsai's concept of self-realization. At the heart of it is the belief that the mind-heart of a self, as the locus of the moral-spiritual qualities, has the self-transcending capacity to unite with or merge into the encompassing whole. This is because, in Chang's view, the human mind is capable of two kinds of knowledge: "the knowledge of seeing and knowing"

---

69. For a lengthy discussion of Chang Tsai's thought, see Ts'ai Jen-hou (1977: 77–216). See also Mou Tsung-san (1968: 417–570).

70. Ts'ai Jen-hou (1977: 77–126).

(*chien-wen chih chih*) and the moral-spiritual insight (*teh-hsing chih chih*). The former refers to empirical knowledge, the latter to an intuitive, a priori kind of knowledge that provides one with the capacity for moral and transcendent experience.[71]

In this regard, Chang Tsai's thought echoed a strain of ethical mysticism in Confucianism that can be traced back to the Mencian idea that the human mind has the capacity to develop to the fullest its innate moral-spiritual potential and thereby to unite with the encompassing whole. Chang Tsai's ethical mysticism is summed up in his vision of a universal *gemeinschaft* in which the whole of mankind, all being parts of the encompassing whole, would form a single community of love and care on earth. He spells out this vision in a short work entitled *Hsi-ming* (Western inscription), which became an unfailing source of moral-spiritual inspiration within the neo-Confucian tradition.[72]

Chang Tsai's thought had echoes in the late Ming, especially in Wang Fu-chih's philosophy. Reacting against both the dualism of the Ch'eng-Chu School and the "idealism" of the Lu-Wang School, Wang came to accept Chang Tsai's *ch'i*-based, monistic interpretation of the belief in the unity of Heaven and man.[73] However, within the framework of *ch'i*-based monism, Wang's thought went beyond Chang's in two ways. First, Wang's world view featured a cosmic dynamism and moral activism, both of which stem from the dynamic view of the cosmos rooted in the *I ching* and constitute a striking characteristic of Chang Tsai's philosophy. In both, the cosmos is pictured as an organic whole, not in stasis but vibrant with movement, creativity, and growth. In brief, unending and incessant change is seen as the dominant mode of existence of the cosmos. This change takes the form of either dialectical movement or generative activities of life. Because both modes of change differ from the unilinear temporal mode, the cosmos is viewed as engaged in a universal, perennial process of cosmic renewal or vitalistic regeneration.[74]

For this reason, in neo-Confucianism the ideal of *jen* represents not only a human world of love and care, but also a cosmos overflowing with life, with the vitality to "generate and regenerate" (*sheng sheng pu-i*). Such a world view inevitably has a moral-spiritual import: to live in tune with the changing, dynamic, encompassing whole, human individuals should engage in constant moral-spiritual renewal. This moral activism is embodied in the concept of *jih-hsin* (daily renewal), which is integral to the *I ching* and Chang Tsai's philosophy.[75] In conscious reaction against what he considered to be

---

71. Mou Tsung-san (1968: 532–56).
72. Ts'ai Jen-hou (1977, chap. 4: 77–101).
73. Chang Ch'i-chih (1965: 266–84).
74. T'an Shuang-ch'üan (1965: 25–39).
75. T'ang Ming-pang (1965: 87–136).

quietist tendencies in the neo-Confucian tradition, Wang Fu-chih made both metaphysical dynamism and moral activism the focal concerns of his thinking.

In Wang's thought, however, both notions are given new significance. Carrying the idea of metaphysical dynamism to its logical conclusion within the framework of the belief in the unity of Heaven and man, Wang developed a dynamic concept of human nature. Because the encompassing whole is constantly evolving and changing, the endowment that an individual receives as his inner nature (*hsing*) from the encompassing whole inevitably also changes and evolves all the time. Thus, instead of being something static and fixed at the beginning of one's life, the inner nature of any human individual is constantly being renewed. In order to let this always-changing inner nature manifest itself, the individual must make unceasing efforts at self-cultivation and moral-spiritual renewal. Further, in this concept of daily renewal, the human being is seen as more than an inert vessel passively receiving and manifesting moral commands from Heaven via his inner nature; primarily he is an agent actively engaged in expanding and furthering the moral will of Heaven. It is in this sense that Wang speaks of "building up Heaven's endowment" (*tsao-ming*) or "building up Heaven" (*tsao-t'ien*).[76] Thus, Wang's cosmic dynamism and moral activism result in a concept of the moral-spiritual creativity of human beings as participants in the process of cosmic renewal.

Closely related to the notions of cosmic dynamism and moral activism is an ethical realism that also stands out in Wang's thought. Like the former ideas, it grew out of his *ch'i*-based monism. For Wang, it followed from his view of cosmic principles as inherent in the material force that moral-spiritual qualities reside in emotional needs and biological desires as part of the material force. As a corollary, Wang held a positive view of the instinctual components of the human self, which neo-Confucian orthodoxy tended to decry as inimical to the cosmic principles and to human nature. Thus, to him human nature embraced moral virtues as well as instinctual drives. He believed that this legitimation of instinctual fulfillment distinguished the Confucian affirmation of life from the other-worldly asceticism of Buddhism.[77]

Wang's ethical realism is certainly at odds with the premium placed on instinctual repression by the orthodox school of neo-Confucianism. However, Wang's realism is far from unqualified, because his thinking in this regard is marked by inconsistency and ambiguity. For one thing, Wang still sometimes evinces tendencies to see a sharp antithesis between principle (*li*) and desires (*yü*) and to see the instinctual self in negative terms.[78] Even when

76. Ibid.: 109–21.
77. Hou Wai-lu (1958, 5: 99–104).
78. Chang Ch'i-chih (1965: 282–84); see also Chi Wen-fu (1962: 89).

he insists on the inseparability of principles and desires, he stops short of drawing the logical conclusion that all desires are legitimate. In fact, he sometimes begs the question, maintaining that only those desires that prove to be endurable, fair, and humane are legitimate. Given all the inconsistencies and ambiguities in his thinking, then, it is no surprise that Wang's *ch'i*-based monism and the accompanying positive view of the instinctual self did not lead him to moral radicalism. All they gave rise to was a moderate realism contained within the framework of neo-Confucian moral values.[79]

The Vision of Reality

As we have seen, Wang Fu-chih's ethical realism and activism as well as his metaphysical dynamism were part and parcel of the *ch'i*-based monism that he developed from Chang Tsai's ontological vision of the unity of Heaven and man. It was through this avenue that T'an Ssu-t'ung first approached the *jen* ideal. However, by the time he spelled out his understanding of *jen*, ideas from other sources, most notably from Mahayana Buddhism, had made their influence felt in the formulation of his world view.[80]

A fundamental premise of T'an's view of *jen* was an unbounded faith in the spiritual power of the human mind—a faith that he professes in his letter to his teacher before writing *Jen-hsüeh*. Confucianism, Mahayana Buddhism, and Christianity all contributed to this faith. Although he continues in *Jen-hsüeh* to echo Henry Wood's idea of mental sway over body and the Christian idea of priority of soul (*ling-hun*) over body (*t'i-p'o*), he draws more upon the teachings of Mahayana Buddhism and Confucianism in articulating his belief in the spiritual power of the human mind.[81]

This combination of Confucian and Buddhist influences is clearly seen in the way T'an conceives of the nature and function of the human mind. On one hand, he accepts the dualistic concept of mind found in the thought of Chang Tsai and Wang Fu-chih, and in neo-Confucian thought in general. Thus, he writes of the distinction between the "human mind" (*jen-hsin*), that is, the mind in its given, natural form, and the "mind of *tao*" (*tao-hsin*), the

---

79. Chi Wen-fu (1962: 90–93).
80. In a long poem K'ang Yu-wei wrote in 1898 to mourn T'an Ssu-t'ung's martyrdom (1954: 527), he implied that T'an had developed his ideal of *jen* under his influence. Liang Ch'i-ch'ao, in his preface to the first edition of *Jen-hsüeh* (ibid.: 515–16), also claimed that T'an's book was basically a further development of K'ang's philosophy of *jen*. T'an may have been indebted to K'ang in some ways, but it must be remembered that, when T'an heard about K'ang's philosophy through Liang, he was already heavily influenced by the writings of Chang Tsai and Wang Fu-chih, in which *jen* was also a pivotal ideal.
81. See T'an's letter to Ou-yang Chung-ku (1954: 316–29). See also a poem T'an wrote after hearing some lectures by Yang Wen-hui on the teachings of Mahayana Buddhism (ibid.: 485). *Jen-hsüeh* itself is replete with the evidence of his faith in the spiritual power of the human mind (ibid.: 6, 7, 11, 29, 47–48, 48–50, 73, 74–75, 80–83, 88–90). For the particular influences of Buddhism and Confucianism, see ibid.: 48–50.

mind that enables one to see the moral-spiritual reality and, therefore, serves as the vehicle for the moral-spiritual transformation of the self.[82] On the other hand, he merges this distinction with the dualism of the Yogacara Buddhist conception of mind. Thus, he also speaks of two kinds of consciousness in the human mind: perceptual and conceptual knowledge (*vignana*) which is the source of human illusions about the existence of the phenomenal world, and transcendental consciousness (*prajna*), which enables one to discern illusions and, by the same token, to see the transcendental, ultimate reality.[83] For T'an, then, both neo-Confucianism and Mahayana Buddhism share a dualistic concept of mind and, correspondingly, also a dualistic conception of world: the world we perceive and a higher reality. The wonder of the human mind is its ability to elevate itself through moral-spiritual cultivation from a lower level to a higher level of vision and thereby merge one's self-ego into the reality—the selfless whole.

How should one go about the cultivation of mind? Although T'an does not give any systematic, clear answer, scattered discussions of the issue in his *Jen-hsüeh* leave little doubt that his concept is primarily a synthesis of the Confucian notion of self-cultivation (*hsiu-shen*) with the Buddhist idea of spiritual discipline of mind. In this synthesis, particular emphasis is given to Yogacara Buddhism's idea of transformation of consciousness from *vignana* into *prajna*. Thus, according to T'an, the cultivation of mind required for achieving a vision of reality involves more than the exercise of a higher moral-spiritual faculty of mind; it also involves the inducement of a suprasensory consciousness, implying the ineffability of envisaged reality and pointing to a strain of transcendentalism in T'an's thinking.[84]

This transcendentalism exists not only in T'an's conception of moral-spiritual cultivation as a means to achieve his vision of reality, but also in the vision itself. In his attempt to characterize the vision of reality as represented by the ideal of *jen*, he often draws heavily upon the concepts of mystic oneness in philosophical Taoism and Mahayana Buddhism.[85] Because these concepts carry some transtemporal and transmundane connotations, T'an's vision inevitably takes on a transcendental, other-worldly coloration, which explains why a certain ambiguity exists in T'an's vision of reality in *Jen-hsüeh*. On one hand, there is the inner-worldly perspective stemming from the neo-Confucian ideal of *jen*, as handed down by Chang Tsai and Wang Fu-chih. On the other, strains of transcendentalism crop up in his characterization of reality. However, whatever ambiguity there is in the overall orientation of T'an's vision of reality, the organic oneness of a selfless whole, as presented at the center of his vision, takes on the coloration of a this-

---

82. Ibid.: 50.
83. Ibid.: 34, 48–50.
84. Ibid.: 32–34, 47–50.
85. Ibid.: 28–34.

worldly mysticism. We can see this in the way he conceived of how the world is constituted.

For T'an, the cosmos and every existence therein are made up of a fundamental constituent substance, which is seen as a basic force of attraction (*hsi-li*), a force that binds together the whole cosmos and everything, however small, in it:[86]

> Throughout the different realms of the universe there is something that is very large but at the same time also very small, and penetrates, permeates, and fills up everywhere. This is something, the color of which one cannot see with one's eyes, the sound of which one cannot hear with one's ears, and the smell and taste of which one cannot perceive with one's nose and mouth. Since there exists no better word to name it, we call it *i-t'ai*.[87]

It is significant that T'an used the word *i-t'ai* to name what he considers the basic material substance. *I-t'ai* is an exact transliteration of the English word "ether"; it must be remembered that ether was a central concept in the physical sciences in the nineteenth century. It refers to a hypothetical invisible substance postulated to pervade all space and serve as the medium for the transmission of light waves and other forms of energy. It was a basic tenet of nineteenth-century scientific materialism that all happenings of nature can be explained in terms of the locomotion of the material ether. T'an's usage of the word ether and some other scientific terms like electricity and mechanical force in his *Jen-hsüeh* have led a number of scholars, especially certain Marxist historians, to consider him a materialist.[88]

Doubtless, there are places in T'an's writings where his thinking lends itself to a materialist interpretation. For example, at times he indulges in a tendency to describe human mind and spirit and their functions in materialistic and mechanistic language.[89] However, a closer examination of T'an's writings reveals that his concept of ether owes more to the neo-Confucian conception of *ch'i*, as developed in the thought of Chang Tsai and Wang Fu-chih, than to nineteenth-century scientific materialism. For T'an, ether is at once both a substance and a force. Sometimes he regards it as a kind of constituent substance (*yüan-su*); sometimes he sees it as a kind of force or energy, like light or heat.[90] This notion of ether is reminiscent of the neo-Confucian view of *ch'i* as a combination of substance and force. But, more significantly, ether is deemed to be the carrier of a vitalistic, empathic quality.

In *Jen-hsüeh*, T'an draws upon the dominant moral-spiritual ideals of

---

86. Ibid.: 6, 9–12; see also pp. 119–21.
87. Ibid.: 121; see also p. 9.
88. See Li Tse-hou (1958: 174–83).
89. 1954: 119–21; see also pp. 9–11, 21–23, 80–81.
90. Ibid.: 9–11, 21–22, 80–81; see also pp. 119–21.

various religious traditions to characterize this empathic quality of ether: "In Mohism it is called undifferentiated love, in Buddhism *dharma* and compassion, in Christianity [it is] the kind of feeling that enables one to love one's neighbor as oneself and to regard one's enemy as a friend." In Confucianism, he emphasizes, "it is called *jen*, *yüan*, and *hsing*."[91] In an essay titled "I-t'ai shuo" (On ether), which T'an wrote at about the same time as *Jen-hsüeh*, he singles out the ideal of *jen* and its metaphysical counterpart, namely, the world view of "forming one body with Heaven, earth, and mankind," to sum up the moral-spiritual qualities inherent in ether.[92] Obviously for T'an ether is no more material than *ch'i*.

T'an's concept of ether as substance-force infused with moral-spiritual qualities is thus perhaps best seen as an outgrowth of Wang Fu-chih's and Chang Tsai's idea of *ch'i*, and it is best understood in the framework of Wang's interpretation of the relationship between *li* and *ch'i* or *tao* (way) and *ch'i* (vessel). In fact, in affirming the ontological primacy of ether, T'an was implicitly—if not explicitly—following Wang's metaphysical monism.[93] The latter concept stemmed largely from a reaction against the predominant tendency in the Ch'eng-Chu School (but sometimes also present in the Lu-Wang School) to ascribe ontological priority to the cosmic principle vis-à-vis material force. However, this reaction was not so much a denial of the existence of the cosmic principle as a subsumption of it under the category of material force. As a corollary, it reversed the orthodox neo-Confucian way of conceiving the relation between the cosmic principle and the material force, viewing the former as function and the latter as substance. T'an's point here is as much to affirm the substantiality of the universe as to affirm the inseparability of substance and moral-spiritual qualities. Seen in this light, T'an's concept of ether, though sometimes couched in the language of nineteenth-century scientific materialism, nevertheless basically retains one distinguishing characteristic of neo-Confucian *ch'i*-based monism—it fuses materiality and moral-spirituality.

Thus, in T'an's view the world is made up of something "really real." The overriding attribute of this primordial substance is its ideationality (or perhaps spirituality). This is what he means when he says that such terms as "ether" and "electricity" were terms borrowed to define the mental force in a superficial and crude way. In another place, he says that one could even do without the word *i-t'ai*, because it is nothing more than what the Yogacara philosophy of Buddhism calls *hsiang-fen* (forms of phenomena as revealed in human consciousness). This was also why, in the same section of his *Jen-hsüeh*, in which he identifies ether as the constituent substance of the universe, he also characterizes *jen* without a qualm as the primary source of

---
91. Ibid.: 9.
92. Ibid.: 119–21.
93. Ibid.: 16, 24.

the whole universe and thereby characterizes his whole world view as "idealistic."[94]

T'an, then, holds that the world is ultimately made up of a primordial substance believed to permeate everywhere to form an all-encompassing whole. In this whole, all existences, through the medium of the primordial substance, interpenetrate and fuse. T'an puts great emphasis on the concept of *t'ung* as the key to the nature of the encompassing whole. The Chinese word *t'ung* defies an exact English translation. Its closest equivalent is "interpenetration" or "fusion." In T'an's *Jen-hsüeh*, this word is often associated with another Chinese word, *i* (oneness).[95] Combining the two concepts, one gets a vivid image of organic oneness, which runs through T'an's text. Consequently, it is safe to assume that, with such words as *t'ung* and *i*, T'an is trying to use the image of organic oneness to convey his vision of reality.

T'an's concept of organic oneness is strongly reminiscent of Chang Tsai's thought, in which *ch'i*-based monism projects a vision of reality in similar terms. But T'an goes beyond Chang Tsai in this regard, because his depiction draws on strains of mystic oneness in both philosophical Taoism and Mahayana Buddhism. In the first place, he consciously assimilated his concept of organic oneness to a similar concept that is central to philosophical Taoism. This concept is pithily expressed in a phrase he borrowed from *Chuang Tzu*: "*Tao* penetrates everywhere unimpeded to form a oneness" (*tao t'ung wei i*).[96] Underlying this phrase is the idea that *tao* is present in all the existences to make possible the fusion and interpenetration of all into a unified, organic whole. In T'an's treatise on *jen*, this notion of organic oneness is at times joined by two similar notions from Mahayana Buddhism: "the interpenetration of the one and the many" (*i-to hsiang-yung*); and "the collapse of the distinction between the three modes of temporality [future, present, and past]" (*san-shih i-shih*).[97] These Taoist and Buddhist notions of mystic oneness inject a note of transcendentalism into T'an's vision of reality. They also have the effect of turning T'an's vision into a vision of undifferentiated, seamless oneness rarely found in the neo-Confucian tradition.

This vision of reality militates against any concept of individuality, multiplicity, or indeed distinction of any sort. In T'an's vision, only the whole is real, and any distinction or individuality that might impair the oneness of the whole is illusory. The implication is clear: all the separate, individual existences are epiphenomenal and therefore ultimately unreal and meaningless. As T'an argues—in a way strongly reminiscent of Chang Tsai and Wang Fu-chih—in the final analysis, there is nothing in this world

---

94. Ibid.: 6, 48, 7.
95. Ibid.: 6, 9, 22, 28.
96. Ibid.: 6. For this pivotal concept of philosophical Taoism, see Chuang Tzu, "Ch'i-wu lun" [Discussion on making all things equal] (1968: 36–53).
97. Ibid.: 28–34.

but the all-pervading ether. The coming-to-be and passing away, the birth and extinction of any individual existence, are all nothing but the concentration and dispersion of the ether. Thus, in an ultimate sense, one never dies. One's death is just one's immersion into the all-encompassing whole from which one originally came.[98]

With this vision of reality, T'an was finally able to dispel the dark shadow of his preoccupation with death. Moreover, the vision gave him a new insight into life: individual life has no meaning other than participating in the encompassing whole, and love and compassion are the only way to transcend one's own ego and to merge back into the whole. For T'an, this was an insight confirmed by all the teachings he had studied, especially the three he most admired: Buddhism, Confucianism, and Christianity.[99] In the meantime, as reflected clearly in T'an's own preface to the *Jen-hsüeh* and the preface written by Liang Ch'i-ch'ao, T'an began to see himself in the image of someone dedicated to the service and salvation of mankind out of love.[100] Out of his vision of reality grew a self-image wrought by such varied cultural ideals as the Confucian sage, the Mahayana Bodhisattva, the Mohist knight-errant, and the Christian missionary: in short, a suffering hero living solely for the ideal of love and compassion.

The Critical Spirit of T'an's Vision

In this way, T'an found a new meaning and purpose in life. But his vision of reality did not just provide a fresh source of meaning for him. It also embodied the supreme virtue of *jen*, thus furnishing a new source of moral guidance. To be sure, *jen* was not the only Confucian virtue that he embraced; he also speaks in his text of the three Confucian cardinal virtues (*chih, jen, yung*) and the five Confucian constancies (*jen, i, li, chih, hsin*). But in his view, all these other virtues could be subsumed under the controlling ideal of *jen*.[101] In this way, *jen* became a new value center that allowed him to take a fresh look at the society around him, and the result was a radical outlook that was almost diametrically opposed to the outlook dominant in his essay "Chih-yen."

One manifestation of his radical outlook is his libertarian view of human instinctuality. We have seen that the influence of Wang Fu-chih's *ch'i*-based monism resulted in a strain of moral realism in T'an's thinking: human

---

98. Ibid.: 22–24, 28–30.
99. Ibid.: 9, 24–25. Although T'an saw the three teachings all converging on a belief in the human individual's ability to transcend ego through the spiritual power of love, he was sometimes inclined to see Mahayana Buddhism as a teaching superior to the other two. T'an wrote *Jen-hsüeh* when he was in the midst of studying Mahayana, and hence he was more strongly influenced by it than by the others. For T'an's criticism of Christianity and Confucianism from a Buddhist standpoint, see ibid.: 26–27, 50–51.
100. Ibid.: 3–5, 515–16.
101. Ibid.: 13.

desires are as inseparable from human nature as the material force is from cosmic principles. Echoing Wang's view, T'an refuses to speak of a separate, inner human nature on the ground that it was nothing more than a function of ether or human desires. He quotes approvingly from Wang Fu-chih: "The principle of Heaven resides in no other place than human desires; without human desires the principle of Heaven could find nothing to manifest itself in." [102]

Wang Fu-chih did not push his moral realism to its logical conclusion and thereby stopped short of any attack on Confucian moral and social values. T'an goes further and launches a radical critique of the existing moral order. The impetus to his critique, of course, stems partly from the moral realism flowing from his ether-based monism, but much of his radical impulse can also be ascribed to influences he received from outside the Confucian tradition, most notably from the secular culture of the modern West.

The thrust of T'an's critique was that the Confucian moral order involves too much affective and instinctual repression. This repression is clearly manifested in the traditional morality, which regards sexual activities as something shameful that must be curbed and repressed by taboos. In T'an's view, the only basis for this kind of morality is the arbitrary conventions inherited from the past. If the sexual organ were located in a different part of the human body, T'an surmises, different conventions probably would have grown to govern our sexual mores, and, considering the variety of mores in different societies, it is entirely conceivable that conventions could just as naturally have developed in China to make sexual behavior a more open type of activity. Thus, for T'an there is nothing inherently shameful about sex; the feeling of shame simply derives from the negative sexual morality of the Confucian *li*, which T'an dismisses as arbitrary and hence as not inherently moral.[103]

In challenging traditional sexual morality, T'an makes it clear that he has no intention of advocating sexual indulgence. He is concerned only to point out that sexual activities are the natural functioning of the human organism. To attempt to repress what is natural would be not only futile but dangerous, because the natural force of sexual drives, when repressed, does not just die away but, like water dammed up, has a destructive potential. Look at the traditional Chinese society, T'an says, where, despite the plethora of taboos regarding sexual activities, carnal indulgence and perversion were still widespread.[104]

In contrast, T'an writes, the West has fewer sexual prohibitions and much greater freedom and openness in expressions of love and intimacy

---
102. Ibid.: 16, 21–22.
103. Ibid.: 16–21.
104. Ibid.: 20–21.

between men and women. Contrary to the Chinese practice, male doctors are even allowed to perform midwifery! Even so, T'an observes, the West has fewer sexual crimes than China. The moral T'an draws from these contrasting developments in China and the West is that the right attitude toward sex is openness and realism rather than an inhibitory negativism. To promote this attitude, T'an calls for dissemination of such knowledge about sex as can be gained from the Western medical sciences and emphasizes the need for publications and institutes devoted to the specialized study of human sexuality. He even goes so far as to suggest creating wax models of the human body to facilitate popular understanding of the structure and functioning of the sexual organs.[105] Some of the moral realism of Western secular culture toward sexuality had apparently affected T'an's outlook.

T'an's revolt against the orthodox Confucian idea of instinctual repression leads him to indict not only traditional Chinese sexual morality in general, but also the particular irrationality of traditional sexual mores regarding women. T'an notes that traditional sexual prohibitions were the most stern against women. No recognition was given to their sexual needs; sexually, a woman was considered to be merely a plaything for a man. Thus arose the abominable practices that warped women's bodies just to satisfy the perverse sexual pleasures of men. The custom of foot-binding was only the most notable example of these practices. The intensity of T'an's outrage against the practice is gauged by his assertion that, to the extent that Westerners as well as Manchus and Mongols did not practice foot-binding, they were justified in establishing dominion over China.[106]

This inhibition of female sexuality, in T'an's view, exemplifies a larger deplorable aspect of Chinese tradition, namely, the unequal status of men and women. Women are made of the same cosmic material as men; they have the same capacity for moral and practical achievements. What, then, are the grounds, T'an asks, for sexual discrimination against them? From this standpoint, T'an goes on to attack Chinese society and culture in a radical tone that suggests the iconoclasm of the later May Fourth generation. T'an claims that his radical stand in this regard stems from his sympathy with the egalitarianism of Mahayana Buddhism, which views man and woman as having equal potential for spiritual development.[107] However, one wonders whether T'an's viewpoint is not also partly indebted to the publications of Christian missionaries, a major theme of which was a critique of Chinese male sexism.[108]

Whatever non-Confucian influences may have contributed to T'an's critical outlook, he regarded his own mental openness as dictated by the

---
105. Ibid.
106. Ibid.: 18–20.
107. Ibid.: 19.
108. Bennett and K. C. Liu (1974: 186–88).

exuberant, life-affirming world view embodied in the ideal of *jen*. Another outlook closely related to this mental openness is, he believes, also enjoined by the world view of *jen*: an attitude of moral activism that is epitomized in the ideal of "daily renewal" (*jih-hsin*).[109] As discussed above, *jih-hsin*, which was very important to Wang Fu-chih's thought, is rooted in a metaphysical world view that sees the cosmos as infused with vitality and dynamism and as constantly engaged in a process of movement and change. In Wang's thought, the idea of movement or change is understood primarily in two senses, namely, cosmological and vitalistic renewal.[110] Cosmological renewal presupposes a cyclical time frame, while vitalistic renewal carries the connotation of generating novelty, variety, and abundance, but all in a nontemporal sense. Both lack the idea of unilinear development, in the sense of augmenting value in an irreversible process of time. T'an's idea of metaphysical dynamism, however, though he echoes Wang's concept of daily renewal in the above two senses, takes on some aspects of unilinear development. In T'an's concept of change, there is some millennial expectation of the future, as evidenced in his belief that "the earth is developing from suffering in the past to sweetness and light in the future." In expressing such a millennial outlook, T'an at one place in his text on *jen* consciously draws an analogy with the Christian eschatological concept of the advent of the kingdom of God.[111]

There are also indications that T'an's idea of dynamism was influenced by the ethos of Western industrial society. T'an must have had the ideal of social progress in mind when he called attention to the cult of innovation in the West, which, in his view, made all the difference between the West's prosperity and the social stagnancy in Asia, Africa, and Australia. He speaks enthusiastically of the West's technological achievements and views them in connection with the Western outlook that values time as a scarce and precious commodity. From this perspective, T'an says, modern technological inventions, such as steamships, railroads, and the telegraph, are invaluable time-saving devices that have resulted in prolonging the span of life many times over. T'an was also impressed by the dynamism and vitality exhibited in the character of Western people. He notes that it is mainly because of these character traits that Westerners were capable of their stupendous achievements and their modern worldwide expansion. One further value emphasized in T'an's writings is what he called *she*, which literally connotes lavishness or extravagance. In the context of T'an's writing, however, it means a willingness to spend, to invest, to enjoy, and to live life to its fullness. Thus, it refers not so much to lavishness as to the yearning for abundance or the spirit of exuberance that permeates a booming in-

---

109. 1954: 34–36.
110. Lin Kuo-p'ing (1965: 135–51).
111. 1954: 5, 35.

dustrial society. T'an's glorification of the ideal *she* bespeaks his unbounded enthusiasm for the energy and dynamism of a commercial-industrial society.[112]

All of T'an's observations reflect a spotty, limited knowledge of modern Western civilization, but they do represent an awareness of what Benjamin Schwartz calls the Faustian-Promethean ethos of the modern West. It is the fulfillment of a strain of dynamism and vitality that he had already admired in the philosophies of Chang Tsai and Wang Fu-chih. These philosophies, in short, provided a standpoint from which T'an was able to view the exuberant and expansive Western view of life and the world as something not entirely extraneous to Chinese cultural tradition.

This did not prevent him from criticizing the Chinese tradition. To him, the predominant tenor of Chinese society, despite some tendencies to the contrary, was just the opposite of the Faustian-Promethean ethos; its outlook on life and the world was negative, as evidenced in the widespread acceptance of such values as quiescence (*ching*) and meekness (*jou*). The result was a static, inhibitory order where a dynamic, exuberant outlook withered, and a meek, cautious conformism thrived. T'an lays the blame for this quiescent ethos at the door of Taoism,[113] but one suspects that he was also echoing, to a certain extent, Wang Fu-chih's reaction against the quietist trend in mainstream neo-Confucianism.

Another manifestation of this negative outlook is what T'an calls *chien* (thrift), which, according to T'an, was an acknowledged value extolled from generation to generation by every family in China. From T'an's point of view, it was more a vice than a virtue, because its usual effect was to concentrate people's attention on conserving, rather than on creating and expanding, wealth. Consequently, it contributed directly to the economic stagnancy and backwardness of China. Physical poverty aside, it resulted in intellectual poverty. Dampening any incentive to think beyond the mental horizon of the existing culture, *chien* thus unwittingly fostered the conservatism of mind that lay at the root of China's pervasive intellectual obscurantism.[114]

In addition, T'an sees a grim logic growing out of the ideal of *chien* that runs counter to the flourishing of civilization. His premise is that the ideal of *chien* implies contentedness with the minimum conditions of human life. The corollary is that civilizational developments beyond these minimum conditions are deplored as superfluous and wasteful. For T'an, this negative, inhibitory view, inasmuch as it was taken for granted as a universal virtue and hence had an even greater hold on the Chinese mind than the values of quiescence and passivity, is at odds with the affirmative spirit of *jen*.[115]

---

112. Ibid.: 36, 46, 37, 38–44.
113. Ibid.: 36–38.
114. Ibid.: 38–40, 40–42.
115. Ibid.: 38–44.

T'an's Iconoclastic Protest

So far, we have seen how T'an's philosophy of vitality and dynamism, which evolved from the philosophies of Chang Tsai and Wang Fu-chih, had taken on some of the character of the Promethean ethos of the modern West. This exuberant outlook led to a radical critique of traditional society and culture; it also led him to enthusiastically embrace Western commercial-industrialism. Significantly, his enthusiasm is largely free of the nationalistic rhetoric of wealth and power prominent in the writings of many contemporary intellectuals who share his economic values. In a time when China's very existence was threatened by foreign economic imperialism, T'an has nothing but scorn for defensive tariffs or protectionism. In an era when Chinese intellectuals were becoming increasingly aware of the "commercial war" (*shang-chan*) on the international scene, T'an recommends an unreserved policy of "open door" to foreign trade. True, T'an's attitude in this regard may have been influenced by the nineteenth-century Western doctrine of free trade, but a deeper reason must be sought in the life-affirming outlook that he developed on the basis of the ideal of *jen*.[116]

Precisely because of the traditional source of this aspect of his world view, T'an cherished the values of raw energy and dynamism, but not without qualification. Indispensable as they may be to human achievement, they are not always necessarily a blessing from a moral-spiritual perspective. Without the guidance of moral-spiritual goals, in fact they can be harnessed to evil purposes and magnify the destructive power of human beings. He insists that raw energy and dynamism must be subject to control by the moral ideal of *jen*.[117] In his view, the ideal of *jen* represents not only a cosmos vibrant with dynamism and vitality, but also a world united by love into a universal *gemeinschaft*. This leads us to the most important aspect of T'an's critical outlook, the ideal of organic oneness that lay at the heart of his philosophy of *jen*.

This image of organic oneness is also a prominent image in much of neo-Confucian literature, centering on the ideal of *jen*. This is certainly true of Chang Tsai's *Hsi-ming*, a philosophical tract that was significant in T'an's intellectual background. An analysis of *Hsi-ming* reveals that the image of organic oneness, typically neo-Confucian, here takes on a distinctive form that reflects the influence of three central neo-Confucian ideas. The first of these ideas is the community of feeling. For Chang Tsai, as for many other neo-Confucian philosophers, a genuine human community is possible only when it is welded by an unimpeded flow of feeling. In such a community, human relationships cannot be abstract and impersonal; interpersonal contact, to borrow Martin Buber's terms, is necessarily an I-thou encounter rather

---
116. Ibid.: 44–45, 45–47.
117. Ibid.: 80–81.

than an I-it meeting. Thus, from a neo-Confucian perspective the prototypical human community is the family. Indeed, in *Hsi-ming* and kindred works, the emotional immediacy of human encounter is emphasized to such a degree that an interpersonal relationship is often expressed in terms of an organismic metaphor. A human community is structured like a human body. Therefore, the members of a human community are related in the same way that the different parts of a human body are.[118] The logical corollary of this organismic analogy is that relationships in a human community should have the same immediacy and intimacy that characterize the organic relationships within a human body.

The neo-Confucian emphasis on the unimpeded, immediate flow of feeling does not imply that such a flow is possible only within the confines of a small community. Instead, it is a basic assumption of neo-Confucianism that the ideal of organic oneness requires the furthest possible extension of feeling. To be sure, this extension of feeling, as every neo-Confucian philosopher would insist, must start with the nuclear community—the family, but the full realization of the ideal of organic oneness demands the extension of feeling beyond family, beyond any natural primary community, to all the people in a state and ultimately to the whole world. This is what Confucianism means by "all under heaven within one family" (*t'ien-hsia i-chia*).[119] Implied in this ideal is the moral vision of a universal *gemeinschaft*. This constitutes the second aspect of the neo-Confucian image of organic oneness.

This second aspect held a prominent place in the neo-Confucian ideal of universality, but universality was fused with a strong measure of particularism, which stands out as the third aspect of the image of organic oneness. The classic Confucian source of this particularism was the Mencian ideal of "graded love." In refuting the Mohist ideal of universal love, Mencius held that love is something that can be extended to the furthest extent but cannot, and therefore should not, be felt for all people in the same way. By its very nature, love then had to be graded or differentiated in accordance with the different social relationships between people. This Mencian conception of graded love later became predominant in the Confucian tradition.

However, when the mainstream of neo-Confucianism crystallized in the northern Sung, the acceptance of this view was at first not so unequivocal, as evidenced in Chang Tsai's *Hsi-ming*, where the idea of organic oneness was central. It must be remembered that *Hsi-ming* was only one part of Chang Tsai's major philosophical work, *Cheng meng* (Correct teaching for beginners).[120] In this larger context, Chang Tsai's idea of organic oneness sometimes carries connotations that sound closer to the Mohist ideal of

---

118. Ts'ai Jen-hou (1977: 44–101).
119. Ibid.
120. *Hsi-ming* was originally a part of *Cheng meng*; Chu Hsi singled it out and made it into a separate piece of text.

universal, undifferentiated love than to the Mencian concept of differentiated love. In fact some neo-Confucian philosophers of the early Sung already took this view.[121] The idea of graded love came to be accepted as the main theme of Chang Tsai's idea of organic oneness only through the interpretations of Ch'eng I and Chu Hsi, both of whom elaborated further on this idea in the well-known doctrine of *li-i fen-shu* (distinctions and differentiations in the unity of principle). To Chu Hsi, it was a Heaven-endowed universal principle that all people on earth should form one community, like a single family. It was in the nature of such a community that there exist distinctions, hierarchical and otherwise, stemming from differences in kinship relationship and social status. Obviously, the harmony Chu Hsi envisaged for the "universal *gemeinschaft*" was a differentiated, hierarchical harmony.[122] Thus, the particularistic norms, known as *Li*, that spelled out all the social and hierarchical differences in the community, had a central place in neo-Confucianism. At the heart of the *Li* was the Confucian doctrine of the three bonds and five relationships, which summed up the principle of differentiation and saw it as built into the structure of the cosmos. In this way, particularism was fused with the ideal of universality in neo-Confucian ethics.

An examination of T'an's idea of interpenetration and fusion as epitomized in the concept of *t'ung* in relation to the neo-Confucian concept of organic oneness indicates both significant continuity and discontinuity. The continuity is, first, shown in the fact that T'an sometimes understood *t'ung* and its underlying idea of harmony in the sense of an unimpeded flow of feeling that makes human community possible. In consequence, for T'an a human community inevitably takes on the character of an organic interdependence; he drives this view home by using various metaphors and analogies. Using the metaphor of electricity, he tries to suggest the directness and immediacy of the flow of feeling or of the bonds of sentiment that should exist in an ideal community.[123]

Another metaphor he uses is of the human nervous system, controlled in the brain and spreading throughout the body. By dint of the nervous system, any sensation that occurs to any part of a human body would immediately be transmitted to the brain and thus be felt no less immediately by the rest of the body. T'an sees a direct analogy between human body and human community. People in a human community should have the organic closeness and direct interdependence of the different parts of the human body. T'an observes that, when a human body suffers paralysis and the organic

---

121. E.g., Yang Shih saw Chang Tsai's view as close to Mo Tzu's ideal of undifferentiated love. See Ch'ien Mu (1978: 85–112). See also Ts'ai Jen-hou (1977: 94); Chan Wing-tsit (1963: 497–500).

122. Ts'ai Jen-hou (1977: 94–96).

123. 1954: 6, 10–12.

interdependence of its parts is lost, this bodily state is traditionally described in Chinese medicine as lack of *jen*. Similarly, because the human community basically has the same organic character as the human body, the inability of one person or a group of people to communicate and empathize with fellow human beings should also be described as lack of *jen*.[124] One might be reminded here of the philosophies of Chang Tsai and Ch'eng Hao, in which almost the same vitalistic metaphor and analogy are used to describe the organic harmony of a human community, but T'an's concept of flow of feeling and organic interdependence should not be regarded as entirely an outgrowth of the neo-Confucian idea of organic harmony. When he wrote *Jen-hsüeh*, T'an had already been exposed to influences from Buddhism, Mohism, and Christianity, where the bonds of love and feeling were also viewed, in different ways, as cementing the human community.

Another continuity between T'an's idea of harmony and those of his neo-Confucian predecessors is in the universalistic scope of his ideal community. For T'an, as for Chang Tsai, the ultimate human concern is not with the fate of any specific social or ethnic group, but with what T'an calls "order on earth" (*ti-ch'iu chih chih*).[125] The terminal community is not any individual country (*kuo-chia*), but the universal community of all-under-Heaven (*t'ien-hsia*). As T'an says in *Jen-hsüeh*, "the order on earth would come with the emergence of the universal community of all-under-Heaven and the disappearance of separate, individual countries."[126] True, this element of universalism in T'an's thinking may not stem entirely from his neo-Confucian background; his exposure to non-Confucian influences may have also played a part. Whatever the intellectual sources of his universalistic outlook, T'an's *Jen-hsüeh* is permeated by this outlook and is therefore marked by a singular absence of sympathy for nationalism.

The universalism in T'an's ideal of harmony is reflected not only in his lack of sympathy with nationalism, but, more surprisingly, in a favorable attitude toward imperialism. First in his private correspondence and then in *Jen-hsüeh*, he completely reverses a hostile, condescending attitude toward foreign peoples and cultures he had expressed in his essay "Chih-yen," resulting in an unabashed condoning of imperialist aggression.[127] Appearing in an age of rampant imperialism, this astonishing attitude can only be understood in the light of his radical outlook, which stemmed from yet another aspect of T'an's ideal of organic oneness.

This third aspect, in contrast to the other two, which were basically outgrowths of Chang Tsai's concept of organic oneness, was marked more

---

124. Ibid.: 10–11.
125. Ibid.: 85.
126. Ibid.; see also T'an's observations, pp. 73, 75.
127. See T'an's letter to Ou-yang Chung-ku (ibid.: 285); his letter to Pei Yüan-cheng, p. 423; and pp. 19, 61–63, 75–76.

by discontinuity than by continuity with the neo-Confucian mainstream. Reading Chang Tsai with Mohist rather than orthodox neo-Confucian interpretations in mind, T'an was able to recapture the connotation of undifferentiated love that was already present in Chang Tsai's thought. Because he was, in the meantime, also exposed to other non-Confucian influences like philosophical Taoism, Mahayana Buddhism, and Christianity, he began to look at other aspects of Chang Tsai's philosophy in a new light.

One such aspect is Chang Tsai's underlying world view in *Hsi-ming*, which is embodied in the idea of the "unity of Heaven and man," in which all human beings are seen as creatures of Heaven and earth. Drawing a logical conclusion from this world view (rarely drawn by neo-Confucian scholars in the past), T'an was led to believe that as children of Heaven and earth, all human beings should be equal.[128] Another aspect is the dualistic conception of self that is implicit, if not explicit, in Chang Tsai's philosophy. T'an now drew on nomenclature from both Confucian and non-Confucian sources to characterize his conception of the dual self. Sometimes he uses Christian terminology, calling the two aspects of self *ling-hun* (soul) and *t'i-p'o* (body); or he categorizes the two in Buddhist and neo-Confucian terms, such as *chih-hui* (the higher wisdom) versus *yeh-shih* (sense-consciousness), or *jen-hsin* (human mind) versus *tao-hsin* (the mind of *tao*).[129] Whatever the terms used, underlying them all is his awareness of a moral-spiritual depth within every person—a higher, inner self as distinguished from the outer, physical self.

For T'an, this dualistic concept of man entails the ideal of equality, because all the distinctions and discriminations that separate human beings from each other and make human community a hierarchical structure occur only when people look at the world from the standpoint of their empirical selves. However, when looked at from the perspective of the spiritual self, these distinctions and discriminations would evaporate, because all human beings share the same endowment from Heaven as their inner natures and hence exist as equals.[130]

The ideal of undifferentiated love and the new social implications that T'an draws from it are reinforced by his acceptance of Western liberal ideals, often neatly summed up in a phrase like "Everyone has the right of self-determination" (*jen jen yu tzu chu chih ch'üan*), which was then being propagated by Christian missionaries like Alexander Williamson.[131] The result is a radical egalitarianism that represents a discontinuity with the mainstream neo-Confucian ideal of *jen*. More significantly, in *Jen-hsüeh* T'an is led by this egalitarianism to an unrelenting critique of the Confucian social ethics of *Li*.

---

128. Ibid.: 51, 55, 65, 68.
129. Ibid.: 26–27, 50.
130. Ibid.: 28, 65.
131. Ibid.: 51.

The radicalness of T'an's critique can be gauged by the fact that it challenges the core of *Li*, namely, the doctrine of the three bonds and five relationships. Among the three bonds, it was the ruler-subject relationship that bore the brunt of T'an's impassioned attack.[132] The attack in itself was nothing special at the time: by the mid-1890s, criticism of the ruler-subject relationship and its institutional foundation—the cosmological kingship—was often heard among the small circle of avant-garde Chinese intellectuals. What distinguished T'an's attack, however, is the fact that it was not motivated by the nationalistic, pragmatic considerations of wealth and power that fuel most of his contemporaries' ideological challenges to monarchy. Instead, T'an's standards of judgment came mainly from the radical universalistic values that stem from his interpretation of the ideal of *jen*. Obviously, T'an is questioning the value of the traditional Chinese rulership not so much from the pragmatic standpoint of political viability as on the grounds of moral legitimacy.

T'an's moral perspective is seen, first of all, in his critique of the dominant political virtue of the Confucian tradition—loyalty (*chung*). In T'an's view, loyalty, as understood in the framework of the Confucian doctrine of three bonds and five relationships, is an entirely one-sided virtue, demanding total and unconditional submission on the part of the subject, while giving license to total arbitrary power on the part of the ruler. The consequence is a strange and perverse phenomenon in Chinese history in which people willingly submitted themselves to domination and enslavement by any tyrannical ruler. All this, he emphasizes, resulted from a gross misunderstanding of the ideal of *chung* as conceived originally by Confucius. *Chung*, in its ancient, genuine sense, means exactly what *chung* as a compound character should mean. The character is made up of two components that signify "middle" and "heart," respectively. Literally, the combination of the two should be understood as "placing the heart in the middle." Derivatively, it may be rendered as "impartial reciprocity." Thus, in T'an's understanding, the concept of loyalty means that one's attitude toward any other individual person is contingent on the latter's attitude toward oneself. The implication is clear: in any social relationship, loyalty should not appear on either side unless it is mutual. For T'an, the social relationship of ruler-subject is no exception and hence must be governed by the principle of reciprocity.[133]

Admittedly, the concept of reciprocity does not necessarily imply egalitarianism. It may simply mean equity in the Mencian sense that people of different social statuses owe different moral obligations to each other. However, T'an's discussion of the concept of loyalty explicitly identifies the principle of reciprocity with that of equality. This identification of the two

---

132. Ibid.: 3–4; see also pp. 53–55, 56–61, 65.
133. Ibid.: 58.

arises from T'an's iconoclastic concept of the origin and nature of rulership:

> In the beginning when human beings first appeared on earth, there was no distinction between ruler and subjects. They were all just people. However, people did not have the ability to govern themselves, nor did they have time to cope with the task of government. Therefore, they elected among themselves one person as the monarch. When we speak of election by all, we do not mean selection of people by the monarch but the election of the monarch by the people. When we speak of election by all, we mean that the monarch is not very distant from the people and hence can bring himself down to stand on the same level with people. When we speak of election by all, it is because the monarch comes only after the existence of the people. So the monarch is the branch while the people are the trunk. If it is illogical in this world to hurt the trunk for the sake of the branch, by the same token how can we let the people get hurt for the sake of the monarch? When we speak of election by all, we mean that he can also be abolished by all. The monarch is he who serves the people. The minister is he who helps the ruler to serve the people. Taxes are levied on the populace to finance public services for the sake of the people. From these premises, we can draw a universal principle, that a ruler should be removed if he does not fulfill his duty and get his work done.[134]

Such a secular, instrumental, and liberal conception of rulership completely strips the traditional cosmological kingship of its mystique and legitimacy. Thus, it is no surprise that T'an went on to launch an impassioned indictment of the traditional monarchy. One central element in this indictment is the Confucian moral condemnation of *ssu* (selfishness).[135] However, T'an's language of government by election and political egalitarianism also reveals the influence of the Western ideal of popular sovereignty. Thus, both Western liberal ideals and Confucian moral views lay behind T'an's challenge to the moral legitimacy of the ruler-subject relationship as formulated in the doctrine of the three bonds and five relationships.

From T'an's moral perspective, the other two traditional social relationships that are prescribed in the doctrine of three bonds are just as much a perversion as the ruler-subject relationship is. To begin with, the father-son relationship, as governed by the Confucian virtue of filial piety, is entirely one of domination and submission. This authoritarian relationship seems to have been unalterably sealed in the popular consciousness by the will of Heaven. In fact, however, the authoritarian character of this relationship is arbitrary and adventitious. Its presence is an unfortunate consequence of people's excessive preoccupation with their empirical selves to the neglect of their spiritual selves. Here T'an is arguing from the premise of his dualistic conception of self. From the standpoint of one's empirical self, the relation-

---

134. Ibid.: 56.
135. Ibid.: 56–59.

ship may take on an authoritarian character, but, from the standpoint of one's spiritual self, it takes on an egalitarian character. Underlying T'an's argument is the idea that the authority of a true father belongs only to Heaven. Because basically the son is as much a child of Heaven as the father, a son can claim spiritual equality with his father before Heaven.[136] In taking such a radical view of the father-son relationship, T'an is obviously drawing an implication from a central idea in Chang Tsai's *Hsi-ming*, namely, that all human beings are creatures of Heaven and earth.[137] However, it must be added that an egalitarian implication is exactly what the neo-Confucian philosophers in general avoided drawing.

True to his radical egalitarianism, T'an, having rejected the Confucian virtue of filial piety, recommends the Taoist ideal of mutual forgetfulness to govern the father-son relationship. For him this Taoist ideal consists of a spiritual relationship characterized by equal status and mutual enjoyment. Citing *Chuang Tzu*, T'an observes, that "mutual forgetfulness is of the highest importance, while filial piety is only of secondary importance. To attain [this spiritual relationship of] mutual forgetfulness is to achieve equality."[138]

T'an's critique of the husband-wife relationship is equally unrelenting. He takes a pessimistic view of the marriage institution itself, feeling that forcing two strangers to live together for their whole life was bound to bring suffering to the couple concerned. The doctrine of three bonds brought more suffering to marriage by reducing the wife to a subhuman status. The doctrine not only allowed a husband to unconditionally dominate his wife, it imposed an abominable concept of chastity, binding a wife to her husband even after the latter's death. As T'an puts it, it is most unfortunate that family for a Chinese woman is practically a prison.

The father-son and husband-wife relationships were only the most glaring irrationalities that perverted the Chinese family system. There were others, as can be seen from the many inequities and ill feelings in the relationships between mother-in-law and daughter-in-law, between stepmother and stepson, between master and servants, and among wife and concubines.[139] For T'an, these irrationalities stand as an irrefutable moral indictment of Confucian family ethics as a whole.

Given such moral indignation against both Confucian political ethics and Confucian family ethics, T'an launched an unreserved, frontal attack on the doctrine of three bonds. He asked people to muster courage to rip apart and burst all the ropes that the doctrine created around them. He held the doctrine responsible for the Chinese social and political tradition that he denounces as a record of robbery and hypocrisy.[140] Because of his indigna-

---

136. Ibid.: 28, 65.
137. Ts'ai Jen-hou (1977: 84, 86).
138. 1954: 65.
139. Ibid.: 65–66.
140. Ibid.: 4; see also p. 54.

tion against what he considered the abysmal depravity of the traditional Chinese order, he condoned the aggressions by Japan and Western nations. He even went so far as to call the invading troops of foreign countries the "forces of humanity and righteousness" (*jen i chih shih*) sent by Heaven to give China the punishment she deserves.[141] The impassioned, radical tone of T'an's indictment of his own culture was unrivaled in the intellectual world of the late Ch'ing; in some ways, it even surpasses the iconoclasm of the May Fourth generation at its height.

T'an's critique of the Confucian five relationships was somewhat less vehement than his blasts against the three bonds. T'an found one saving element in the five relationships, namely, friendship. For T'an the relationship between friends, in contrast to the other four, is inherently an egalitarian one and hence has the virtue of preserving the autonomy of the individuals involved. Thus, in his view, the relationship between friends should be placed above the other four and replace the three bonds as the primary social relationship: "Friendship should not just be valued more than the other four relationships. It should also be the model for the other four. When the latter are all pervaded by the spirit of friendship, it means that they can be abolished."[142]

Apparently, T'an understood friendship in a very broad sense; he uses it to mean any social tie formed on the basis of voluntary devotion. It is in this sense that he saw friendship as what made possible those social movements that led to the creation of the religions he admired. In his view, Jesus' following was made up of those who were willing to cut off all their family ties and obligations to the state to join him. This was even more true of Buddha's followers, who were willing to sever all social ties and worldly entanglements to be with him. In his view, Confucianism was no exception in this regard.[143] His view was, then, that only on the basis of friendship can people get together in ways characterized by love, equality, and voluntarism.

For T'an, thus, at the core of the ideal of *jen* lies an ethical outlook that runs counter to the doctrine of the three bonds and five relationships. In fact, it is not just the doctrine but the whole traditional normative order, the *Li* (or what has been traditionally called the *ming-chiao*), that he found incompatible with his ideal of *jen*. However, in his impassioned denunciation of the traditional order, T'an sometimes went even further. In his view, the spirit of *jen* is at odds with and hence can be upset (*luan*) by the very existence of *ming* itself. Literally, *ming*, of course, means "name," but, in the context of T'an's writings, it refers to rules or norms. Implied in T'an's opposition to *ming*, then, is the idea that *jen* symbolizes certain generalized ideals, which, once accepted by people, constitute a moral-spiritual inwardness that can

---

141. Ibid.: 61–63.
142. Ibid.: 66–68.
143. Ibid.

not be bound by any external rule or norm. In short, any normative order or conventional rule constricts and undermines the spirit of *jen*.[144] Underlying this revolt against *ming* per se is something that borders on what may be called moral "antinomianism."

This antinomian impulse is a reflection of the strain of mysticism that runs through T'an's interpretation of *jen*. Mysticism carried within itself a tendency to look on ultimate reality as ineffable. As a result, words and concepts were suspected of being inadequate to describe this reality. T'an's portrayal of his vision of organic oneness leaves one with the impression that he had a strong sense of the ineffability of what he attempted to describe. Thus, it is not surprising that T'an's vision of reality does not lead to any systematic depiction of the institutional structure of the ideal order he envisaged.

This strain of mysticism in T'an's thinking also explains why the presence of his concept of time as a process of unilinear development fails to blossom into a dominant outlook in his philosophy of *jen*. Although T'an considered himself a convert to K'ang Yu-wei's reformism, he made only vague, oblique references to K'ang's historical doctrine of "three ages" in *Jen-hsüeh*, without embracing it enthusiastically.[145] As I discussed above, both Christian and Western secular concepts of progress left an imprint on T'an's critique of the traditional order. However, the presence in T'an's mysticism of concepts of organic oneness stemming from Mahayana Buddhism and philosophical Taoism can also be seen. These concepts carried transcendental and ahistorical connotations that militate against the view of history as a temporal process directed toward the future. In fact, they point to a clear tendency in T'an's vision of organic oneness to view ultimate reality as transcending the flow of time. This inhibition of a futuristic outlook, along with his antinomian suspicion of the externalization of moral-spiritual vision in any institutional order, may explain why his philosophy of *jen*, while involving a millennial vision of perfection for the future and a sense of the imperfection of the existing order, does not issue (as K'ang Yu-wei's philosophy did) in any futuristic utopianism.

When seen in the context of his *Jen-hsüeh*, T'an's martyrdom clearly represents more than a dedication to political reformism. It also testifies to his devotion to a vision of reality that was the end result of a lifelong quest—a quest that not only compelled him to protest against the existing sociopolitical order, but also enabled him to accept death without fear.

---

144. Ibid.: 13–15.
145. Ibid.: 51–54, 87–88.

4

Chang Ping-lin (1869–1935)

AFTER THE failure of the reform movement in 1898, K'ang Yu-wei's intellectual preeminence among the early Chinese intelligentsia was soon challenged by a young scholar who opposed not only K'ang's political cause of reformism, but his New Text interpretation of Confucianism as well. This young scholar was Chang Ping-lin, the scion of a wealthy scholar-gentry family of Yü-hang County in Chekiang Province.[1] Little is known about his early life other than a few facts about his education. During his childhood, he received some of his education from his maternal grandfather. Under the latter's tutelage, Chang at an early age was exposed to the intellectual influence of such Ming loyalist thinkers as Ku Yen-wu and Wang Fu-chih and was also made aware of the ethnic tensions between the Manchus and the Han Chinese in Ch'ing history. Chang later credited his grandfather with being the first one to give him an anti-Manchu consciousness.[2]

A CHOICE BETWEEN TWO CAREERS

Chang spent his early life largely in his hometown and the neighboring cities, all in the general area of eastern Chekiang, where an intellectual tradition of historical scholarship had long flourished. Inasmuch as the writings of Ming loyalists were an important part of this historical scholarship, it featured a strain of anti-Manchu ethnic consciousness and was distinguished by an emphasis on the practical function of historical knowledge. In the closing decades of the nineteenth century, some of the local literati were actively engaged in trying to revive this regional intellectual tradition.

---

1. T'ang Chih-chün (1979, 1: 1–4).
2. 1965: 1; T'ang (1979: 5–6).

Chang had close intellectual ties with some of these literati.³ Thus, the scholarly climate of his native place had the effect of reinforcing and also broadening the education he received from his family.

In his late teens, Chang was exposed to an intellectual influence of a different nature, when he discovered the attractions of the "evidential scholarship" of the School of Han Learning.⁴ In his early twenties, he began to attend a famous Confucian academy at Hangchou, the Ku-ching ching-she, a citadel of Confucian evidential scholarship in the late Ch'ing. The presiding scholar of the academy, Yü Yüeh, was a friend of Chang's father and a master of Han Learning with a nationwide reputation.⁵ Meanwhile, Chang also had the opportunity to become acquainted with some other renowned scholars of Han Learning in his home region, such as Huang I-chou, Kao Hsüeh-ch'ih, and T'an Hsien.⁶ Thus, during his youth he was pulled by two different ideals of scholarship, one emphasizing the moral-practical function of scholarship and the other stressing scholarship as a purely intellectual pursuit divorced from politics.

It was the moral-practical ideal that eventually proved stronger; when the reform movement got under way after 1894, Chang became involved. He enlisted in K'ang Yu-wei's Self-Strengthening Study Society (Ch'iang-hsüeh hui) in 1895. The next year he left Ku-ching ching-she and joined the reformist newspaper *Shih-wu pao* (Chinese progress), edited by Liang Ch'i-ch'ao.⁷ In 1897 Chang, along with some of his fellow literati from eastern Chekiang (such as Sung Shu, Ch'en Ch'iu, and Ch'en Fu-ch'en) founded a journal at Hangchou with the Confucian ideal of *ching-shih* (practical states-manship) in its title—*Ching-shih pao* (Journal for practical statesmanship). Chang began to plunge wholeheartedly into the politics of reform.⁸

Chang's involvement in politics incurred the disapproval of his teacher, Yü Yüeh, a scholar with a conservative bent who wanted to maintain the tradition of political noninvolvement established in the School of Han Learning. When Chang quit Yü's school in 1896, Yü was already upset. The

---

3. Ch'ien Mu (1964, 1: 28–33, 386–92). Scholars from eastern Chekiang, such as Sung Shu, Ch'en Ch'iu, Sun I-jang, and Ch'en Fu-ch'en, were trying to resuscitate the local tradition of scholarship for practical statesmanship. Chang's chronological autobiography indicates that he was a close friend of Sung Shu's and was also acquainted with Ch'en Fu-ch'en (1965: 5–6). Chang was also a personal friend of Sun I-jang's and probably knew Ch'en Ch'iu; see "Sun I-jang chuan" [A biography of Sun I-jang], in Chang (1919, *Wen-lu*, chüan 2: 74b–76a). When *Ching-shih pao* [Journal on practical statesmanship] was published in Hangchou in 1897, Chang Ping-lin was its editor along with Sung Shu and Ch'en Ch'iu; see T'ang Chih-chün (1957: 251).
4. 1963: 3.
5. Ibid.: 4–5. See also Chang, "Yü hsien-sheng chuan" [A biography of Yü Yüeh] (1919, *Wen-lu*, chüan 2: 73a–74b).
6. Chang, "Huang hsien-sheng chuan" [A biography of Huang I-chou], (1919, *Wen-lu*, chüan 2: 76a–78b). "Kao hsien-sheng chuan" [A biography of Kao Hsüeh-chih] (ibid.: 71b–72b). See also T'ang (1979, 1: 11–13).
7. T'ang (1979, 1: 36–37); Chang (1965: 5).
8. T'ang (1979, 1: 45–49); Chang (1965: 4–5).

tension between teacher and student finally erupted in an open split between them in 1902 when Chang defied his teacher's moral authority by invoking the example of Ku Yen-wu, the revered founder of Han Learning who combined scholarship with politics as a justification for political engagement.[9] Though renouncing the political quietism of Han Learning, Chang never gave up the other side of that school's heritage, namely, the exaltation of pure scholarship as a primary value. In fact, throughout his life, he managed to combine political activism with a strong sense of the vocation of scholarship.

Chang's scholarly bent led him to develop wide-ranging intellectual interests during his youth, especially with regard to the Chinese cultural heritage.[10] Consequently, the voluminous writings he produced present a bewildering variety of ideas that, when juxtaposed, often appear incomprehensible. Much of the incomprehensible look, however, is reduced, if not eliminated, if we keep in mind the distinction between Chang as a scholar and Chang as an engaged intellectual. Not all of the intellectual interests that he developed as a young scholar had a bearing on his outlook as an engaged intellectual. Difficult as it may be to draw the line between the two facets of his thought, it is nonetheless necessary if we are going to make sense of his moral and social thinking during this period.

One of his intellectual interests during his mid-twenties was Mahayana Buddhism, which was to have an important bearing on the later development of his thinking.[11] But, at the time, it was the revival of the noncanonical classical philosophies that appealed to him most.[12] His fervent interest in them is owed largely to his background in Han Learning. The revival of noncanonical classical philosophies was an offshoot of internal developments in the tradition of Han Learning since the late eighteenth century. For Chang's own involvement in this development, his teacher, Yü Yüeh, was an important channel. For instance, one of Yü Yüeh's major works, *Chu-tzu p'ing-i* (Commentaries on the pre-Ch'in noncanonical texts) was a masterpiece of textual scholarship on these ancient philosophies.[13] Through Yü Yüeh, Chang also came to know other important scholars in this field. One notable example among the latter whom Chang greatly admired was Sun I-jang, a prolific writer of textual commentaries on the ancient noncanonical philo-

---

9. Chang (1965: 8); see also Chang, "Hsieh pen shih" [A farewell to my teacher] (1981: 121–23).
10. A quick glance at his writings before 1911 shows that his interests ranged from such abstruse subjects as phonetics, etymology, and Chinese medicine to such popular subjects as literature, philosophy, and sociology.
11. Chang (1965: 5–6); see also T'ang (1979, 1: 20–21).
12. Chang (1965: 6, 54); T'ang (1979, 1: 13, 14). Most of the writings that Chang published in *Ch'iu shu* (1978) reflect his interest in noncanonical classical philosophies.
13. Chang (1919); see also Liang Ch'i-ch'ao (1963: 87).

sophies.¹⁴ Thus, it was in Yü Yüeh's circle that he entered into the intellectual world of ancient philosophical texts.

Chang's interest in many of these texts was largely scholarly, but some of them had more than a scholarly significance for him. This was especially true of *Hsün Tzu*, which, as he admits in his autobiography, had a particular intellectual attraction for him.¹⁵ The attraction was by no means accidental, because a philosophical preference for *Hsün Tzu* had been an undercurrent in the School of Han Learning since the mid-eighteenth century.¹⁶ In fact it ran particularly strongly in Yü Yüeh's thought, as reflected in his emphatic endorsement of Hsün Tzu's heterodox concept of human nature.¹⁷ Unsurprisingly, given the prominence of Hsün Tzu's thought in Chang's background, Chang already took a strong pro–Hsün Tzu stand in the early reformist journals that he contributed to. In fact, the first edition of his earliest published major book, *Ch'iu shu* (Book of raillery), both opened and concluded with chapters promoting Hsün Tzu's standing in the Confucian tradition.¹⁸

THE FORMATION OF CHANG'S EARLY THOUGHT

The decade of the 1890s was thus a pivotal period of Chang's life. During these years, he not only became politically engaged, but also expanded his mental horizons beyond the established boundaries of Confucian scholarship. Inevitably, he came into contact with an important intellectual trend of his time—Western learning. During the 1890s, Western learning spread from the treaty-ports to the intellectual world of Chinese inland cities. Living in Hangchou, a city close to the sea and close to Shanghai, Chang was naturally exposed to these influences from abroad. In consequence, Chang's writings in the early reformist journals (which mushroomed in China after 1895) bear the strong imprint of Western learning, in addition to that of *Hsün Tzu* and other indigenous influences.

The combination of these influences is clearly shown in a major article of his that appeared in fall 1899 in the reformist journal *Ch'ing-i pao* (Journal of

---

14. Sun I-jang was Yü Yüeh's disciple; see Chiang Wei-ch'iao (1972: 75); and Chang, "Sun hsien-sheng chuan" [A biography of Sun I-jang]; and "Shui-an Sun hsien-sheng shang-tz'u" [An essay mourning the death of Sun I-jang] (1919, *Wen-lu*, chüan 2: 86b–89a).
15. 1965: 6.
16. Ch'ien Mu (1964, 1: 357–58; 2: 491–93).
17. Chiang Wei-ch'iao (1972: 70–75).
18. In an article published in the newly founded reformist journal, *Shih-hsüeh pao* [Journal of practical learning], Chang put Hsün Tzu forward as the figure second only to Confucius in the Confucian tradition and openly attacked Mencius as unworthy of the lofty place he occupied in the tradition (T'ang [1979, 1: 51–52]). See also Chang, "Tsun Hsün" [Putting Hsün Tzu on a pedestal] (1978: 1a–2a); "Tu Shen" (1978: 97a–100a).

disinterested discussion), with two lengthy supplements.[19] Its title, "Ju-shu chen-lun" (Truthful disquisition on Confucianism), suggests that the piece was written in response to the heated debate then being waged among Chinese scholar-officials about the meaning and import of Confucianism.[20] A major focus of the debate was, of course, the interpretations of Confucianism put forward by such leading figures of the reformist circles as K'ang Yu-wei and T'an Ssu-t'ung. Although Chang at that time was politically sympathetic toward the cause of K'ang and T'an, he had long felt uncomfortable with K'ang's New Text teachings. In fact, he had already done some writings to dispute K'ang's interpretations, albeit largely on textual grounds.[21] Now the publication of his interpretive essays on Confucianism revealed profound philosophical differences that separated Chang's early thought from that of K'ang Yu-wei and T'an Ssu-t'ung.

One major difference stemmed from their divergent points of departure in the Confucian tradition. Whereas K'ang and T'an often championed Mencius' thought, which they thought represented the true brand of Confucius' teachings, Chang's point of departure was Hsün Tzu's thought.[22] Following the latter's "naturalistic" view of the world, Chang saw the cosmos from disenchanted eyes, in striking contrast to the moral, teleological world view of Mencius. The greatness of Confucius, Chang says, lay primarily in his ability to transcend superstitions and to view the world as free of gods and spirits.[23] It is from this "naturalistic" perspective that Chang rejects the Christian theistic belief and the Buddhist belief in reincarnation.[24] It is also from this perspective that he takes sharp exception to T'an Ssu-t'ung's *Jen-hsüeh*, which was then being published in the reformist journals in both Shanghai and Tokyo.[25] T'an Ssu-t'ung, despite his copious use of vocabulary borrowed from the nineteenth-century Western sciences, took a basically spiritual view of the world that owed a great deal to his study of Mahayana Buddhism. Chang viewed such a spiritual world view as woefully erroneous, because he believed the ultimate reality of the world was not the Buddhist's all-containing, immaterial *Dharmakaya* but something physically substantial, such as ether or atoms with shape and mass.[26]

---

19. 1977: 118–25. The two supplements were "Shih t'ien lun" [On the sky as seen through our eyes] and "Chün shuo" [On bacteria].
20. Ibid.
21. See the letter Chang wrote in spring 1897, "Chih T'an Hsien shu" [A letter to T'an Hsien] (1977: 14–15), and his "Chin ku wen pien i" [On the distinction between the New Text and the Old Text teachings] (ibid.: 108–15). Although the latter article was written to refute Liao P'ing's writings on the New Text School, it may also be seen as an indirect attack on K'ang Yu-wei's New Text teachings.
22. See K'ang Yu-wei (1968b: 1a–3a); T'an Ssu-t'ung (1954: 9).
23. 1977: 120–21.
24. Ibid.: 135–36; see also pp. 125–27.
25. See T'ang Chih-chün (1974b: 166–75).
26. 1977: 133–35.

The reference to such concepts as ether and atoms suggests that Chang was exposed to the influence of Western sciences. A close examination of his writings indicates that Hsün Tzu's "naturalistic" perspective allowed Chang to make an easy transition from his Confucian background to Western scientific materialism, as evidenced in his refutation of the traditional view of heaven (*t'ien*).[27] Heaven, in his view, was neither ultimate reality nor the source of light, as was commonly believed. What is conventionally envisaged as heaven is in actuality nothing but the reflection of various astronomical phenomena in our eyes. Thus, Chang believes, we may as well dispense with the concept of Heaven and replace it with that of nature, which is explainable in terms of energy and mass.[28]

Apart from scientific materialism, another major theme of his essays is evolutionary cosmology, which he picked up from Western learning, largely through the influence of Yen Fu.[29] In fact, the two Western world views above dominated not only the three essays under consideration but various editions of *Ch'iu shu* in the early 1900s.[30] On the basis of these two world views, he was able to develop further Hsün Tzu's moral and social thought.

According to the theory of natural evolution, Chang notes, all of nature constitutes a chain of evolution, at the end of which stand human beings.[31] Because human beings evolve from the lower species, they naturally share a great deal with the latter in terms of physical endowment and basic biological needs. Of course, this does not mean that no differences exist between human beings and subhuman animals, but it does mean that human nature is both good and evil. Mencius made the mistake of concentrating on the good side and neglecting the evil. Hsün Tzu, on the other hand, was aware of both sides of human nature and hence developed a more balanced concept of man.[32]

Apart from Hsün Tzu's concept of human nature, Chang also inherited the latter's overriding moral concern: how to create a moral order on the basis of human nature as envisaged by Hsün Tzu. Chang's solution again owes considerably to Hsün Tzu's thought. He echoes Hsün Tzu by emphasizing moral order as a function of channeling and nurturing, rather than suppressing, human desires. But, more importantly, Hsün Tzu's idea of social integration and organization, centered around the idea of *ch'ün*

---

27. Ibid.: 125–27.
28. Ibid.: 120, 134.
29. Ibid.: 128–37.
30. The different editions of *Ch'iu shu* were collections of essays Chang wrote in the late 1890s and the early 1900s, in which he spells out his world views and presents his views on his two other major concerns, namely, the noncanonical classical philosophies and the burgeoning protest movement against the Manchu government. But, as far as Chang's world views were concerned, they were largely outgrowths of the views he puts forward in the three articles under discussion here.
31. 1977: 128–37.
32. Ibid.: 134–35, 137–38.

(grouping), became the point of departure for his social and political thinking.[33]

The idea of *ch'ün* was a focus of discussion among the reformist intellectuals at that time, reflecting the fact that many were fundamentally rethinking the nature of social and political organization in China.[34] The discussion of *ch'ün* was a clear sign of the emerging crisis of the sociopolitical order. Seen in this context, Chang's appropriation of Hsün Tzu's idea of *ch'ün* must also be seen as a response to the intellectual crisis. But, in responding to this crisis, Chang again found Hsün Tzu's thought converging with some of the Western thought he was studying, especially with the kind of Social Darwinism he was absorbing from Yen Fu's writings.[35]

For one thing, Hsü Tzu's concept of *ch'ün* fits very well into a Social Darwinian picture of the world. According to Hsün Tzu's observation, Chang notes, a human being is no match for a cow in terms of strength and no match for a horse in terms of speed, but human beings control cattle and horses. Why? Hsün Tzu found the answer in the capacity of human beings for grouping. However, quoting Hsün Tzu to this effect, Chang goes further and draws a broader lesson. Chang perceived that the capacity for grouping explains not only why human beings are able to dominate horses and cattle, but also why they are able to control all the lower species. Moreover, it helps us to understand how the law of survival of the fittest operates in the kingdom of animals. For example, he notes, the development of this capacity for grouping explains the survival of such small animals as bees, while the lack of this capacity explains why such large and ferocious animals as lions are killed by human beings and have become vanishing species.[36]

More important, Hsün Tzu's concept of *ch'ün* enabled Chang to make sense of the competition and struggle currently going on among the human races. Chang views *ch'ün* as one of the critical human capacities that determine the varying fortunes of different races: it was why the yellow people, who achieved a higher level of social integration and organization as groups, fared better than the black, the brown, and the red; and also why the yellow races were being trampled under by white people, who were better organized as groups than they were.[37] Apparently starting from Hsün Tzu's concept of *ch'ün*, Chang arrived at a Social Darwinian picture of the world that might have come from the pen of Yen Fu.

Despite Social Darwinism's impingement on Chang's concept of *ch'ün*, Chang retains some distinctive features from Hsün Tzu's thought. One was

---

33. Ibid.: 135, 138–39.
34. For a discussion of the emergence of the concept of *ch'ün* in the intellectual context of the era, see Chang Hao (1971: 105–12).
35. For Chang's relationship with Yen Fu, see his letter to Hsia Tseng-yu, also a friend of Yen Fu's, and the letter Yen Fu wrote to Chang (1981: 109–13).
36. 1977: 137, 139.
37. Ibid.: 139.

Hsün Tzu's idea of fate (*ming*). According to Chang, Hsün Tzu's wisdom in this regard began with the distinction he made between individual and collective fate. Regarding the fate of the individual, Hsün Tzu took the view that "fate depends on Heaven," but, as Chang points out, "Heaven" in this connection must be understood in the context of Hsün Tzu's "naturalism." Seen in that light, Hsün Tzu's dictum could not mean that fate is controlled by supernatural force. It was then open to two interpretations: one was that the fate of an individual depends on pure accident in the outside world; and the other was that the fate of a person depends on the past behavior of his own ancestors. Because retribution for the ancestral activities of a family usually was worked out over many generations, one could never be sure exactly how ancestral behavior would affect the fate of a certain specific descendant. Either interpretation, in Chang's view, supported Hsün Tzu's belief that the human individual had no control over his personal fate.[38]

On the other hand, Hsün Tzu's thought also featured a strain of anti-fatalism, which was expressed most clearly in his famous chapter, "T'ien-lun p'ien" (On Heaven), in the book *Hsün Tzu*. There, the ancient thinker urged people to harness Heaven as nature to human uses rather than sing praises to Heaven as a mighty supernatural force. In Chang's view, Hsün Tzu made his point here with the sole reference to the collective will and effort of a whole nation or society. In this way, Chang arrives at the moral he drew from Hsün Tzu's anthropological thought: "In short, an individual person has no control over his fate. However, if a whole group of people can work together, then the fortune of the group completely hinges upon the collective effort of the members of the group. Therefore, one can speak of fate with regard to an individual, but not to a nation."[39]

One further stamp of Hsün Tzu's thought on Chang's concept of *ch'ün* came from its moral thrust. True, there were some strains of tough-minded realism in Hsün Tzu's thought that could fit into the amoral world view of Social Darwinism. Nevertheless, Chang was aware that Hsün Tzu's overall concern was the creation of a moral order. In fact, he repeatedly quoted Hsün Tzu to this effect in the essays under consideration. For this reason, too, although Chang's concept of *ch'ün* led him to recognize the need for tough-minded realism in conceiving social organization, he sometimes spoke of this need with misgivings and irony.[40]

So far, Chang's focal concern, as embodied in the idea of *ch'ün*, was how to integrate and organize China as a viable sociopolitical order, and his thinking in this direction reflected the combined impact of Hsün Tzu's thought and Western ideas. Chang's intellectual horizons continued to expand. He reports that, at this time, he also became intensely interested in

---

38. Ibid.: 141–43.
39. Ibid.: 142–43.
40. Ibid.: 135, 139–40.

Legalist thought.[41] But, by and large, Western learning played a greater role in the evolution of his sociopolitical thinking in the late 1890s and early 1900s. Largely with the help of Western thought, he was able to articulate his concern more fully and clearly in new ideas and values regarding the state and society. In the meantime, the moral perspective that he inherited from Confucianism via Hsün Tzu maintained its subtle hold as his sociopolitical thinking unfolded.

BEYOND ETHNIC NATIONALISM: A MORAL PERSPECTIVE

Chang's involvement in the reform movement turned out to be a short interlude in his life. Soon after the movement failed in late 1898, he began to move gradually away from the K'ang-Liang reformist circles. By the early 1900s, he was already known as a radical intellectual of a clearly revolutionist stamp.[42] From then on up to the revolution of 1911, Chang was a major intellectual spokesman for the revolutionist group.

In the early 1900s, Chang was best known among the Chinese intelligentsia for his ethnically oriented nationalism—anti-Manchuism. Indeed, on the surface at least, anti-Manchuism had become the most striking characteristic of his concept of *ch'ün*. He felt that the Chinese people had a cultural distinctiveness that was biologically rooted and geographically conditioned. Biologically, the Chinese descended from the ancient cultureheroes, the Yellow Emperor (Huang-ti) and Shen-nung. Geographically, although the Chinese people might have originated in the land west of what later came to be known as China, they had moved into and settled in this land longer than any other. In short, his version of ethnically oriented nationalism revolves around one basic idea, that the uniqueness of the Chinese people lay in their pure blood and sacred land.[43]

Chang did not fully articulate his ethnic nationalism until after he went into exile in Japan in 1906.[44] When he did so in the journal *Min pao* (The people), his ethnic nationalism was not entirely couched in the language of blood and soil but also carried a strong moral tone. In his view, the existence of the Manchu regime represented the domination of a people made up largely of Han Chinese by an ethnic minority. Hence, the struggle against the Manchu regime was no mere revolution (*ko-ming*) in the traditional sense

---

41. See sections on Legalism in *Ch'iu shu* (1978: 4a–5a, 74a–77b); see also "Ch'in cheng chi" [Notes on the politics of the Ch'in dynasty] (1919, *Wen-lu*, chüan 1: 63b–65b).

42. T'ang Chih-chün (1979, 1: 108–14; 1974b: 182–88; 1975: 59–74).

43. Chang's ethnic nationalism is expressed mainly in the essays that he published in *Min pao*, esp. in "Chung-hua min-kuo chieh" [A definition of the Republic of China], "P'ai-Man p'ing-i" [On expelling the Manchus], and "Fu-ch'ou shih-fei lun" [On the rights and wrongs of revenge] (1919, *Pieh-lu*, chüan 1: 1a–13b, 14a–22b, 30a).

44. The major articles spelling out his ethnic nationalism were all published in *Min pao* after 1906; see n. 43.

of overturning a dynastic regime. It was primarily an act of revenge on the part of the Han Chinese to recover their collective honor and dignity (*fu-ch'ou* or *kuang-fu*).⁴⁵ Hence, this struggle was no wanton outburst of racial hatred and hostility, but a moral act—what he called a "righteous protest and resistance" (*cheng-i chih fan-k'ang*) directed not against all the Manchu people, but specifically against the Manchu government.⁴⁶

In defending ethnic nationalism, Chang was also asserting the general principle of revenge and revolution, which he believes should be applied all over the world (and even to all the species on earth), wherever racial-ethnic domination and oppression occur. He realizes that some would denounce revenge as a reversion to ancient barbarism, and he grants the validity of this denunciation in the case of revenge between individual persons, because violent revenge within a civilized society is unnecessary: the law usually exists to maintain justice. But the logic of this argument does not apply to the situation among nations and races, because no effective higher law exists to maintain justice among countries and racial-ethnic groups. Thus, for Chang, revenge between racial-ethnic groups is entirely justified, so long as it is carried out as an act of "righteous protest and resistance" against alien aggression or domination.⁴⁷

In his view, the moral thrust of racial-ethnic revenge is no different from that of revolution in defense of human rights. Both are morally justified violence directed against oppression. He vividly expresses this tone of moral protest and condemnation in his idea of "perfect nationalism" in *Min pao*:

> [However] there is something in [nationalism] which is grand and great. What we embrace would not merely apply to the Han people. As for those other weak nations who are conquered, ruled, and enslaved by powerful nations, we should try to recover the independence of them all as long as we have enough strength left. Alas! India and Burma were swallowed by England; Vietnam was annexed by France. All the intelligent and good-natured people are now trampled underfoot. Therefore ... we should return them [to their former independence]. As for those who are not part of us, can we bear to let the descendants of the old civilized people stay in shackles? We who want to [uphold] the perfect nationalism should extend our sympathy so as to save [all] those who suffered and to gain complete independence for them. As for those peoples who, following the model of the devilish [American president] McKinley, engaged in expansionism under the pretext of helping others, we should make it a principle to kill them without pardon.⁴⁸

Clearly, underlying Chang's ethnic revenge is a moral vision of universal racial-ethnic liberation.

---

45. 1919, *Pieh-lu*, chüan 1: 22b–30a; 13b–22b; and "Ko-ming tao-teh shuo" [On the revolutionary morality] (ibid.: 30a–b).
46. Ibid.: 20a, 21b.
47. Ibid.: 26b–30a.
48. "Wu wu lun" [Five theses of nihilism] (ibid., chüan 3: 43a–44a).

This moral language of justice and righteousness not only has a place in his concept of anti-Manchuism, but it also pervades the vision of the postrevolutionary order that he was developing at the time. On the surface his vision bears strong imprints of Legalist influences. At the time, Chang was engaged in rehabilitating the ancient Chinese Legalism against a longstanding Confucian bias. His efforts are nowhere more clearly seen than in the way he portrays the two central figures in the Legalist tradition, Shang Yang and the First Emperor of Ch'in. Confucian historiography paints the two as archvillains in Chinese history, but Chang presents both as model statesmen who practiced government by law.[49] Government by law, in his view, provides a despotic system with certain redeeming advantages: it is more rational because it can counteract the arbitrariness of despotism; and it promotes social equity, insofar as only one person, namely, the king, is allowed to be above the law, while all other persons are equally subjected to its control. Largely for these reasons, he preferred the Legalist ideal of government by law to the Confucian ideal of government by virtue.[50]

However, some historians have exaggerated the influence of Legalism over Chang. Whatever the differences between Legalism and Confucianism, Legalism shares the latter's basic monarchical concept of political system, but this was exactly what Chang had come to reject. Under the same ideal of government by laws, he had made the switch from Legalist monarchy to constitutional democracy. In fact, the political institution that he envisioned for the new order after the overthrow of the Manchu government was constitutional democracy. One of the most important characteristics he expected to see in the future new republic was the supremacy of law. He was certainly aware of the difference between the supremacy of law in a democratic republic, where even the chief executive must obey the law, and the government by law in a traditional monarchy, where the monarch was above the law. It was by no means accidental that, when he borrowed the Western concept of separation of powers in his design of a new government of China, he attached special significance to the ideal of judicial independence.[51]

An examination of his concept of republican government in other aspects also shows that his Legalist leanings were not so strong as one might expect from his occasional glorification of the role of Legalist statesmen in Chinese history. Legalism, it must be recalled, is distinguished by a concept of politics free of moral concern. Chang's vision of the future democratic order, however, is not couched in the Legalist language of wealth and power that colors the concept of democracy of many of his contemporary intellectuals. Instead, it is often spelled out in terms that bespeak strong moral impulses.

---

49. See *Ch'iu shu* (1978: 74a–77b); 1919, *Wen-lu*, chüan 1: 63b–65b.
50. 1919, *Wen-lu*, chüan 1: 63b–65b.
51. "Tai-i jan-fou lun" [On the legitimacy of a parliamentary system] (ibid., *Pieh-lu*, chüan 1, 60a–73b).

Moral impulses clearly underlie the most striking characteristic of Chang's concept of the future democratic order, namely, his repudiation of the parliamentary system. The basic reason for this repudiation was his moral revulsion against what he had learned about the electoral process and party politics in the United States and Japan.[52] He notes that the records of the electoral processes and party activities in both countries show the overriding role of wealth as a determinant in politics. Men elected to parliament are usually the local wealthy and powerful (*t'u-hao*), who, after being elected, act in a way that promotes their own interests. Parliamentary democracy, then, is a political system that usually serves the interest of the wealthy and the powerful at the expense of the poor and the underprivileged; it has an inherent tendency to generate social inequality and class rigidity.[53] It is in this sense that Chang calls the parliamentary system "feudalism in disguise."

Chang does not make the observation gratuitously, because he sees a special historical connection between the two. As he points out, the parliamentary system arose in the West and Japan against a background of feudalism. Consequently, it would come as no surprise that the system in either country reflected the feudal spirit of social inequality and class rigidity. It is this view that Chang uses to refute many of his contemporaries, most notably the reformists, who championed parliamentary democracy in China. He reminds them that, in China, history followed a course different from that of the West and Japan. In contrast to Japan and the West, which went through a feudal stage only in their recent past, China had long outgrown her feudal stage. Consequently, China had far less social inequality than the West and Japan. Indeed, as he observes, if anything could be said for the Chinese tradition, it was that social equality had obtained in China since the decline of her ancient feudalism. For the sake of preserving this tradition of social equality, he is strongly opposed to the idea of introducing parliamentary institutions, which he was afraid might increase the class gap in China.[54]

Underlying his distrust of parliamentary institutions is, obviously, a moral concern with social equality. This moral concern is even more evident in the social program that he envisions for the future republic. For Chang, there were three basic ways in which a new society must be constructed in China: first, land redistribution to eliminate tenancy and to ensure equitable ownership of land; second, the establishment of government-owned industries to let workers share the profit; and third, a ban on the inheritance of property to prevent the concentration of wealth. Although stated in broad and vague terms, these ideas nevertheless demonstrate clearly his concern with social justice. Altogether, Chang's vision of the future reveals less of a Legalist, amoral concern with the state's wealth and power than a moral

---

52. Ibid.: 65b–66a, 67a; see also ibid., chüan 3: 44b.
53. Ibid., chüan 1: 60a–62a.
54. Ibid.: 60a–61b, 67b, 69a–b, 73a.

quest for a just government and society.⁵⁵ It was this moral vision of the future combined with his ethnic nationalism that turned him from a reformist into a fiery rebel against the Manchu government in the decade of the 1900s.

We have seen that Chang's concept of *ch'ün* is articulated in some new ideals regarding state and society, largely due to Western ideological influences. He spells out these ideals not only in the nationalistic idioms of blood and soil, but also in a language with strong moral tones. Although his language bespeaks the strong imprint of Western ideals and values, its moral tone also reminds us of the concern with moral order that he inherited from Hsün Tzu. His moral tone is even stronger when we examine his ideas on how to achieve the revolution he envisions. Perhaps because he was primarily a man of ideas, his writings by and large say little about means and method. To the extent that he expresses himself on this issue, he shows a significant preoccupation with morality, almost completely ignoring the issues of tactics and organization.

Chang's moral approach to the making of revolution is based on the lessons he drew from his own observation of radical politics. As he watched the swelling of the ranks of Chinese intelligentsia of both the reformist and the revolutionist persuasions—what he called the "new party people" (*hsin-tang*)—he felt concern about their lack of moral commitment. Most of them, in his view, were just following a fad or pursuing self-seeking motives. Thus, despite all their talk about new ideas, in mentality and behavior they were still prisoners of the traditional penchant for factionalism and cliquishness.⁵⁶

Chang's revulsion and disappointment were particularly directed at the group of new party people of which he himself was a member—the revolutionists. In an article entitled "Ko-ming tao-teh shuo" (On revolutionary morality) that appeared in *Min pao*, he takes a strongly moralistic view of the social composition of the people involved in revolutionary movements. As he surveys the social scene of China, he finds that the higher a social group stands in terms of status and education, the lower it has sunk morally. Because most of his revolutionary compatriots came from the upper class, it was by no means accidental that their behavior left much to be desired.⁵⁷

Chang sees this lack of moral strength as the most serious problem besetting the cause of the revolution, because, in his view, to carry out a revolution requires the strongest moral fiber on the part of revolutionaries.⁵⁸ His emphasis on the moral requirement for participation in a revolutionary movement leads him to challenge some of the moral concepts in vogue at that time. One concept that was then fervently championed by some in-

---

55. Ibid., chüan 3: 44a.
56. "Chen hsin-tang lun" [On warnings to the new party] (ibid., chüan 1: 44b–56a).
57. "Ko-ming tao-teh shuo" [On revolutionary morality] (ibid.: 35b–40b).
58. Ibid.: 31b–32a, 40b–41a.

tellectual leaders was the distinction between public and private morality. Liang Ch'i-ch'ao, for example, calls attention in his famous *Hsin-min shuo* (On the new citizen) to civic virtues as the kind of public morality most undeveloped in the Chinese tradition, but most essential to nation-building.[59] Chang does not so much reject the concept of public morality as raise the question of whether the distinction between public and private morality can be made, that is, whether people defective in personal morality would have the moral rigor and strength to meet the demands of public morality.[60] For the same reason, he jettisons a time-honored moral distinction in the Chinese tradition, namely, the distinction between morality of principles and morality of literal compliance. Again he questions whether people who are lax in following rules of behavioral propriety for ordinary, day-to-day occasions have the moral strength adequate to maintain basic principles.[61] The purpose of his challenges to these widely held moral conceptions is obvious: to drive home the idea that revolution is an enterprise demanding the highest moral commitment and integrity.

Thus, Chang's ethnic nationalism is undergirded by a moral perspective that colors both his concept of revolution and his concept of postrevolutionary order. The language of blood and soil that he frequently uses in his polemical writings to present his case against the Manchus must not conceal from us his view of revolution as a moral enterprise. On the other hand, his moral perspective did not lead him to develop (as many of his fellow intellectuals did) a utopian vision or chiliastic expectations of the political future of China. Revolution for him was not the final act of redemption to usher in a millennium in China or on earth.[62] Instead, a transcendental world view gradually crystallized in his mind after 1903—a world view that eventually led him to see not only his political radicalism, but everything else in a different perspective. To see how this world view evolved, I will take a close look at Chang's complex relationship with the Chinese tradition.

BEYOND ETHNIC NATIONALISM:
CHANG'S PATH TO YOGACARA BUDDHISM

To consider Chang's relationship with the Chinese tradition in the decade of the 1900s, we must remember his early, extended involvement in the development of Han Learning. This involvement opened doors for him to many aspects of the Chinese tradition that otherwise would have been closed. Despite his diverse scholarly interests in various aspects of the tradition, his philosophical preferences largely centered on the tough-minded

---

59. Chang Hao (1971: 149–219, 272–95).
60. 1919, *Pieh-lu*, chüan 1: 32a.
61. Ibid.
62. Ibid., chüan 3: 42b–45b.

Confucianism of Hsün Tzu. However, as the decade of the 1900s wore on, his early relationship with the Chinese tradition changed. His enthusiasm for Hsün Tzu wore thin by the middle of the decade, as he turned increasingly radical in his outlook. In fact, his pre-1911 years turned out to be the most iconoclastic period of his life.[63] For one thing, neo-Confucianism, especially the orthodox Ch'eng-Chu school, was often the target of his scorn and disapproval.[64] As for Confucius himself, Chang had already cast this sacred figure in an unflattering light in a revised edition of *Ch'iu shu*, which he wrote in 1900.[65] Chang continued his criticism of Confucius in the later editions of *Ch'iu shu*, and also in an important essay written in 1906, "Chu-tzu hsüeh lüeh shuo" (A general discussion of the noncanonical philosophies), in which he painted Confucius as a self-serving and unprincipled scholar. Confucianism was also sometimes depicted as a creed that encouraged muddled thinking and promoted a morality that placed a premium on self-seeking and hypocritical behavior.[66] This sort of unreserved attack on Confucius and Confucianism represented an even more radical stance than that of T'an Ssu-t'ung in some ways and anticipated the iconoclasm of the May Fourth generation. Unsurprisingly, some of the leading radical intellectuals of the May Fourth generation like Lu Hsün and Wu Yü paid tribute to Chang Ping-lin's pioneering role in the modern iconoclastic movement.[67]

Meanwhile, Chang was also actively involved in an intellectual movement for the "rejuvenation of national quintessences" (*kuo-ts'ui*), a movement that began to sweep across China's intellectual world in the early 1900s and soon generated reverberations among scholar-officials in the government as well as among the intelligentsia of both the reformist and revolutionist persuasions.[68] The term "*kuo-ts'ui*" was a neologism borrowed from Japan, where similar movements had been in vogue since the late nineteenth century, but, basically, the *kuo-ts'ui* movement must be seen as a response to the growing impact of the West in China. As such the movement was fed by two powerful, intertwined strains of feeling. One was an angst for cultural identity: Chinese intellectuals had become painfully aware of the deficiency of their own tradition in the course of their country's confrontation with the West but felt compelled by their cultural pride to affirm its value. Such a feeling was doubtless present in Chang's mind when he responds to the

---

63. After 1911 Chang's outlook became increasingly conservative. In 1914 he compiled his own writings and revised his *Ch'iu shu* into *Chien lun* (1919: 16, 17, 18), and in both collections he deliberately left out many of the pre-1911 polemical essays in which he had expressed radical views (T'ang [1979, 1: 481–90, 510–11]).

64. 1968: 2–4, 13–14; "Shih Tai" [An interpretation of Tai Chen's thought] (1919, *Wen-lu*, chüan 1: 120a–24a); "Yen-shuo lu" [A speech text] (1906: 14).

65. 1968: 2–4.

66. 1914, chüan 3: 3a–6b; see also Chang's speech to overseas Chinese students in Tokyo (1906: 5).

67. Lu Hsün (1961: 442–43); Wu Yü (1917a: 9–11; 1917b: 323–26; 1917c: 431–43).

68. T'ang (1979, 1: 200–1); see also Yang T'ien-shih (1974: 34–44).

Western cultural impact in this way: "While [some] people feel ashamed of our differences with Western culture, I rather feel proud of these differences."[69] Closely related to this concern for cultural identity is his belief that consciousness of the value of tradition is necessary for fostering nationalism. Chang says that, just as crops depend on nourishment from outside to grow, the development of a people's nationalistic feeling depends on their knowledge of their cultural heritage. Only those who are aware of the cultural richness of their tradition can love their country.[70]

Out of these feelings often grew wholesale affirmation of China's cultural heritage among people involved in the *kuo-ts'ui* movement. Chang did not go as far as such extremists as Huang Chieh and Teng Shih did.[71] But some of his efforts to define the national quintessence come close to wholesale, indiscriminate affirmation. For instance, at one point he emphasizes the need to become sensitized to the value of three aspects of Chinese history in order to develop nationalistic feeling: the spoken and written languages, the laws and institutions, and the exploits of historical figures.[72]

Chang at this time was also engaged in affirming the value of the noncanonical aspects of traditional thought. Could we then look on his thinking and activities in this direction as no more than a part of his concern to promote the *kuo-ts'ui* movement? Obviously, this concern must be taken into account, but we should not push this consideration too far, because his interest in the noncanonical aspects of Chinese thought had other roots in his mind, as clearly reflected in his fervent study of Mahayana Buddhism and philosophical Taoism.

Chang's interest in the two philosophies began separately in his early years. He started studying philosophical Taoism along with other classical Chinese philosophies when he was 16.[73] In both the early editions of his famous *Ch'iu shu* and his "Chu-tzu hsüeh lüeh shuo" mentioned above, he discussed Taoism in a way that emphasized the purposive and manipulative aspects of Lao Tzu's teachings.[74] Thus, the tone of his comments on philosophical Taoism is critical on the whole. However, when he published a three-section serial on Taoism in *Kuo-ts'ui hsüeh-pao* in 1910, he completely reverses his evaluation and fervently defends Taoism against the charge of political cynicism. He was particularly sympathetic with Chuang Tzu's philosophy and viewed its spiritual teaching as an invaluable source of inspiration and edification.[75] The key to this reversal of attitude, as he

69. Yang (1974: 37).
70. "Ta T'ieh-cheng" [A reply to T'ieh-cheng] (1919, *Pieh-lu*, chüan 2: 69b).
71. Yang (1974: 36, 40–41); see also Schneider (1976: 47–89).
72. 1906: 9.
73. 1965: 3.
74. *Ch'iu shu* (1978: 3a–4a; 6a–b); 1914: 5a–6b.
75. "Yüan Tao" [On Taoism] in *Kuo-ku lun-heng* [Essays on the national heritage] (1919, chüan 3: 120a–31a).

suggests in an autobiographical sketch of his intellectual career, was a new development that took place in his study of Mahayana Buddhism in the mid-1900s.[76]

Chang was introduced to the study of Mahayana Buddhism in the late 1890s by two of his close friends, Hsia Tseng-yu and Sung Shu, who were both pioneers in the revival of Buddhist study in modern China. But, as Chang admitted years later, he did not begin to study Buddhist teachings seriously until the period between 1903 and 1906 when he was imprisoned in Shanghai for publishing anti-Manchu revolutionary writings. During his incarceration, the enforced quietude allowed him to pursue some important Buddhist texts, such as *Yogacaryabhumi-sastra*, *Nyayapravesa*, and *Vidya-matrasiddhi sastra*.[77] Later he claimed that it was then that he really "awakened" to the essential teachings of Mahayana Buddhism.[78]

Chang emerged from prison a Buddhist convert. Thus, when he went to Japan immediately afterward, he told his fellow revolutionists that religion—by which he meant his newly acquired Buddhist faith—and the preservation of national quintessence were his two most important intellectual concerns.[79] In fact, for a while he was even thinking of going into a monastery and becoming a monk.[80]

Like most of his contemporary Buddhist intellectuals, Chang was a devotee of the Yogacara school, especially of its Dharmalaksana sect.[81] But this fact did not preclude his interest in the Mahayana Buddhism of other persuasions like Madhyamika and Zen.[82] They were, after all, the Mahayana sects that shared with the Yogacara school much of the same soteriological ends, spiritual impulses, and metaphysical world view.

Why was Chang converted to Buddhism at this time? First of all, the 1900s were a turbulent period in his life. He was entering the mid-years of his life and was in prison for three years, where, according to his own testimony, he was subjected to physical torture and mental deprivation. In addition to these sufferings, he witnessed a close friend of his, Chou Yung, languishing to death in prison.[83] These "boundary situations" in his life naturally put him in a frame of mind more responsive to the spiritual messages of Buddhism.

Equally important in explaining his embrace of Mahayana Buddhism were certain historical circumstances of his times. During the decade of the 1900s he lived mostly in Shanghai and Tokyo, the two nerve centers of the

---

76. "T'ai-yen hsien-sheng tzu-shu hsüeh-shu tz'u-ti" [Mr. Chang Ping-lin's own account of his intellectual career] (1965: 53–54).
77. 1965: 5–6, 10.
78. Ibid.: 10; see also pp. 5a–6b.
79. 1906: 4, 6–9.
80. T'ang (1979, 1: 296–97).
81. 1919, *Pieh-lu*, chüan 2: 58a–60a; see also 1965: 10–11, 53–54.
82. 1919, *Pieh-lu*, chüan 2: 58a–60a.
83. T'ang (1979, 1: 191–93, 201–3).

intellectual world of the Chinese intelligentsia, and became a leader among this group, to whom people looked for intellectual guidance and orientation. The cultural environs of Shanghai and Tokyo and the role he played in them made him naturally sensitive to the crisis of the orientational order that was engulfing the Chinese intelligentsia. (See chap. 1 for discussion of this crisis.) Like Liang Ch'i-ch'ao and many others, Chang was among the group of avant-garde intellectuals in the transitional generation who found in Mahayana Buddhism a perspective that allowed them to combine political activism with a comprehensive philosophy to make sense of life and the world.

A BUDDHIST WORLD VIEW

Chang spells out his reading of Yogacara teachings in an extended commentary he wrote on the second chapter of the *Chuang Tzu*, entitled "Ch'i-wu lun" (Discourse on making all things equal).[84] Significantly Chang chose "Ch'i-wu lun," generally regarded as the most characteristic and the most important chapter of *Chuang Tzu*, as the medium for elucidating his Buddhist views. Chang not only writes to this effect in the preface to his commentary,[85] but also frequently refers to other chapters of *Chuang Tzu* as corroborations of the spiritual truths he found in "Ch'i-wu lun." These facts suggest that Chang's commentary on "Ch'i-wu lun" is tantamount to an interpretation of the philosophical Taoism of *Chuang Tzu* as a whole. More important, he was convinced that *Chuang Tzu* was kindred in spirit to Yogacara Buddhism. True, he was aware that it does not contain the philosophical categories and arguments used in Yogacara teachings, but he felt that this should not be allowed to obscure the fact that the different terminologies of the two convey the same truth and spirit. His commentary on "Ch'i-wu lun" is thus an attempt to show the homology between the philosophical Taoism of *Chuang Tzu* and Yogacara Buddhism and thereby to assimilate the former with the latter by way of interpreting the often cryptic, ambiguous ideas of the former in terms of the systematic phenomenological analysis of the latter.[86]

Two different readings of the title "Ch'i-wu lun" suggest two divergent interpretations of the whole chapter. According to Wang An-shih and

---

84. The commentary on "Ch'i-wu lun," entitled *Ch'i-wu lun shih* [An interpretation of "Ch'i-wu lun"], was published in 1910 (1919, 11: 1a–63b). The previous year he published a volume of textual commentaries on the book of *Chuang tzu*—*Chuang tzu chieh ku* [Textual commentaries on *Chuang Tzu*] (1919, 9: 1a–40b). Apparently, these volumes were the result of Chang's scholarly labor over a number of years in the late 1900s; see T'ang (1979, 1: 315, 346, 348).

85. See Chang Ping-lin, "Ch'i-wu lun shih hsü" [Preface to *An Interpretation of "Ch'i-wu lun"*] (1919, 11: 1a–b).

86. Ibid.: 1a.

others, the title can be read to mean "Unifying all the different views of things." But Chang prefers a much older reading that renders the title as "Discourse on the equality of all things," because this reading brings out Chuang Tzu's crucial idea of undifferentiated oneness that, in his view, runs through the whole chapter from beginning to end.[87] Indeed, Chang looked on the whole chapter as a skein of themes woven around this idea of oneness. One central theme is a skepticism about the reality and meaning of the mundane world. For Chuang Tzu, the visible world is in a constant flux wherein all the existences incessantly transform themselves from one form into another and no particular form of existence is more real than any other. This vision of the phenomenal world is what is called *wu-hua* (transformation of things) in "Ch'i-wu lun."[88]

This concept points to Chuang Tzu's main thesis: the phenomenal world has only a relative, conditioned reality. In a famous analogy, Chuang Tzu compares all beings in the phenomenal world to shadow and penumbras that have only contingent existence (*yu-tai*) in the sense that they have no substance of their own and depend for their existence on conditions external to them. Unconditioned reality (*wu-tai*) belongs only to the *tao* or ground of being.[89]

In the background of "Ch'i-wu lun" is Chuang Tzu's idea of the immanence of *tao* in every individual. This immanent *tao* constitutes the true self or true controller (*chen-tsai*) in the individual human being, as distinguished from his biological self.[90] The indwelling *tao* or true self still preserves its transcendence, as seen in a certain spirit of negation that permeates Chuang Tzu's philosophy. This spirit is, first, directed toward the self-ego of any human individual as something that stands in the way of the realization of *tao*. Chuang Tzu spoke of "losing one's self-ego" (*sang-wo*) in "Ch'i-wu lun."[91] The spirit of negation is also shown toward the ubiquitous human tendency to evaluate and to discriminate. At the root of this tendency, Chuang Tzu sees an intellectual and moral sophistication that inevitably arises with the development of human culture and society. This sophistication, as well as the attachment to self-ego, makes for what Chuang Tzu calls the "given mind" (*ch'eng-hsin*) and the "boundaries and distinctions" (*feng*) that human beings draw everywhere. For the realization of *tao*, the given mind and the inveterate human tendency to discriminate must all be discarded. In other words, the ultimate reality can be made manifest only after self-ego and mundane sophistications are transcended.[92]

---

87. *Ch'i-wu lun shih ting-pen* [The final edition of an interpretation of "Ch'i-wu lun"] (1919, 12: 1a).
88. Ibid.: 1a, 58b–62b.
89. Ibid.: 38b–40b, 51a–58b.
90. Ibid.: 9b–10a.
91. Ibid.: 4b.
92. Ibid.: 11b–19a.

In "Ch'i-wu lun," such self-transcendence is believed to be possible. When it is achieved all the differences and distinctions that used to matter for the self-ego now become meaningless and disappear from view. All that is left is the unconditioned, ultimate *tao*. That oneness is celebrated in "Ch'i-wu lun" and in the *Chuang Tzu* as a whole. Hence, the thesis of "Ch'i-wu lun" is that anyone who achieves self-transcendence will see the oneness and thereby the universal equality of all things in the world.[93]

All these spiritual truths of *Chuang Tzu*, Chang believed, are echoed in Yogacara Buddhism. As Chang says in his commentary on "Ch'i-wu lun," "the gist of 'Ch'i-wu lun' in large measure jibes with the Buddhist canons."[94] In his eagerness to elucidate and elaborate these Taoist ideas in terms of the systematic philosophy of Yogacara Buddhism, Chang inevitably blurs some differences between the two, consciously or unconsciously. For instance, the other-worldliness of Chuang Tzu never went as far as that of Mahayana Buddhism. The Taoist concept of transcendence, while certainly devaluing the human world, still allowed a positive view of the nonhuman, "natural" world. On the other hand, the natural world, being part of the phenomenal world, was viewed as just as illusory as the human world by Buddhism. Yet our main concern here is not to judge whether Chang misinterprets Taoism or Buddhism. It is to see how he interpreted the philosophy of Chuang Tzu in a way that assimilates it into Yogacara Buddhism.

First of all, Chang finds Chuang Tzu's devaluation of the mundane world echoed in Yogacara Buddhism. As with the Taoist idea of "transformation of things," the Yogacara teaching also views the phenomenal world as a perpetual flux, as reflected in the doctrine of reincarnation (*liu-ch'u sheng-ch'en*), which the Yogacara school assumes in common with every other sect of Buddhism.[95]

Underlying this doctrine of reincarnation is the pivotal Buddhist concept of conditional causation (*yüan-ch'i*), which Chang regarded as kindred in spirit to Chuang Tzu's concept of contingent existence (*yu-tai*). Like the latter, the Buddhist concept of conditional causation sees the world as locked in an endless chain of causes and effects. Everything in this world is merely a concatenation of causes and effects, and nothing has any independent nature of its own. Even the chain of causation as a whole does not have any more substance than the individual existence in it. As Chang observes, the chain not only has no end; it has no beginning in any independent, substantial first cause. Here he obviously interprets Chuang Tzu's relativistic world view in terms of Mahayana Buddhism's concept of emptiness.[96]

A natural corollary of this nihilistic world view is the gloomy, negative

---
93. Ibid.: 18b–24a.
94. Ibid.: 23a.
95. Ibid.: 58b–62a.
96. Ibid.: 16a–b, 51a–58b.

outlook on human existence that Chang intimates in his commentaries. Individual life invariably has its inception in a primordial ignorance, runs its course as determined by the karma of its activities, and ends in suffering and death, only to be reborn to go through the dreary cycle again and again. In this way, life is caught in a perpetual flux made up of endless rounds of birth and rebirth. In short, according to Chang, both Mahayana Buddhism and philosophical Taoism basically share the same view of the "emptiness" of the ego-self and the phenomenal world (*jen wu-wo, fa wu-wo*).[97]

True to the teachings of the Yogacara school, Chang believes that an awareness of the "emptiness" of self and world approaches but has not quite reached the highest wisdom of the Mahayana Buddhism, because this awareness leaves unanswered the problem of the origin of the ignorance and illusion that prevent people from realizing the truth of emptiness. To answer this problem, he devotes a large portion of his commentaries to elucidating the transcendental concept of ultimate reality that underlies the Mahayana philosophy of emptiness.[98]

In Yogacara Buddhism, such a transcendental, spiritual reality is variously termed *alaya-vijnana*, *tathagatagarba*, or *bhutatathata*.[99] Whatever its name, this ultimate reality is characterized as a sort of repository consciousness in which are stored two kinds of seeds (*vija*) or senses: the pure, uncontaminated and the contaminated. The latter is the ultimate source of the phenomenal world.[100] More specifically, the phenomenal world is seen as the result of the joint, cumulative working of seven contaminated senses rooted in the *alaya-vijnana*. The first five senses are seeing, hearing, smelling, tasting, and touch. The sixth, called *mano-vijnana*, is the mental sense in charge of synthetic apprehension, and the seventh, *klista-mano-vijnana*, is the discriminating and constructive sense. The seventh sense is given special importance because it is considered the cause of the individualization and ego-formation of human beings (and indeed of all existences) and therefore is the root of all delusions that mistake the apparent for the real.[101]

According to the Yogacara world view, then, the emergence of an individual human mind is nothing more than the activation of a series of senses that issue from the *alaya-vijnana*. From the transcendental source, the human mind is equipped with certain innate perceiving, categorizing, and conceptualizing capacities furnished by the first six senses of the *alaya-vijnana*.

---

97. Ibid.: 18a, 23b–24a, 51a–62b.
98. Ibid.: 9b–10a, 54b–55a.
99. Ibid.: 10b–11a, 12a–13a. Chang presents the basic teachings of Yogacara Buddhism in a series of articles in *Min pao* from late 1906 to late 1907. Especially important are "Chien-li tsung-chiao lun" [On establishing religion] (*Min pao*, no. 9, Nov. 15, 1906); "Jen wu-wo lun" [On the nonexistence of the human self] (*Min pao*, no. 11, Jan. 25, 1907).
100. 1919, *Ch'i-wu lun shih*: 12a–13a, 53b–54a; see also 1919, *Pieh-lu*, chüan 3: 10b–11b, 31b–41b.
101. 1919, *Ch'i-wu lun shih*: 5b–9a, 12b–13a; see also 1919, *Pieh-lu*, chüan 3: 10b–11b.

At one place in his commentary, Chang mentions five such innate capacities of mind: the temporal sense (*shih-shih*), the spatial sense (*ch'u-shih*), the sense of sensual qualities (*hsiang-shih*), the sense of number (*shu-shih*), and the sense of causality (*yin-kuo shih*). He compares these innate mental capacities to the twelve a priori categories that Kant sees as inherent in the human mind.[102] Because of these innate senses, the human mind is able to project self and world as if they are independent objective realities.

This "idealistic" view of the individual self and the phenomenal world, Chang believes, corresponds to what Chuang Tzu called *ch'eng-hsin* (the given and preconceived mind) in the "Ch'i-wu lun."[103] However, what is suggested and intimated by way of metaphors, parables, and paradoxes in Chuang Tzu's philosophy is systematically spelled out in the Yogacara analysis of names (*ming*), forms of phenomenon (*hsiang*), and mental differentiation (*fen-pieh*). The Yogacara teaching inherits the basic Mahayana view that one cannot speak of a phenomenon in itself, because a phenomenon is invariably expressed in "names," that is, words. But words cannot exist independently of mental constructions. Hence, from the Mahayana point of view, names, phenomena, and mental constructions are always bound together.[104]

A major concern of Yogacara teaching (and of Mahayana Buddhism as a whole) is to demonstrate that the three entities, being entirely the products of subjective consciousness, do not and cannot reflect the existence of an independent, objective reality. This explains why Chang devotes a good portion of his commentary on Chuang Tzu to carrying out the same demonstration. For instance, in his elucidation of Chuang Tzu's idea of the relativity of language, Chang emphasizes the Mahayana argument about the lack of necessary correspondence between a name and the phenomenon to which it refers.[105] As examples, he points to three kinds of nouns we commonly use to name phenomena. One is the ordinary noun. Does any necessary correspondence, he asks, exist between a proper noun like the word "fire" and what it refers to? Obviously not, he says, for the simple reason that different peoples and cultures use different words to denote the same phenomenon. Another kind of noun is the "derivative noun" that denotes a noun formed by combining two or more other nouns. Chang points out that the meaning of a derivative noun usually has nothing to do with the meanings of those constituent nouns together or separately. This fact again goes to show that the meaning of the derivative noun is arbitrary and has no intrinsic relationship to what it refers to. A third type of noun consists of terms like *tao* or *t'ai-chi* or *pen-t'i* that refer to ultimate reality. An examina-

---

102. 1919, *Ch'i-wu lun shih*: 12a–13a.
103. Ibid.: 11a–15a, 15a–18b.
104. Ibid.: 1a–b.
105. Ibid.: 1a–9a, 12a–18b, 19a–20a.

tion of these "ultimate terms" again gives no particular reason why they are chosen to refer to the ultimate reality. For Chang, these examples and many others he discusses in his commentaries serve to demonstrate that there is no objective reality corresponding to any type of names or mental concepts.[106]

Chang also sees the nature of definition, involved in any use of language, as a good example to illustrate his point. Any word, he says, can be made intelligible only by defining it in terms of some other words. Because words in any language are limited in number, the definition of them inevitably becomes circular. This circularity of the process of definition serves to demonstrate a central thesis of Mahayana Buddhism, namely, that the meaning of any word is derived from its relationship with other words, rather than from any intrinsic relationship with an existing objective referent.[107]

In Chang's view, the consciousness of a differentiating mind is the source not only of linguistic naming and categorization, but also of the basic forms commonly assumed to be inherent in the external world. Consequently, the objectivity usually accorded these forms is completely unfounded.[108] For illustration, he points to time as one basic form that represents nothing objective but is a function of our subjective senses. This is why, he said, time is usually felt to move slowly in our childhood, but after middle age it is felt to move quickly. When we are enjoying ourselves, it is often our experience that "time is up" before we know it. On the other hand, for those who do hard work, time often appears endless. In the same way, the measurement of space, Chang argues, is as much a function of our subjective senses.[109] To drive home his points in this regard, he does not just argue by example but draws on Yogacara Buddhism's detailed, technical analysis of the formation and operation of our mental processes.[110]

Another example of a basic form believed to be imbedded in the external world is substance, assumed to underlie any attribute or appearance of a phenomenon. As Chang argues, there are only two ways of proving the existence of such substance, and either way runs into logical difficulty. On the one hand, if the substance is of a material nature, we can never find the ultimate irreducible elements that make up its material substance. Because any material entity, however small, can be broken down into smaller elements, theoretically the process of breaking it down is endless. Thus, we would never find the ultimate constituent elements of any substance. On the other hand, if the substance is of an immaterial nature, we cannot use sense-perceptions as the basis for inquiry into its underlying substance, nor can we discover the substance by inference, because any inference has to depart

---

106. Ibid.: 25b–31a.
107. Ibid.: 19a–20a.
108. Ibid.: 5b–9a.
109. Ibid.: 8a, 8b–9a.
110. Ibid.: 5b–9a, 12a–18b.

from sense-perceptions that do not exist to start with. Obviously, substance is an illusion that exists only in the minds of people who blindly cling to a belief in the objective reality of the self and the world.[111]

According to Chang, another innate function of the differentiating mind is an evaluative disposition, which makes a distinction between right and wrong and between true and false. It is the view of Yogacara Buddhism that this disposition is rooted in the "seventh sense" mentioned above—the sense that generates individual identity and self-awareness. Consequently, Chang regards the evaluative disposition as being bound up with the subjective consciousness of self-ego. By the same token, the distinctions people commonly make between right and wrong or between true and false cannot have any objective validity: "The distinctions between right and wrong do not descend from heaven; nor do they arise from earth. They all spring from human consciousness.... To look upon evaluative distinction as something determined from the beginning of the world is tantamount to mistaking nothing for something."[112]

In arguing the lack of objective validity in the "names, forms of appearances and mental discriminations," Chang often resorts to paradoxical reasonings and uses examples that are puzzling and farfetched. Yet throughout it is clear that his efforts were inspired by the typical approach of Mahayana Buddhism to the problem of the self-existence of the phenomenal world. That is, he uses all kinds of discursive as well as dialectical arguments to drive home the pivotal Mahayana idea of *sunyata*—the illusory quality of the ego-self and thereby of the phenomenal world that the ego-self projects.[113]

But, as indicated above, Chang is a Yogacarin. Typically, he sees the Mahayana notion of *sunyata* as inseparable from an awareness of an ineffable ultimate reality. The thrust of all his relentless critiques of the illusoriness of self-ego and the phenomenal world is to show that all the mental processes responsible for projecting a self-ego and the external world have nothing whatsoever to do with the transcendental, ultimate reality—*bhutatathata*. That Chang affirms such a transcendental reality is not surprising, because the belief in such a reality is integral to the Yogacara notion of *alaya-vijnana* that he accepted. Whereas *alaya-vijnana* is believed to carry the contaminated seeds that give rise to the phenomenal world, it also has its pure, uncontaminated part that constitutes transcendental reality.[114] This also explains why Yogacara Buddhism developed a dualistic concept of the self that, in Chang's view, corresponds to the dualism implied in Chuang Tzu's concept of self in the "Ch'i-wu lun." Just as Chuang Tzu spoke of a spiritual

---

111. Ibid.: 21b–22a.
112. Ibid.: 14a–19b.
113. Ibid.: 5b–9a, 12a–18b, 19b–24a.
114. Ibid.: 10b–11a, 12a–13a, 24b, 56b–58a.

self deep within the bodily self as its true prince (*chen-chün*) or true governor (*chen-tsai*), Yogacara teaching also discerned a "true mind" (*chen-hsin*) in the self. Just as Chuang Tzu believed in the possibility of transcending the bodily self to become identified with its spiritual "true governor," so did Yogacara teaching also believe in such a possibility. Indeed, the burden of the whole Yogacara teaching is to demonstrate the possibility of transforming the false consciousness into transcendental insight or, in Chang's own words, of "eradicating all the contaminated 'seeds' and consciousness and thereby becoming spiritually awakened to the purest mind (*tsui ch'ing-ching hsin*)" that was embedded in the self.[115]

From the perspective of this "purest mind" or the *bhutatathata*, the phenomenal world is of course "empty." Following Mahayana Buddhism, Chang's commentaries recognize two ways in which the idea of emptiness can be understood. One is the Madhyamika approach, whereby the idea is understood to refer to the endless process of dependent causation responsible for the appearance of the phenomenal world. The other is the Yogacara approach preferred by Chang, that is, the approach built around a concept of dependent causation that is not endless but ultimately rooted in the "foundation consciousness" of the *alaya-vijnana*. Both approaches, Chang believes, provide perspectives that can homologize with the gist of the "Ch'i-wu lun" specifically and Chuang Tzu's philosophy in general.[116] First is the perspective that grows out of the Madhyamika concept of dependent causation. To illustrate the affinity between the latter and the central ideas of Chuang Tzu, Chang refers to the philosophy of Fa-tsang (643–712), a master of Hua-yen Buddhism, whose concept of dependent causation was turned into a world view of radical relatedness, as seen in Fa-tsang's doctrine of unlimited causation (*wu-chin yüan-ch'i*). According to this doctrine, the phenomenal world is so bound together by the ties of mutual causation that it constitutes a seamless organic whole of "all in one and one in all." Chang says that he does not necessarily accept all the paradoxical arguments that Fa-tsang employs to evolve his monistic world view; however, Chang views the philosophy of organic oneness as a natural corollary of the Mahayana concept of radical relatedness. Because of this view, Chang sees the world view of Buddhism converging with that of philosophical Taoism.[117]

Apart from a perspective focused on the emptiness of the phenomenal world, the Yogacara world view provides, Chang believes, another perspective, one focused on the transcendental ultimate reality.[118] As he emphasizes, once we have transcended all the forms of appearances, the linguistic categories, and the conceptualizations that fill a mortal mind, we would

---

115. Ibid.: 9b–11b.
116. Ibid.: 31b–32a, 37a–38a.
117. Ibid.: 32a–38b.
118. Ibid.: 9b–11b.

enter the state of the "true mind" and thereby awaken to the ultimate reality of the *bhutatathata*. From the transcendental perspective of the latter, "there are no human beings and no 'ten thousand things' outside the *tathagata-garba*; what distinctions and differences can we then speak of [regarding the phenomenal world]?"[119] It is this vision of transcendental oneness that Chang also finds at the core of the "Ch'i-wu lun." As Chang sums up the gist of the latter at the beginning of his commentaries,

> the uniformity of all things means universal equality. If we inquire closely into its real meaning, [we will find that] it means not just equal regard for [all] the sentient beings without making distinctions between the superior and the inferior among them. This is because ultimate equality emerges only when one transcends all the phenomena we can speak of, all the phenomena we can name and categorize and all the phenomena we can construct through our mind. It is this ultimate equality that is meant by the uniformity of all things.[120]

In this way Chang again comes to see Chuang Tzu sharing the same vision of reality with Yogacara Buddhism—a vision of an all-encompassing, undifferentiated, selfless whole where everything is interfused and interpenetrated with everything else.

A CULTURAL CRITIC FROM THE BUDDHIST VANTAGE POINT

It was thus Chang's discovery of Yogacara Buddhism that not only allowed him to see philosophical Taoism in a new light, but also to develop a transcendental outlook on life and the world. Not surprisingly, he now became convinced that in Yogacara Buddhism he had found the perfect teaching on earth. He spells out the rationale for this conviction in a framework that takes its departure from the Yogacara doctrine of three self-natures.[121] According to this doctrine, there are three different modes of existence. The first is the illusory mode that springs from the all-too-human tendency to cling to what things appear to be and to mistake appearance for reality. The second is the contingent mode that refers to those beings whose existences are completely contingent on, or derivative from, other forms of existence. Finally, there is the absolute, unconditional mode of existence characteristic of the ultimate reality.[122]

Underlying this concept of the three basic modes of existence is Yogacara Buddhism's "idealistic" world view that sees the phenomenal world as nothing but a process of emanation or flowing forth of consciousness from the ultimate *alaya-vijnana*.[123] Thus, according to Chang, the illusory mode of

---

119. Ibid.: 38a.
120. Ibid.: 1a.
121. 1919, *Pieh-lu*, chüan 3: 10a–30a.
122. Ibid.: 10a–11b.
123. Ibid.: 30a–43b.

existence is attributable to the sixth sense that derives from the *alaya*, the so-called *mano-vijnana*, which synthesizes all the perceptions of the lower senses and projects them as independent objective reality. As for the contingent modes, they are the creations of all the rest of the senses, including the first five and the seventh, that is, the *klista-mano-vijnana* and the contaminated parts of *alaya* itself, all of which do not make judgment about reality on their own but cogitate and infer on the basis of the sixth sense. Finally, responsible for the absolute mode of existence is the transcendental insight that the *alaya* is capable of achieving when it cuts itself off from the flow of contaminated consciousness.[124] Consequently, in the final analysis the three basic modes of existence reflect three modes of consciousness rooted in *alaya*.

In Chang's view, most of the religions in the world have sprung from the illusory and contingent modes of consciousness. Because illusory consciousness, with its tendency to look on anything it perceives as real, is apt to seize on a conditioned existence in the phenomenal world and to identify it with unconditioned reality, it is the shaping force behind lower types of religions like fetishism, animism, and various forms of anthropomorphism. Such a tendency even underlies some high religions like Hinduism, Christianity, Islam, and the Pure Land sect of Mahayana Buddhism.[125]

For Chang, more important in shaping people's mentality is the tendency to combine the illusory with the contingent consciousness. People affected by this tendency are apt to fall into either of two mental traps. One is to build up all sorts of mental associations and inferences on the initial illusion created, thus resulting in three false views. The first is to look on one's self as something of a real substance, oblivious of the truth that, outside of the *alaya*, nothing is real. The second is to reify the outside world, without realizing that all existences in the phenomenal world are mere manifestations of the subjective consciousness of the individual minds. The third takes the form of religious worship. Chang notes that, although there are different kinds of religious worship ranging from primitive cults of nature to advanced religions like monotheism and pantheism, all are rooted in the same psychological needs. On the one hand, he sees a need to ascribe all the sufferings, afflictions, and troubles in human life to an external power who can be expiated through religious worship. On the other, he sees a natural proclivity of the human mind, being impressed and awed by the size, complexity, and regular rhythm of the cosmos, to see all as being controlled and dominated by an all-powerful agent.[126] This powerful agent is then pictured as an infinite being who serves as the source of all the laws that govern the functioning of the universe. Chang emphasizes, however, that divine attributes, such as infinity and law-giving, are just as much the

---

124. Ibid.: 10a–11b.
125. Ibid.: 17a–18a.
126. Ibid.: 14a–16a.

creations of the subjective consciousness of the human mind as are the psychological needs that underlie every religion. Like our belief in the independent nature of the outside world and self-ego, most religious world views grow out of nothing but the illusion bred by certain forms of consciousness in the human mind.[127]

All the foregoing false views are consequences of a mental trap that tricks a person into seeing something where there is nothing in actuality. Chang points out that another mental trap lurks in the contingent consciousness that leads people to see nothing where there is really something, that is, to mistake reality for illusion. People who think along the track of contingent consciousness are apt to get carried away by the logic of nihilism once they become aware of the unreality of the outside phenomenal world and ego-self. But they fail to realize that, though the latter two are nothing but the projection of subjective consciousness, consciousness itself does have a source. Whatever else may be unreal, the source itself cannot be unreal. In this way, Chang comes back to the fundamental thesis of Yogacara Buddhism, namely, that in the final analysis there is an ultimate spiritual reality (*alaya*) lying behind all the illusions that constitute the phenomenal world. It is just as mistaken to believe that no ultimate reality exists behind the illusory phenomenal world as to believe in the reality of the phenomenal world.[128]

For Chang, all these arguments point inexorably to the conclusion that only Mahayana Buddhism is free of these two mental traps. Meanwhile, all other forms of religion, whether theism or pantheism, are handicapped by one or the other of the two traps. Hence, they all express themselves in a blind faith in something outside the individual mind that does not exist and in the meantime they fail to have trust in the ultimate spiritual reality that lies within the individual mind.[129] Chang, however, is not entirely without sympathy for pantheism, inasmuch as he discovered in it something approaching Yogacara teaching, namely, the belief that there is no supernatural being except the spiritual force inherent in all the beings in the world. This explains why his critique of pantheism is not so harsh as his critique of theism.[130]

The main target of his critique of theism is, of course, Christianity, and here he uses logical and paradoxical arguments typical of a Mahayana dialectician. First, he sees the Christian concept of monotheism as full of contradictions. One such contradiction is between the Christian concept of Jehovah's relationship with the world and that of God as the infinite, ultimate power. There are two ways of conceiving the relationship between God the creator and the created world, Chang maintains. One can conceive

---

127. Ibid.: 19a–22a.
128. Ibid.: 12a–14a.
129. Ibid.: 12a–15a, 19a–24b.
130. "Wu-shen lun" [On atheism] (1919, *Pieh-lu*, chüan 3: 7a–7b); see also pp. 19a–24b.

of them as identical. In that case, the existence of God would have a beginning and an end, inasmuch as the world is usually thought to have been created at a definite point of time in the past and to come to an end at a certain point in the future. On the other hand, if Jehovah is conceived as separate from the world, this would mean that the world begins and ends arbitrarily, reflecting an erratic mind on the part of God. This sort of erratic mind would certainly detract from the perfection of God. Thus, whether Jehovah is considered as identical with or separate from the created world, either concept contradicts the concept of God as a timeless, infinite power.[131]

The Christian description of Jehovah as omnipotent and omniscient, in Chang's view, also undermines the Christian concept of God as the creator of human beings. If Jehovah is really omnipotent and omniscient, he must have the ability to create human beings totally free of evils. But we know for a fact that evils exist among human beings. The Christian explanation could attribute evil to the existence of the devil, but this explanation does not really make sense. Ultimately, one has to ask why devils exist in this world. The answer has to take one of the following forms: either God on purpose created the devil to trick and mislead human beings; or the devil is something independent and hence beyond the control of God; or the devil, although a creature of God, turned rebellious against God; or that God created the devil to test human nature. Any one of these possible answers, in Chang's view, goes against the Christian concept of an omnipotent and omniscient God.[132]

Another Christian theological concept that Chang found logically untenable is that of a transcendental, absolute, and self-sufficient God. Again he found this concept incompatible with the Christian notion of God the Creator. Chang points out that there are only two ways in which God could be conceived to have created the world. He could have created the world out of materials outside himself, but the fact that materials exist outside God would imply that God is not an absolutely self-sufficient being. On the other hand, if God is believed to have created the world just out of himself, it would be difficult to explain why God, according to the Christian explanation, creates human beings only once rather than going on creating them continuously. Either way, the concept of an absolute and self-sufficient God would not hold water.[133]

Logically, then, the Christian concept of God is riddled with cracks and contradictions. But, in Chang's judgment, more fatal is the proof of God's existence by the argument that all the existences in the world must have a final maker. Theoretically speaking, anything, including Jehovah, can be shown to have its cause, and nothing can ever be proved to be the final maker of other existences. Consequently, this sort of argument can never locate the

---

131. Ibid.: 2a–b.
132. Ibid.: 2b–3a.
133. Ibid.: 3a–4a.

so-called final maker unless it is stopped arbitrarily. Hence, the whole proof of Jehovah as the final maker is an exercise in futility and falls into what Buddhist logic calls the "fallacy of endless argument."[134]

Chang's critique of theism is part of his efforts to prove Mahayana Buddhism to be the best religious faith on earth. From his viewpoint, the Yogacara teachings have none of the weaknesses that beset the theistic religions.[135] Yogacara Buddhism avoids the trap of theism by seeing neither God nor gods in any form whatsoever behind the phenomenal world, and it also steers clear of the trap of radical nihilism by affirming the ultimate reality of *alaya*. Consequently, in Chang's view, Yogacara Buddhism has the virtue of viewing salvation as dependent not so much on the saving power of God or gods as on the capacity of the individual human mind. Indeed, it is this spiritual self-reliance that more than any other characteristic of Mahayana Buddhism elevates it above all the others.[136]

With his faith in Yogacara Buddhism, Chang acquired a new value center, so to speak. At the heart of this new value center was the Buddhist other-worldly orientation, with its "logic of negation," so called because the other-worldly orientation relentlessly dissolves any meaning and value that one can find in existence in this world.[137] In the Chinese tradition, however, this logic of negation was rarely, if ever, carried through because of the tendency to accommodate the central values and institutions of Chinese society.[138] In Chang's newly found Buddhist faith, however, this logic of negation is given free play. An immediate victim of this logic is the ideas and theories that he had previously adapted from Western sciences and incorporated into his early intellectual outlook, built on the basis of Hsün Tzu's tough-minded Confucianism.

One such idea that Chang found incompatible with the Buddhist world view was materialism. However, departing from the transcendental perspective of Yogacara Buddhism and pursuing its logic of negation, he often draws on arguments and language from Western philosophy to drive home his refutation. He observes that all a materialist can incontrovertibly establish regarding any existence in the outside world is nothing but a string of sense-perceptions. To assert that this string of sense-perceptions represents something out there in the world is itself an inference whose validity cannot be established by sense-perceptions. In short, according to Chang, a logically consistent materialism could not go beyond sense-perceptions to establish the objective reality of the external world.[139]

---

134. Ibid.: 5a.
135. Ibid.: 18a–24b.
136. Ibid.; see also 1906: 6–9 and 1919, *Pieh-lu*, chüan 2: 58a–60b, 61b–62a, 65a–b.
137. For a discussion of the logic of negation in Buddhism, see Bellah (1965: 369–423).
138. Ch'en (1973: 14–124).
139. "Ssu ho lun" [On four dubious concepts] (1919, *Pieh-lu*, chüan 3: 69b–70b).

If Chang's arguments here sound like George Berkeley's idea that "to be is to be perceived," indeed he sometimes explicitly borrows David Hume's classic analysis of the law of causality for his refutation of the scientific world view. In must be noted that the crux of Hume's analysis is the idea that causality is not an "objective" necessary relationship. As Hume sees it, the idea of causality rests on nothing more than a habitual association of "impressions" in the "imagination," which are set up when events of type A have been constantly observed without fail to be conjoined with events of type B. This habitual association of impressions would then give rise to a felt expectation that, whenever we observe a new A, a new B will arise. In this light, then, the causal relation is in no way inherent in the objective situation but is a subjective expectation projected by the human mind into the external world.[140]

From Chang's standpoint, Hume's analysis of causality is welcome support for the idealistic thesis of Yogacara Buddhism. Chang also borrows Hume's example of the heat and light of the sun or a flame to push further his own argument. Chang's explanation of the example runs like this: We remember having seen the phenomena of the sun or a flame before. We also remember that our perception of these phenomena has always been accompanied by the sensations of heat and light we felt before. We then project the associations that take place in our minds between what we have seen and what we have felt into things outside ourselves. And we then regard the former as cause and the latter as effect as if the relationship of cause and effect between the two is objectively constitutive of the external world.[141]

So far Chang claims that he is merely following Hume's reasoning, but then he takes Hume to task for not pursuing his arguments far enough. Strictly speaking, Chang notes, only the sensations of heat and light are present in our sense impressions. The sun and the flame are something we arrive at in our mind through mental construction. Thus, if we can only trust our sense-impressions, we cannot look upon the phenomena of sun and flame on the same par with those of light and heat, let alone establish the relations of cause and effect between them.[142]

Here Chang is in effect questioning the validity of any scientific explanation by induction. He notes that such an explanation usually takes the following form: "If this is so, then that is so." If one asks on what ground the inductive explanation holds, the answer has to be that it has always held in the past. If one further asks why it has always held in the past, an inductive explanation would then reach the end of its tether. Given his critiques of materialism and of the idea of causality, it is no surprise that he views as untenable the closely related scientific belief in the "uniformity of nature."

---

140. Ibid.: 70a–b.
141. Ibid.: 70b–71b.
142. Ibid.: 70b–71a.

For him, the so-called nature is neither an independent reality nor does it reveal the kind of uniformity imputed to it by science, and the so-called laws of nature (*tzu-jan kuei-tse*) are nothing inherent in the objective reality of the cosmos but are creations of human consciousness.[143]

Chang not only assails the general idea of the laws of nature; he also singles out for refutation an idea that was increasingly accepted in China as a scientific law—universal evolution. He points out that evolution is not even a universal phenomenon in nature. It may exist as such in the organic realm of nature, but it does not in the inorganic realm, where things usually move in a cyclical way rather than in a unilinear, developmental way. Now, he further argues, even in the organic world, evolution, on close examination, is nothing but an illusion. To prove his point, he employs a paradoxical argument borrowed partly from ancient Chinese dialecticians and partly from the Eleatic philosopher of ancient Greece—Zeno. According to this argument, at any point of time an arrow in flight occupies a space equal to itself. Therefore, an arrow in flight is basically nothing more than repetitions of an arrow at rest at different points. For Chang this argument demonstrates that movement is no different from being at rest. Hence, the notion of evolution that is built on the idea of forward movement is what he calls a hallucination (*huan-hsiang*).[144]

The primary target of Chang's anti-evolutionist polemic, however, is evolution understood in the sense of progress toward a perfect society. His refutation is based on his observation that nothing is an absolute value in this world. Everything has its positive as well as negative aspects. This is as true of the phenomena of evolution as of anything else.[145] He points out that intellectual progress in the sense of accumulation of knowledge may in fact exist, but evolution in the sense of moral progress is open to question.[146] If evolution means moral progress, he argues, then animals higher on the evolutionary scale would have a better moral character and be less prone to evildoing than those lower on the scale. Actually, this is not necessarily the case. For example, in intellectual ability, human beings are certainly superior to the rest of the animal kingdom, and so is the capacity of human beings for moral conduct and social organization. On the other hand, the human capacity for evildoing is equally greater. Chang points to the massive killings and destruction that frequently occur among human beings. Ironically, these killings and destructions, which are far beyond the ability of the fiercest and cruelest animals, are exactly the results of the social sophistication and intellectual ingenuity of human beings.[147]

---

143. Ibid.: 70b, 73a–76a.
144. Ibid.: 66b–67a.
145. Ibid.: 67a–b.
146. Ibid.: 58b. Chang's arguments in this regard were mainly presented in "Chü-fen chin-hua lun" [The divergent outcomes of evolution] (ibid., chüan 2: 77b–87b).
147. Ibid., chüan 2: 78b–79b.

For Chang the moral ambiguity of evolution is clearly borne out by human history. Since ancient Greece, he points out, class differences between nobility and commoners have been steadily decreasing in Europe, so have the status gaps between ruler and subjects, men and women. This may indeed be taken as a sign of improvement in social morality. In the meantime, however, European civilization has become increasingly materialistic, and wealth has been increasingly accepted as the determinant of social status. In consequence, the class division between the wealthy and the poor has widened. Similarly, in modern Europe religious freedom and toleration have made remarkable headway, but this trend has been accompanied by a decline in moral-spiritual commitment to principles. In Japan, too, one finds the phenomena of moral improvement and deterioration growing simultaneously. On one hand, the law-abiding spirit and loyalty to the state spread more widely in society after the Meiji reform. On the other hand, individual moral independence and chivalrous spirit declined sharply. Turning to Chinese history to confirm his point, Chang expresses even greater skepticism about identifying evolution with moral progress. In his perception, Chinese history since the Sung dynasty has been a moral slide all the way.[148]

Just as evolution does not necessarily mean moral progress, neither does it necessarily coincide with the increase of happiness in society. Subhuman animals' ability to acquire happiness certainly cannot compare with that of human beings. However, subhuman animals also go through far less suffering in their lives than human beings do, on the whole. But the kind of happiness that human beings are able to experience is doubtlessly beyond the ken of the rest of the animal kingdom in terms of both its variety and quality. Beyond sensual pleasures are all kinds of happiness made possible only by society and culture, for instance, the happiness of enjoying honor, wealth, and power and the satisfaction derived from achievements of all kinds. Yet the price human beings pay for their happiness is also enormous. People are willing to go through all manners of suffering to get the happiness they want; furthermore, often the sacrifices and deprivations they undergo in pursuit of happiness turn out to be in vain in the end. For human beings, then, evolution obviously involves as much suffering as happiness. Therefore, one cannot simply identify evolution with progress in the sense of a better life.[149]

Chang makes it clear that his view of evolution as a mixed bag of good and evil is rooted in the Yogacara concept of man. This concept is susceptible to two related, but still somewhat different, interpretations, which combine to account for Chang's misgivings about evolution.[150] One interpretation is based on one particular notion of *alaya-vijnana*. As indicated above, Yoga-

---

148. Ibid.: 82b–83a, 83b–84b.
149. Ibid.: 79b–81a.
150. Ibid.: 81a–82b.

cara Buddhism sees *alaya-vijnana* as the ultimate reality of the world that stores in itself "seeds" (*chung-tzu*) of all beings. This ultimate reality exists simultaneously in two states, "pure" and "contaminated." In its pure state, *alaya-vijnana* contains only "primordial seeds" (*pen-yu chung-tzu*), which have a pristine character transcending good and evil. In its contaminated state, *alaya-vijnana* is the root cause of all the concrete existences in the world. Inasmuch as the *alaya-vijnana* has this contaminated aspect, it also contains "origination seeds" (*shih-ch'i chung-tzu*) that carry within themselves the potential for good and evil. In the framework of this world view, an individual person has an innate tendency to be morally good and evil at the same time. Because this innate tendency is inevitably manifested in the life activities of each human being, it is unavoidable that evolution would turn out to be Janus-faced in a moral sense.[151]

Another interpretation of the Yogacara conception of man that is responsible for Chang's critical view of evolution lies in its idea that *alaya-vijnana* has the inexorable tendency to evolve, out of itself, the outside world. *Manas* is the first stage of the *alaya* in its outward evolvement, and marks the dawn of self-consciousness. This *manas* or, rather, *alaya* in its self-consciousness inevitably generates a tendency toward individuation and thereby gives rise to individual will, passions, prejudices—to all the manifestations of what Chang called the "mind of egotism" (*wo-man hsin*).[152]

This egotism is also called the mentality of competitiveness (*hao-sheng hsin*); it grows out of the self-consciousness of the *manas* along with three other mentalities typified by love of the good, love of beauty, and love of truth. The mentality of competitiveness takes two forms: competition with a purpose and competition without a purpose. The former refers to those competitions undertaken to satisfy one's basic desires and to acquire wealth, power, and prestige. The latter refers to those competitions undertaken for their own sake.[153] In Chang's view, both forms of competitiveness bespeak an egoistic mentality that is purely evil in nature, whereas the other three mentalities reflect either a purely good nature or a nature that is neither good nor evil. Because the human mind, being a mix of four mentalities, is both good and evil in nature, human activities are naturally a mixed record. In this light, evolution can only mean actualizing potential for both good and evil rather than a straight moral improvement.[154]

Thus, in Chang's view, the idea of evolution makes as little sense as the idea of materialism and causality. In attacking these ideas, he has for all practical purposes come to disown much of his early thought and to refute the scientific world view of his day. Despite all the arguments he borrowed

---

151. Ibid.: 81a–b.
152. Ibid.: 81b–82b.
153. Ibid.: 81b–82a.
154. Ibid.: 82a–b.

from Western philosophies, the driving force of his refutation is still the logic of negation inherent in the transcendentalism of Mahayana Buddhism. That logic is carried further in an essay entitled "Wu-wu lun" (Five theses on nothing) that he published in *Min pao* in 1907. In it he reaffirms his belief in the validity of his sociopolitical radicalism, but only for the near future. Over the long haul, however, his revolutionary vision of the future is just as meaningless as his reformist opponents' concern with the wealth and power of the state. Nothing but transcendentalism made sense to him.[155]

Chang's world-denying outlook must be seen in the context of the anarchism that prevailed at that time in radical revolutionist circles. In his essay he gives qualified endorsement to anarchism but says it does not get to the bottom of the problem.[156] His world-rejecting view consists of two phases of argument. The first phase gives some provisional credit to anarcho-individualism, inasmuch as it contains the insight that there is no need for the formation of any social group. Chang observes that, as long as human settlements (*chü-lo*) exist on earth in whatever form, the settlements that are better located and endowed in terms of natural conditions inevitably are subject to aggressions from poorly located and poorly endowed settlements. Conflict and violence attend the very existence of human settlements.[157]

Such anarcho-individualist arguments quite naturally led Chang to single out the institution of the territorial state for attack. He considers unfairness to be built into the institution, inasmuch as it tends to hide from view the social contribution of individual citizens. People everywhere are apt to reify the institution of state, Chang avers, with the consequence that collective achievements, which involve the efforts of a large number of individuals, are often credited to the state or to its leader.[158]

Chang's anarcho-individualism does not just rest on moral grounds. It also reflects a nominalist perspective that recognizes only individual human beings as real and refuses to see any human group or organization as having a reality of its own other than as an aggregation of its members. In this view, then, a state is merely an abstraction that represents no reality sui generis. Quite naturally, Chang emphatically rejects the statist idea that a state is something concrete that can serve as the locus of sovereignty for a whole body of citizens.[159]

Not surprisingly, Chang's nominalistic view is accompanied by a radical individualism. In his view, every person comes into this world with no strings attached and hence owes no obligation to anyone but himself. "[Human

---

155. Ibid., chüan 3: 42b–75b.
156. Ibid.: 43b–48a.
157. Ibid.: 46a–48a.
158. "Kuo-chia lun" [On the state] (1919, *Pieh-lu*, chüan 3: 80a–82b).
159. Ibid.: 76a–80b.

beings are born] not for the sake of this world, nor for the sake of their society, nor for the sake of their country, nor for the sake of other people. Therefore, every human being at bottom has no obligation to his world, society, country, or other persons." It is all fine and good if someone has done something to benefit other people without getting any reward in return. But altruism is something one can expect only from extraordinary people; it cannot be expected as an obligation from every person.[160]

Chang, however, accords anarcho-individualism only relative validity because, though it can deal with problems and troubles that come with such human institutions as state, society, and government, it offers no remedy for problems and troubles that are inherent in life. A basic shortcoming of anarcho-individualism lies in its naively optimistic view of human nature. For one thing, it takes no note of the sensual lust and murderous impulses in human nature that bulk so large in the Buddhist picture of man. More important, it is blind to an all-important phenomenon pointed out by the ancient Greek thinker Heraclitus, namely, that conflict and struggle are found everywhere in the universe. Although Chang makes it clear that he disapproves of Heraclitus' glorification of conflict, he nevertheless accepts conflict as a perceptive, empirical observation of the actual condition of the universe.[161] In fact, here Chang finds another corroboration of Buddhism's negative concept of man. Again, he refers to the instinctive competitiveness rooted in the self-consciousness of ego (*manas*) that inevitably attends the evolvement of individual existence out of the cosmic *alaya* consciousness. As long as individual human beings exist, competitiveness and conflict are bound to remain.[162]

In this way, Chang was led back to the Buddhist view that the basic solution to problems in life and society lies in transcending the self-ego of human individuals. Thus, Buddhist transcendentalism again lies at the base of his nihilistic critique in "Wu-wu lun." From the Buddhist perspective, he is able not only to endorse the Taoist ideal of withdrawal from society (*yin-tun*), but also to echo Schopenhauer's idea of the extinction of will.[163] Like Schopenhauer, Chang grants an individual person the right to commit suicide, but he also shares Schopenhauer's misgivings about suicide as a means to the extinction of will.[164] Chang writes that Schopenhauer's misgivings make good sense from the Buddhist perspective. After all, the ultimate goal of suicide is the extinction of will and the attainment of *nirvana*, but the attainment of *nirvana* is determined more by how one sets one's will and

160. Ibid.: 60a–61b.
161. Ibid.: 48a, 50b–54a, 55b–59b.
162. Ibid.: 50b, 58b.
163. Ibid.: 63a–b.
164. Ibid.: 63b–64a.

attitude than by what one does to one's physical life. Chang notes:

> As for death by way of suicide, it can terminate one's life, but not one's life-seeking mind. This life-seeking mind is one's own will. If one dies by suicide but still preserves his will [to live] he would later be reincarnated only in a different form in the world. Therefore, the avoidance of the sufferings of the world lies not in the annihilation of one's physical body, but in the extinction of one's will [to live].[165]

For Chang suicide is not the solution to the problem of transcending the self-ego. The key still lies in the Buddhist insight into the illusoriness of self-ego. Here again Chang draws on the view of Yogacara Buddhism that one's attachment to self-ego is fortified by two forms of consciousness. One form of consciousness called "conceptual self" (*fen-pieh wo*) is rooted in the fact that an individual human mind is endowed with a general mental sense (*mano-vijnana*) on top of five special, immediate senses of perception—seeing, hearing, smelling, tasting, and touching.[166] The general mental sense is capable of linguistic categorization and conceptual reasoning and consequently can make all kinds of mental projections, such as distinction, inference, characterization, and comparisons. These mental projections give rise to the belief that each individual human being, along with other existences in the world, is made up of indestructible permanent substance and hence represents an independent, objective reality. Out of this belief grows a strong sense of self-ego that, in the final analysis, is nothing but an illusory creation of the human mind.[167]

The second form of consciousness is more deeply rooted; this consciousness is called by Yogacara Buddhism the "in-born self" (*chü-sheng wo*). This form of consciousness has a sort of relative and derivative reality in the sense that the self-ego of any individual being, though nonexistent in itself, is nevertheless a reflection of reality, in the same way that a rainbow, though nothing solid and real itself, reflects a compound of sunshine and air that is real.[168] Underlying this recognition of the relative reality of the self-ego is the pivotal Buddhist conception of the phenomenal world as a concatenation of conditional causations. Every being in the phenomenal world is nothing but a complex of conditions supplied from sources other than itself. Inevitably, this chain of conditioned causations can be traced to what Yogacara Buddhism regards as the ultimate source, the *alaya-vijnana*. Every being then owes its conditioned existence ultimately to the *alaya-vijnana*. To be sure, Yogacara Buddhism looks on the whole phenomenal world as an unfortunate aberration, because all the individual beings are seen as nothing but projections of delusions generated from within the *alaya-vijnana*. However, to the

---
165. Ibid.: 64a.
166. Ibid.: 30a–41b.
167. Ibid.: 30b–36b.
168. Ibid.: 30a, 36b.

extent that all the individual beings are linked by a chain of conditioned causations to the *alaya-vijnana*, an attachment to self-ego as something real inevitably lingers on. Herein is rooted the sense of the inborn self.[169]

To transcend this sense of the inborn self is more difficult than to overcome the sense of the conceptual self. The latter can be overcome by persistent, rigorous philosophical analysis. To transcend the sense of the inborn self, philosophical understanding, though still necessary, is no longer adequate. What is required is a combination of philosophical understanding and Yoga practices, such as mental concentration and breath control—a spiritual awareness that comes only from the *samatha-vipasyana* so much emphasized in the philosophy of T'ien-t'ai Buddhism.[170]

Chang's critique of the belief in the reality of a self-ego is throughout based on the assumption that this belief is a function of the development of subjective consciousness. If one's mind is filled with false consciousness, one believes in the reality of a conceptual self. If one's mind is dominated by conditioned consciousness, one believes in the reality of an inborn self. However, when one transcends both false and conditioned consciousness and achieves what Yogacara Buddhism calls the ultimate perfect consciousness (*bhutatathata*), one is then awakened to the truth that the human sense of self-ego has no basis in objective reality.[171]

True to the spirit of Buddhist transcendentalism, Chang not only sees no substance to the self-ego of an individual human being, but also sees all beings in the phenomenal world as devoid of substance. The truth of the latter view is a necessary complement to that of the former. A philosophical nihilism based on the former view without the support of the latter would not only be incomplete, but futile as well. Borrowing an argument from Darwinian evolutionism—the idea that beings of higher species evolve from those of lower species—he takes the view that, even if human beings disappear from earth, they are bound to reemerge, as long as sentient beings of other types still exist. In short, a full-blown nihilism must have a logical conclusion in the view that the phenomenal world as a whole has no meaning and reality in ultimate terms.[172]

Thus, in pursuing the Buddhist logic of negation, Chang launched a cultural critique far more radical than those of K'ang Yu-wei and T'an Ssu-t'ung. The cultural critiques of K'ang and T'an led them to reject the ideological core of the traditional order. But Chang went beyond that to question and challenge not only some basic assumptions of the then-fashionable Western learning, but also the very meaning of human existence.

---

169. Ibid.: 36b–41b.
170. Ibid.: 30a, 41a–b.
171. Ibid.: 41b.
172. Ibid.: 48b–49b.

THE JANUS FACE OF CHANG'S BUDDHIST WORLD VIEW

Paradoxically, although Chang relentlessly pursued the Buddhist logic of negation, he does not view Buddhism as simply a negative, pessimistic teaching.[173] For, in Mahayana Buddhism, the logic of negation was designed to help the believer see beyond the illusoriness of the existing world to a spiritual reality where he might find ultimate solace and salvation. Also, the character of Mahayana Buddhism is such that it allows an affirmative outlook on human life to grow within its transcendental world view.

Chang's view of Buddhism in this regard was based on his interpretation of a distinction he considers central to the Buddhist world view, namely, the distinction between the "world of inanimate things" (*ch'i-shih-chien*) and the "world of sentient beings" (*yu-ch'ing shih-chien*). In Chang's mind, the Buddhist pessimism and negativism are directed at the former rather than at the latter. Buddhism has a soteriological intent, inasmuch as it perceives sentient beings as all caught in the suffering inanimate world. Chang uses the analogy of a sinking boat to illustrate this distinction. People on a sinking boat are, of course, all eager to leave the boat. Although they would all certainly look upon the sinking boat as dangerous, they do not have antipathy toward each other. In fact, they would all have sympathy and love for each other and work together to save themselves from being drowned. Similarly, although Buddhism is negative about the suffering inanimate world, it enjoins commiseration and love for the people on earth. Thus, in contrast to eremitism, which advocates withdrawal from the human world, Buddhism is characterized by an affirmative outlook toward the human world.[174]

Chang was obviously inspired here by the Mahayana ideal of Bodhisattva.[175] To him, the world-affirmative outlook embodied in it is a natural corollary of the Yogacara teaching that all the sentient beings partake of the same reality—*alaya*. Inasmuch as they all stem from one single spiritual reality, individual salvation cannot be separated from universal salvation. Hence, one should take the vow of Bodhisattva, staying on in this suffering world indefinitely in order to provide help and succor to all sentient beings. By the same token, the Mahayana teachings sometimes recommend the idea of keeping our self-attachment after we cut off our attachment to the inanimate world, insofar as the self in this instance is interpreted as referring to the larger self, embracing all sentient beings.[176]

In this light, Chang's ideal of revolution and his vision of a new postrevolutionary order are not necessarily a contradiction of his Buddhist faith.

---

173. Ibid.: 25a–b.
174. Ibid.: 26a–b.
175. 1906: 7–8, 9; 1919, *Pieh-lu*, chüan 3: 25a–26a.
176. 1919, *Pieh-lu*, chüan 3: 25a–26a.

Given his self-image of a Bodhisattva, it would be perfectly logical for him to see the envisaged revolution and the establishment of a new order as an act of compassion to relieve suffering in the world. This is why he views his political radicalism as a necessary preliminary step to the final transcendence of the world.[177]

Mahayana Buddhism, however, provided him not only with a conceptual framework to put his political cause in a cosmic perspective, but was also an invaluable source of moral energy for carrying out his ideal of revolution. Revolution for Chang was a moral enterprise requiring selfless commitment and highest integrity. Yet, where are the beliefs and values that could motivate the necessary moral strength? Chang at this time was often critical of Confucianism, especially of the neo-Confucian orthodoxy. Thus, not surprisingly, he takes the view that Confucian ethics, though suited to the moral needs of a simpler age in the past, can not serve as the motivational source of revolutionary commitments for the present.[178] Chinese people, he notes, were shackled by a psychology of demoralization created by their experience of repeated defeats by foreign powers and by a Darwinian belief in the natural domination of the strong over the weak. To counter this psychology of demoralization, Chang points out that

> even [such Buddhist beliefs as] reincarnation and hell would not do. One has to propagate the Buddhist ideal of renunciation of life in order to get rid of people's fear of death; one has to spread the Buddhist ideal of selflessness in order to rid people of obsession with money; one has to disseminate the Buddhist ideal of equality in order to rid people of a slavish mentality; one has to imbue people with the Buddhist ideal of the Buddhahood in all in order to rid people of a passive and withdrawn outlook; one has to uphold the Buddhist ideal of purity of deeds, words and ideas in order to rid people of lust and rapacity.[179]

Mahayana Buddhism thus supplied a moral heroism that, in Chang's view, was rooted in its idealistic world view. Inasmuch as this Buddhist idealism views the human mind as the source and determinant of everything in this illusory world, it induces voluntarism and self-confidence to a degree otherwise impossible. Insofar as this idealism sees the individual life as something illusory to be transcended, it inspires people to defy death and to disregard pragmatic calculation of self-interest. In this way, a moral heroism is generated that arouses people to the sustained, courageous, and vigorous action indispensable to the success of revolution or any other type of political enterprise.[180] Chang believes that his view in this regard is supported by lessons drawn from history. It is not accidental that many of the late Ming

---

177. Ibid.: 45b.
178. Ibid.: 42a–b.
179. Ibid.: 29a.
180. 1919, *Pieh-lu*, chüan 2: 58a–b.

literati who tenaciously fought the Manchu invasion to the bitter end were adherents of Ch'an Buddhism. Followers of Wang Yang-ming also contributed significantly to the late Ming struggle against the Manchu conquest, but, as Chang points out, Wang's spiritual teachings owed much to Buddhism. And, insofar as Wang's philosophy featured an idealistic view of the world, Chang looks on it as a sort of analogue of Buddhism. Hence, for him it is just as instructive that Wang's teachings played an important part in the success of the Meiji Restoration in Japan. All these historical experiences served to prove how much the idealism of Mahayana Buddhism could function as a motivation for revolutionary action.[181]

The reason that Ch'an Buddhism could have such motivational significance lies in the idealistic world view that Chang believes it shared with most of the other Mahayana sects, an idealistic world view that could "discipline character and still the mind." Although he saw the practical value of Ch'an Buddhism, like many other Buddhist intellectuals of the modern era, he had serious misgivings about it. For one thing, he is critical of the excesses that the antiformalism and iconoclasm of Ch'an often engendered. His reservations also have to do with the fact that the mainstream of Ch'an Buddhism, under the influence of the Madhyamika teachings, did not give full articulation to an idealistic world view.[182]

This idealistic world view, in Chang's judgment, resides not so much in the later mainstream phase of Ch'an Buddhism as in its early phase, a phase that depended on the *Lankavatara sutra*, a sutra of Yogacara persuasion, for the main source of its teachings.[183] Much as he appreciated the early developments of Ch'an Buddhism, Chang makes it clear that it was the Hua-yen and Fa-hsiang sects—the traditional core of the Yogacara Buddhism—that he valued most.[184] It was the intensely idealistic views of Yogacara teachings that appealed to him more than any other branch of Mahayana Buddhism. This idealistic world view not only put life and the world in perspective for him, but also functioned as an invaluable source of motivation for political engagement and social action.

Thus, Chang was no simple nationalist or "nativist," as some historians have tended to characterize him. This was especially true after 1903, when his encounter with Mahayana Buddhism gradually led him to develop a universalistic world view that, though not necessarily contradicting his nationalism, certainly allowed him to see beyond it. In his world view, Chang stands much closer to his reformist opponents than in his political stance. In fact, the concept of selfless oneness at the core of Chang's Buddhist

---

181. Ibid.: 58b–60a, 65a.
182. Ibid.: 58b–59b.
183. Ibid.: 59a–60a.
184. Ibid.; see also 1906: 7–8; 1919, *Pieh-lu*, chüan 3: 42b.

world view is strongly reminiscent of the vision of an all-encompassing undifferentiated whole that is expressed in T'an Ssu-t'ung's ideal of *jen*.

To be sure, significant differences separate the two concepts of selfless oneness. For one thing, T'an Ssu-t'ung's concept derived from more diverse sources than Chang's, which stems almost completely from Mahayana Buddhism. Further, T'an's was charged with passions of love and moral indignation that are absent from Chang's philosophical concept of self-transcendence into the primordial unity. These differences perhaps help to explain why Chang, having read T'an's *Jen-hsüeh*, did not find it congenial.[185]

These differences, however, must not lead us to overlook the broad parallels between the two concepts. To begin with, both concepts owed their basic motivating impetus to indigenous sources. Although in either case the concept did not issue in any vision of a utopian society for the future, both provided their authors with a critical standard that led them to become radical critics of their own society. Further, the concepts furnished each with a new life-ideal—of a selfless hero who lives solely for a cosmic cause. In short, Chang Ping-lin, like T'an Ssu-t'ung, found in the ideal of mystic selflessness not only a new source of meaning and identity, but also a fresh center of values.

---

185. 1919, *Pieh-lu*, chüan 3: 42b.

5

Liu Shih-p'ei (1884–1919)

THE ONLY person among the revolutionist intelligentsia to rival Chang Ping-lin's intellectual prestige was Liu Shih-p'ei. Born in 1884 into a well-known scholarly family of I-cheng, a district in Yangchou prefecture in Kiangsu Province, he was something of a boy wonder.[1] We know little about his early life, but in his teens he began to climb the traditional ladder of success by taking the civil service examinations. By the end of 1902, at the tender age of 18, he had already acquired the esteemed *chü-jen* degree.[2] In 1903 he went to Peking to take the metropolitan examination but failed.[3] In the same year he began to emerge into the limelight of history. That fall, he moved from his native town to Shanghai to join the radical circles of revolutionaries,[4] where he soon established himself as a luminary through his powerful pen. He edited various revolutionary journals and wrote prolifically to publicize the cause of revolution. In 1907 he went to Japan, where he continued his career as a radical publicist. However, in 1908 he suddenly changed course, returning to China to serve the Ch'ing government.[5] Still during his brief five years of involvement in the revolutionist movement, he became one of the leading intellectual figures and radical publicists in China.

LIU SHIH-P'EI'S INTELLECTUAL ROOTS

Where did his radical outlook come from? Scant as it is, our information about his early life does provide some clues. First, he came from an in-

---

1. Liu Shih-p'ei (1965, 1: 22–23).
2. Preface by Yin Yen-wu (ibid.: 22).
3. Preface by Ts'ai Yüan-p'ei (ibid.: 23).
4. Ibid.: 15, 23.
5. Ibid.: 5, 23, 34; see also Ch'ien Hsüan-t'ung's preface (ibid.: 37).

tellectual background strongly shaped by indigenous influences from the Chinese tradition. His hometown, Yangchou, had been a principal center of Han Learning ever since the late eighteenth century,[6] and, in Liu's own family, Han Learning ran particularly strong. For several generations, the Liu family had produced scholars who contributed greatly to evidential research of the Confucian classics. By the time of his birth, his family had a long-established reputation in China's scholarly world.[7] Building on this family heritage, he was able to become, at a young age, a master of philological and textual criticism, with a stature comparable to that of Chang Ping-lin.[8]

For Liu, Han Learning was not just a storehouse of philological and textual scholarship, however. It was also a door opening into other realms of Chinese thought. As I discuss in chapter 1, at the height of its development, Han Learning branched out from Confucian scholarship into the study of nonorthodox and non-Confucian pre-Ch'in philosophies. In fact, these heterodox tendencies ran especially strong in the brand of Han Learning that developed in Yangchou, called the Yanchou School. Moreover, a pioneering figure of the Yangchou School in this direction was Wang Chung, a scholar whom Liu greatly admired.[9]

Apart from serving as a bridge to the philosophical heritage of ancient China, the Yangchou School went beyond the technical evidential researches to study the Confucian moral philosophy of self-realization.[10] Following the trail blazed by the great eighteenth-century scholar Tai Chen, who was not a native of Yangchou but lived there for a long time and made his influence widely felt in that area, a galaxy of Yangchou scholars arose to study moral philosophy in the framework of Han Confucianism. These men were in revolt against what they considered the intellectual derailment that took place in the Confucian tradition due to the rise of Sung-Ming neo-Confucianism.[11] Liu was conscious of the distinctive intellectual tradition of his native town in this regard and was a fervent admirer of Tai Chen and other leading scholars of the Yangchou School. In fact, he later would be called the last master of the school.[12]

As Han Confucianism developed in the late nineteenth century, the Yangchou School's philosophical-critical orientation blended with another

6. See Chang Shun-hui (1962: 1–18).
7. Ibid.: 164–82; Liu (1965, 1: 19, 20).
8. Chang Shun-hui (1962: 183–208); preface by Yin Yen-wu in Liu (1965, 1: 22).
9. Chang (1962: 86–91). For Liu's admiration for Wang Chung, see his "Liu-ju sung" [Paeans to six Confucian scholars] (1965, 3: 2143).
10. Chang (1962: 15, 129–36, 158–63); Ch'ien Mu (1964, 1: 435–43; 2: 453–522).
11. Chang (1962: 1–18).
12. Ibid.: 184–85. See preface by Yin Yen-wu in Liu (1965, 1: 22). See also "Tai Chen chuan" [A biography of Tai Chen] (ibid. 3: 2071), where Liu emphasizes that Tai Chen's scholarship was preserved and developed in the Yangchou School. See also "Yang-chou ch'ien-che hua-hsiang chi" [Biographical sketches of some luminaries in the history of Yangchou] (ibid.: 2145–6).

important trend. For many scholars, the days were long gone when people viewed Han Learning and Sung Learning as irreconcilable approaches to Confucian scholarship. Instead, people now tended to view the two kinds of Confucian scholarship as complementary and to blur the distinctions between them.[13] This explains why Liu could be a master of technical evidential research at the same time that he was an avid student of neo-Confucian moral philosophy and, especially, of the philosophy of Wang Yang-ming and his disciple, the T'aichou scholar Wang Ken.[14]

Liu Shih-p'ei was also heir to another legacy of his hometown. In Yangchou anti-Manchu feeling ran particularly strong, mainly because of the memory of the bloodbath that occurred in the city following its conquest by the Manchus in the seventeenth century. These memories were kept alive over the years by the continuous circulation of anti-Manchu tracts. One of these, *Yang-chou shih-jih chi* (Ten days at Yangchou), was a lurid eyewitness account of the Manchus' wanton pillaging and massacres after the fall of the city.[15] Another was *Sheng-ch'ao hsün-yang lu* (The record of martyrdom at Yangchou), a collection of biographical accounts of Ming loyalists, such as the famous Shih K'o-fa who organized a heroic defense of Yangchou against Manchu forces in 1645. The author of this text, Liu Pao-nan, was a local scholar and also a close friend of Liu Shih-p'ei's great-grandfather, Liu Wen-ch'i.[16] Apparently influenced by local anti-Manchu publications, Liu Shih-p'ei during his early youth allegedly wrote a text in a similar vein—*Yang-min ch'üeh-lu lu* (A record of repulsions of barbarians by the Yangchou people).[17]

No less significant an influence on Liu was the strain of ethnic consciousness in the Chinese cultural tradition that filtered down through his family heritage. In the elite thought of the Chinese tradition, this strain of ethnic consciousness had never predominated, but it was strong enough to have formed an articulate pattern of ideas and feelings among the Chinese literati, at least since the Southern Sung. This consciousness found its most eloquent expression in the thought of Cheng Ssu-hsiao of the Southern Sung and

---

13. "Han Sung hsüeh-shu i-t'ung lun" [On the differences and similarities between the Han and Sung learnings] (ibid., 1: 647–48).

14. *Ching-chung jih-pao* (1968 rpt., vol. 4, no. 198 [Sept. 10, 1904], sec. 4). In this issue, Liu published an autobiographical poem in which he expresses his profound admiration for Wang Yang-ming's moral philosophy. He also claims in the poem that he has written a book on Wang, entitled *Wang-hsüeh fa-wei* [An explanation of Wang Yang-ming's scholarship]. See also ibid., 4, no. 204 (Sept. 16, 1904), sec. 4, in which he wrote a lengthy poem dedicated to Wang Ken; *Kuo-hsüeh fa-wei* [An explanation of traditional scholarship] (1965, 1: 595–96); see also "Yang-ming hsiang-tsan" [A tribute to Wang Yang-ming's portrait] (ibid., 3: 1525).

15. We know little about the origin of this work except that its author was Wang Hsiu-ch'u. The book was proscribed during the Ch'ien Lung period but recirculated during the late Ch'ing as an important piece of anti-Manchu literature. See Hummel (1943: 652, under Shih K'o-fa).

16. For a short biography of Liu Pao-nan, see ibid.: 529.

17. *Ching-chung jih-pao* (1968 rpt., vol. 4, no. 198, sec. 4). In the autobiographical poem mentioned in n. 14, he refers to this text.

Wang Fu-chih of the early Ch'ing, the two thinkers who Liu Shih-p'ei claims were most responsible for shaping his ethnic outlook.[18]

Liu first came under the influence of traditional ethnic consciousness through his family. Much in his family scholarship had sensitized him to the relationship between the Han Chinese and the so-called barbarians in Chinese history. His great-grandfather Liu Wen-ch'i, for instance, was an expert on the historiography of the Northern and Southern dynasties (*Nan-pei shih*), a historiography in which Sino-barbarian relationships and the legitimacy of barbarian dynasties were at the forefront of discussion.[19] More important, Liu Shih-p'ei's grandfather Liu Yü-sung was involved in editing the complete works of Wang Fu-chih, probably the most important intellectual source of traditional ethnic consciousness in the late nineteenth century, and also wrote a chronological biography of Wang.[20] Because of this family heritage, Wang Fu-chih became a sort of culture hero for Liu Shih-p'ei from childhood on. He was so conversant with Wang Fu-chih's writings that before he was 20 he reportedly had already written a volume of notes on them.[21]

Equally as important as Liu's traditional background, however, was the fact that Liu's formative years roughly coincided with the post-1895 period. It was then that the cultural impact of the West was beginning to spread beyond the coastal treaty ports into the inland cities on a large scale.[22] Liu's hometown, where he lived until he was 19, was a part of Yangchou, a major city on the Yangtze River. Further, Liu is known to have visited such metropolises as Peking, Shanghai, and Nanking during his trips to take the civil service examinations. Thus, his early mental world, dominated as it was by indigenous trends of thought, was also penetrated by influences from the West.[23]

IN SEARCH OF "COMPLETE MAN" AND "COMPLETE SOCIETY"

Out of such a varied background emerged a structure of radical thinking whose basic features were foreshadowed in Liu's first published book, a book that also made him well-known among the early Chinese intelligentsia—*Jang shu* (The book of expulsion).[24] A major part of the book is dominated by

---

18. Ibid.; see also *Jang shu* [The book of expulsion] (1965, 3: 3b, 8b).
19. Hummel (1943: 534).
20. Chang (1962: 167–69). See also Hummel (1943: 535).
21. *Ching-chung jih-pao* (1968 rpt., vol. 4, no. 198, sec. 4); see also Liu's autobiographical poem (n. 14).
22. For a detailed discussion of the spread of the Western culture outside the treaty ports in the post-1895 years, see Chang Hao (1980: 274–338).
23. Ts'ai Yüan-p'ei, "Liu chün shen-shu shih-lüeh" [A biographical sketch of Liu Shih-p'ei] in Liu (1965, 1: 23); see also a poem Liu wrote in 1903 about his visit to Nanking in *Fei-feng chi* (1965, 4: 2159–63).
24. Preface by Ch'ien Hsüan-t'ung (1965, 1: 34).

Liu's nationalism, which, in its basic features, is analogous to Chang Ping-lin's. For Liu as for Chang, nationalism entails a basic sympathy with state nationalism and with its concomitant anti-imperialism. But the thrust of nationalism in the context of Liu's writings was ethnic nationalism or, more specifically, anti-Manchuism. Again, Liu's ethnic nationalism, like Chang's, was fed by influences from both traditional and Western sources. With this book, Liu joins with Chang Ping-lin to become one of the two most articulate spokesmen for ethnic nationalism among the revolutionist intelligentsia.

Although the bulk of *Jang shu* is concerned with explicating Liu's ethnic nationalism, this is by no means the book's only theme. Toward the end of the book, he blasts the Confucian doctrine of the three bonds (*san-kang*).[25] It is clear that Liu's sociopolitical protest goes much deeper than a mere revolt against the Manchu regime in Peking. It challenges the legitimacy of the whole traditional sociopolitical order.

Significantly, Liu does not justify his repudiation of the doctrine of the three bonds in terms of the need for nationalism, nor does he spell it out in the amoral language of Social Darwinism. Rather, it is couched in idioms that reflect a moral quest for the just society and the virtuous man.[26]

One clue to this moral perspective is a philosophical treatise, published in the *Kuo-ts'ui hsüeh-pao* in 1905 and entitled *Li-hsüeh tzu-i t'ung-shih* (A general exegesis of key terms used in the philosophies of the neo-Confucian school of rationalism).[27] In its preface, Liu says that he wrote the treatise in order to clarify the meaning of some pivotal concepts in the moral philosophy that underlies the Confucian concern for self-cultivation. Liu makes it clear that he owes his inspiration to a methodological principle established by Tai Chen, namely, that Confucian moral truth can only be discovered by rigorous philological elucidation of the terms and concepts of the Confucian classics. To carry out this enterprise, Liu draws mainly upon the tradition of Han Learning as handed down through Tai Chen and the Yangchou School. He believes that these philosophers provide much better guides for understanding the Confucian concern with self-cultivation than the Sung-Ming neo-Confucian philosophers.[28] Liu is continuing the philosophical battle that his predecessors at Yangchou had been waging since the middle of the eighteenth century.[29]

But this philosophical treatise must not be viewed only in the context of a scholarly debate within the Confucian tradition. Like some of Liu's other major writings at this time, it must also be seen as a response to the intellectual crisis that was then emerging. In the middle of the 1900s, the

---

25. 1965, 2: 762–64.
26. Ibid.
27. 1965, 1: 551–68.
28. Ibid.: 551.
29. Chang (1962: 1–18).

intellectual world of the Chinese intelligentsia was being inundated by novel experiences, values, and ideas from outside. How could the new be reconciled with the familiar? How could a unified world view or an overall perspective be forged to help them make sense of this rapidly changing world? A sensitive soul like Liu was likely to have felt the need for a symbolic framework through which to view the world in some meaningful order. Under these circumstances, it is only natural that Liu would look for guidance in an intellectual source with which he was most familiar—the Yangchou School and especially the thoughts of its patron saint Tai Chen.

The way Liu interpreted Tai Chen is indicative of his response to the overall intellectual crisis. Tai Chen's thought was part of the general trend in late imperial China toward a monistic world view based on the concept of *ch'i*, rather than on the metaphysical dualism of orthodox neo-Confucianism. Its cosmological symbolism centered around the belief in *ch'i*; in Tai's world view, for example, the symbolism of *yin-yang* and the five elements occupy a central place.[30] Nevertheless, though Liu claims that he follows Tai Chen's approach to formulating the moral philosophy of self-cultivation, cosmological symbolism does not figure at all in his treatise.[31] In a way, this is no surprise, because Liu wrote the treatise at a time when Western sciences had penetrated deeply among the Chinese intelligentsia and had begun to establish an authority that made it difficult for scholars to continue to believe in traditional cosmological symbolism. In fact, Liang Ch'i-ch'ao, who also wrote at that time about his involvement in the study of neo-Confucian moral philosophy, once stated explicity that the influx of Western sciences compelled him to appropriate the moral insights regarding discipline of character from neo-Confucianism, but not the cosmological symbolism that was usually fused with its moral insights.[32] Living as he did in the same intellectual world with Liang, Liu most likely shared Liang's attitude in this regard.

Although Liu left cosmological symbolism out of his treatise, he still retains some other basic categories of orientational symbolism from Tai Chen's philosophy. Especially important is his appropriation of *li* (principles), the pivotal category of that symbolism.[33] Following Tai Chen, Liu takes sharp exception to the neo-Confucian conception of *li*. Neo-Confucianism, in his view, is marred by a transcendental, abstract turn of thinking that reifies *li* as something that is not only independent of material force, but also has an ontological primacy over it.[34] Liu's preference here, of

---

30. Hou Wai-lu (1958, 5: 430–54).
31. 1965, 1: 551–68.
32. Chang Hao (1971: 274).
33. 1965, 1: 553–54.
34. Ibid.; see also "Tung-yüan hsüeh-an hsü" [Preface to a study of Tai Chen's scholarship] (1965, 2, chüan 17: 2005–7).

course, is for Tai Chen's own concept. Tai had defined *li* as a faculty of reason that embodies what can be endorsed by all human minds and is congruent with the dictates of all human feelings and desires. Liu also accepts the definition of *li* that had long prevailed in the Han Learning tradition and still underlay Tai Chen's philosophy, namely, that *li* is a pattern or order inherent in all existences in the outside world. Consequently, as Liu sees it, there is an order that is as much inherent in our subjective faculty of mind as it is in the objective world.[35] Implicit in this view is a belief in the existence of a universal human nature and a belief that knowledge of that universal human nature will provide guidance for our orientation and conduct in the world. In this way, through the concept of *li*, he retains the fundamental Confucian belief that understanding of our own nature provides a moral compass for behavior.

Thus, Liu's treatise on neo-Confucian concepts is as much an appropriation of tradition in response to a contemporary intellectual crisis as it is a participation in a dialogue within the tradition. Although his appropriation of tradition is focused on the Confucian idea of defining the universal human nature with the goal of self-understanding, he does not undertake any comprehensive systematic definition in this treatise. However, his exegesis of some neo-Confucian categories does bring out several themes that would be sounded in his elucidation of human nature in another major work that he wrote at that time.

Liu's view of *li* as that which is endorsed by all human minds implies a voluntaristic concept of self and points to a strain of moral activism in his thought. Underlying this view of *li* is his concept of *hsin*—the mind-heart—as the mental controller in the individual self. He traces this concept of *hsin* to Chu Hsi's commentary on *Ta-hsüeh*, which defines *hsin* as the seat of the human spirit and the intelligence that gathers together all principles and responds to all external events.[36] Implicit in Chu Hsi's observation is the idea that the mind-heart has two interdependent aspects—an inner substance and an outer functioning. For Liu, this idea is particularly significant from the moral point of view. In its inner substance, the mind-heart is the source of moral thinking; in its outer functioning, it is the controller of moral conduct. Just as both inner substance and outer functioning are indispensable to a full concept of mind-heart, so both are integral to man as a moral being. To be moral, therefore, does not mean merely to have moral ideas present in the mind; it also means to manifest morality in one's outer behavior. In Liu's view, a deplorable tendency of Sung-Ming neo-Confucianism is that it conceived of morality exclusively in terms of its inner substance, to the neglect of its outer, behavioral functioning. For Liu, the thrust of Confucian

---

35. 1965, 1: 554.
36. Ibid.: 554–56, 560–61.

moral thought was not only the idea that human mind is the source and controller of moral conduct but, more important, the notion that morality must ultimately issue forth in the actions of human individuals.[37]

Given this emphasis on the activistic orientation of morality, it will come as no surprise that Liu undertakes a critique of the neo-Confucian idea of *ching* (quiescence) in his treatise. He has no objection to the idea of quiescence per se; in fact, he was well aware of the prominence of the idea in the Confucian repertoire of methods and techniques of mental discipline. He points out that, in Han Confucianism, quiescence means either ordering or examining the mind. Understood in either sense, quiescence can serve as an effective antidote to the two weaknesses of the human mind: its proclivity toward impatience and recklessness; and its susceptibility to confusion and derangement. In Sung-Ming neo-Confucianism, the idea of quiescence became the seed of a host of precepts and techniques, all aimed at coping with these two weaknesses. Chief among them are the twin precepts of *han-yang* (the cultivation of self-possession) and *shou-lien* (withdrawal and restraint). In Liu's view, the former is particularly effective in curing impatience and recklessness, and the latter in preventing emotional disturbance and mental turmoil.[38]

However, the value of these precepts and of the underlying idea of quiescence is not unconditional from the viewpoint of Confucian self-cultivation, because they assume significance only on the assumption that the human mind is actively dealing with the outside world (for the obvious reason that a human mind is apt to become reckless and turbulent only during activity). Thus, from a Confucian standpoint, the idea of quiescence in isolation is meaningless. Quiescence becomes a value only when predicated on an activistic outlook. Regrettably, however, as Liu sees it, Sung-Ming neo-Confucianism, from early on, was often warped by a tendency to put a premium on quiescence as an end in itself. For example, for such neo-Confucian philosophers as Ch'eng I and Li Yen-p'ing, *ching* meant an introspective, contemplative, and withdrawn frame of mind and was prized on the ground that contact with the outside world would confuse the mind and lead it astray. The upshot, in Liu's judgment, was that *ching* had become indistinguishable from quietism, as evidenced by the centrality of quiet-sitting in the neo-Confucian approach to self-realization.[39]

Liu's moral activism finds its fullest expression in his critique of the Confucian concept of *ming*. He points out that *ming*, understood in the sense of control of individual fate by supernatural forces, has had an important place in Confucianism. He calls this concept of *ming ming-shu chih ming* (astrological fatalism). But he also finds in the Confucian tradition other concepts of fate

---

37. Ibid.: 560–61.
38. Ibid.: 565–68.
39. Ibid.: 567–68.

that are at odds with astrological fatalism. For one thing, the concept had also been understood in an ethico-metaphysical sense, referring to the Heaven-endowed capacity for moral actualization. In both Mencius' thought and neo-Confucianism, the latter concept of *ming*, which Liu calls *li-i chih ming* (ethico-metaphysical fate), holds that human fate is not something preordained by the supernatural forces, but something that can be fulfilled by human effort. The nonfatalistic concept of *ming* bulks even larger in Hsün Tzu's world view, which envisages Heaven as merely an order of nature rather than the controlling force in the cosmos. A corollary of this world view is an activistic outlook that is just the opposite of the fatalistic concept of *ming*: a belief that human beings can not only determine their own fate, but have the ability to conquer nature for their own purposes. Backing up his arguments with many references to ancient Chinese classics, both Confucian and non-Confucian, Liu states his belief that voluntarism and activism are as much a part of the Chinese cultural heritage as the fatalism is.[40]

Liu sometimes uses the concept of *tsao-ming* (forging one's fate) to epitomize his voluntarism. Because this was an expression of activism and antifatalism characteristic of the philosophy of Chiao Hsün, a scholar of the Yangchou School whom Liu greatly admired, we may assume that Chiao Hsün influenced him here. In other words, in articulating the antifatalism and activism of Chinese tradition, he is at least partly following a trail blazed by his predecessors at Yangchou.[41]

In Liu's philosophical treatise, *li* is viewed not only as a subjective faculty of reason, but also as the pattern inherent in all concrete existences in the outside world. Liu believes that the latter view needs particular emphasis in order to avoid some serious mistakes in the world view of mainstream neo-Confucianism, as well as in its approach to moral cultivation. Given the tendency of mainstream neo-Confucianism to reify *li* as ontologically independent and separate from the material force, many neo-Confucian philosophers inevitably came to look on *li* as something completely extraneous to emotions (*ch'ing*) and desires (*yü*). These emotions and desires were normally considered an integral part of the material force that constitutes the concrete existence of the individual self. From this, it was but a short step to the view that eventually prevailed in the orthodox Ch'eng-Chu School, namely, that *li* is incompatible with *ch'ing* and *yü*. Because *li* is the source of moral values and norms in the universe, this incompatibility can only mean the moral illegitimacy of *ch'ing* and *yü*.[42]

To Liu, this sort of negative, inhibitory morality has little place in Confucianism if one follows the lead of the Han Confucian philosophers who

---

40. Ibid.: 559–60.
41. Ibid.: 560; Ch'ien Mu (1964, 2: 477–78).
42. 1965, 1: 556.

saw *li* as the internal pattern of any concrete existence. Their view avoids the antagonistic dualism of *li* and *yü* and thereby allows morality to have a more open and positive character. Liu spells out his thinking along this line in his explication of *hsing*, another key category in the Confucian conception of man. In orthodox neo-Confucianism, *hsing* refers to *li* insofar as it resides in the individual mind as its nature. Its nature was therefore pure goodness, separate and distinct from the material endowment of the mind, which, like *ch'ing* and *yü*, is contaminable. Thus, according to this view, running parallel with the dichotomy of the *li* and the material force in the neo-Confucian world view is a further dichotomy between the inner nature and the outer, material endowment of the human mind.[43]

For Liu, it was as wrong to speak of the latter dichotomy as of the former, because just as *li* is inherent in the material force, *hsing* is inseparably immanent in the material endowment of the mind. Hence it is meaningless to speak of good or evil with regard to any nature apart from its material manifestations, such as emotions and desires. As for emotions and desires, he did not look on them as totally evil, either, as the orthodox neo-Confucianist did. Because so-called nature is an inherent part of emotion, emotion can be a good thing, as long as it does not exist in excess. Hence, he points out that, in contradistinction to the orthodox neo-Confucian view, the ancient Chinese classics recommended *chih-ch'ing* (controlling emotions), rather than eradicating them. Similarly, desire too could be a good thing. Liu notes that there are two kinds of desires: biological needs, such as the need for sex or food, and moral, spiritual, and other kinds of aspirations. Without biological needs, there would be no life; without aspirations, life would have no purpose. Again, only in excess does desire become evil. It was Liu's view that the ancient Chinese tradition encouraged curbing or reducing desires but never urged eliminating them altogether. In short, the moderate fulfillment of emotions and the satisfaction of desires are essential to, rather than go against, the moral actualization of man.[44]

So far, both in Liu's critique of the orthodox neo-Confucian concept of *li* and in his interpretation of such concepts as *hsing*, *yü*, and *ch'ing*, he follows the arguments of Tai Chen closely. Eventually, however, he goes beyond Tai Chen's thought to launch a philosophical attack on the traditional Chinese social order. It must be noted that Tai Chen did not merely regard the orthodox neo-Confucian concept of *li* as a source of debilitating asceticism; he also considered it conducive to authoritarian social order. Tai emphasized that if *li* is not defined in terms of the feelings and desires of the common people, it is apt to be given an arbitrary interpretation by people of high social status to serve as ideological justification for dominating people of

---

43. Ibid.: 554–56.
44. Ibid.: 555–56.

lower status.⁴⁵ Building on this observation of Tai Chen's, Liu makes a radical critique of orthodox neo-Confucianism.

For Liu, two aspects of the orthodox neo-Confucian concept of *li* stand out. First, it is totally devoid of humanitarian content, as reflected in the notion that *li* is a total negation of *ch'ing* and *yü*, which, in Liu's interpretation, represent the simple, basic needs of common people.⁴⁶ Second, *li* is usually understood in a way that serves the interests of the powerful and privileged (*i shih wei li*).⁴⁷ These two aspects of the orthodox concept, in Liu's view, add up to an ideological defense of the authoritarian Confucian doctrine of the hierarchical order (*ming-fen*). For Liu, then, Tai Chen's redefinition of *li* in terms of the desires and emotions of the common people has the implication of questioning and challenging some basic aspects of the traditional social order. In drawing this implication, however, Liu pushes Tai Chen's arguments much further than Tai himself ever had.⁴⁸

Viewed in context, Liu's philosophical treatise was only a companion piece to a much larger work that he wrote in the same year: *Lun-li hsüeh chiao-k'o shu* (A standard text on ethics). This work developed further the moral radicalism discussed above and also enlarged on the idea of defining human nature for self-understanding and moral practice in a more comprehensive and systematic way. This book, like the treatise, is, despite its title, not a theoretical, objective disquisition on ethics. In fact, to a greater degree than the treatise, it is a response to the emerging crisis of orientational order. Liu states explicitly that the disquisition was written for the practical purpose of defining a moral outlook to serve as a guide to individual and collective behavior in the modern world. In this regard, he says that he has modeled his book on the *Ta-hsüeh*, which, among the Confucian Four Books, is generally regarded as the fundamental primer on Confucian moral goals and practices.⁴⁹

Liu's book is reminiscent of another popular tract of his time that was also written partly for the purpose of continuing the moral heritage of the *Ta-hsüeh*: Liang Ch'i-ch'ao's *Hsin-min shuo* (On the new citizen).⁵⁰ However, there is a striking difference between the two. Where nationalism permeates Liang's text, there is only a faint echo of it in Liu's. And, whereas Liang wrote his text to foster the ideal of the citizen of the new Chinese nation, Liu penned

---

45. Ibid.: 553–54, 556; see also "Tai Chen chuan" [A biography of Tai Chen] (1965, 3: 2070–71); and ibid.: 2144.
46. 1965, 1: 554, 556; see also ibid., 3: 2144 and "Tsui-kang p'ien" [On condemning the "three bonds"] (ibid., 2: 763).
47. 1965, 1: 554; ibid., 2: 763. See also *Chung-kuo min-yüeh ching-i* [Refined notions of social contract in the Chinese tradition] (ibid., 1: 710).
48. 1965, 2: 763.
49. 1965, 4: 2301.
50. For an analysis of Liang Ch'i-ch'ao's *Hsin-min shuo*, see Chang Hao (1971: 149–219).

his to enunciate the moral ideal of what he called the *wan-ch'üan chih jen* (complete man) and the *wan-ch'üan ti she-hui* (complete society).[51]

Yet Liu's perspective is not exactly that of the Confucian moral tradition; the latter is characterized by a universalistic claim that Confucianism is the source of universal moral truths. It is this universalistic claim, however, that Liu has begun to question, as we can see in the way he defines the concept of *lun-li*. The term is a neologism borrowed by the early Chinese intelligentsia from the Japanese to designate ethical rules and norms. What is important to note is that underlying Liu's concept of *lun-li* is an evolutionary view of morality; for Liu, the Chinese *lun-li* represents an ethical order centered around the five Confucian relationships. However, he draws on his knowledge of anthropology and etymology to show that the Chinese way of ordering these five relationships is not a moral verity that has existed from the beginning of history. It emerged only as the result of a particular historical evolution. Even an ancient Confucian belief, he says, supports this evolutionary view. This belief holds that the teaching of the five relationships was the creation of the ancient sage-king Shun and his minister Shang Chieh. Liu believed that these historical facts and beliefs run counter to the dominant Confucian view that was later developed in the doctrine of the three bonds, which holds that the Confucian way of ordering the three relationships of father-son, ruler-subject, and husband-wife are inherent in the cosmic order of Heaven.[52]

In the same vein Liu redefines the Confucian concept of *tao*. In the Confucian tradition, Liu points out, *tao* does not mean just the moral order: it also represents the cosmic order and hence can be identified with the "principle of Heaven" (*t'ien-li*). As such, it is a cosmic as well as a moral imperative and is both all-embracing and unalterable. It is this concept of *tao* that underlies the doctrine of three bonds, which people "dare not doubt and dare not violate." However, in Liu's view, it is all plainly a myth. For him, the Confucian *tao* merely symbolizes a cluster of moral norms that grew out of the mores and customs of a particular society, with nothing transcendental or universal about it.[53]

Thus, Liu's critique of the Confucian concepts of *lun-li* and *tao* is not so much a repudiation of the belief in the existence of universal values and truths as a rejection of the Confucian normative order embodied in the doctrine of the three bonds and the five relationships. In fact, the underlying assumption of Liu's book is that there is a universal human nature and that a knowledge of human nature would provide guidance for moral orientation

---

51. 1965, 4: 2303, 2349.
52. Ibid.: 2301.
53. Ibid.

and practice in the world. Thus, the text is written in language addressed as much to the individual human being per se as to the individual Chinese. It is this universalistic perspective that distinguishes Liu's text from Liang Ch'i-ch'ao's *Hsin-min shuo*, which was dominated by a particularistic concern for the Chinese nation.

Liu's moral outlook is evident in a notion that he terms the "ethics of the individual" (*chi-shen ti lun-li*). Consciously following the model of the *Ta-hsüeh*, Liu feels that the concern of the ethics of the individual is not only to cultivate a complete man but also to provide the starting point for the construction of a complete society. Again reflecting his Confucian heritage, he considers self-understanding to be a prerequisite for the cultivation of a complete man. Our examination of *Li-hsüeh tzu-i t'ung-shih* has already shown his involvement in the centuries-old internal debate in the Confucian tradition over the cultivation of human nature. In *Lun-li hsüeh chiao-k'o shu*, Liu's involvement in the debate continues.[54] In the meantime, however, his responses to the debate were also being affected by some new ideas of man that were emerging on the intellectual horizon from the West.

Liu's understanding of the self is organized around a threefold concept of the faculties of mind: the cognitive, the affective, and the volitional. Such a concept of mind Liu probably owes to a similar tripartite classification of human faculties that was popular in the West and could easily have been picked up from the publications of Christian missionaries or from Japanese works on the west. In Liu's work, however, this tripartite classification is more apparent than real. A closer analysis of Liu's concept of the volitional function, for instance, shows that to him it means nothing more than emotion focused and directed. For him, volition is not an independent category like the other two. Consequently, the human mind is in effect made up of two faculties: the cognitive and the affective.[55] This dualistic concept of mind is reminiscent of a similar bifurcation—between cognition on the one hand and the emotions and desires on the other—in the thought of the Yangchou School, which was so prominent in his intellectual background.[56]

Liu's analysis of the affective function of the self basically develops the same argument he evolved in *Li-hsüeh tzu-i t'ung-shih*: moral cultivation means self-realization; the latter involves not repression, but fulfillment, of the emotions and desires, that is, of the natural self. Hence, in this book he arrives at the same radical critique that his treatise on neo-Confucianism

---

54. Ibid.: 2299, 2303–6.
55. Ibid.: 2306–7.
56. As pointed out earlier, the Yangchou School's moral philosophy and underlying concept of man are basically an outgrowth of Tai Chen's thought. Central to Tai's concept of man is the bifurcation of mind into cognitive and affective faculties; see Hou Wai-lu (1958, 5: 437–42).

made of the tendency of the mainstream neo-Confucianism to define human nature in Manichean terms.[57]

Liu's elucidation of the cognitive function of mind, however, leads him to evolve some new themes in *Lun-li hsüeh chiao-k'o shu*. By cognitive function, he means not just the ability to conceptualize for comparison and analysis, but, more important, the capacity for moral knowledge and judgment. He emphasizes the innateness of this ability, ascribing the source of his belief in this regard to Mencius' and Wang Yang-ming's idea of the innate sense of the good.[58] Thus, just as with his concept of the affective function of self, his concept of the cognitive function was conceived largely under the influence of the Chinese intellectual tradition.

Liu's analysis of the functions of mind provides the basis for his definition of the process of moral cultivation, which is necessary for becoming a complete man. Because of his emphasis on the innate moral sense of the mind, he endorses the Confucian view that mind is "the lord of self" and gives a central place to the idea of establishing the primacy and control of mind over body in his definition of moral cultivation.[59] Further, in his elucidation of the process of establishing the control of the mind over the body, he draws heavily on the Confucian and neo-Confucian repertoire of methods of mind cultivation and character discipline. The result is an unabashedly eclectic approach to defining the process of moral cultivation, in which he adopts and combines ideas from different schools within the Confucian tradition. But the point to note is that the process of moral cultivation that emerges from this eclectic formulation still basically follows the Confucian format, namely, a format that begins with goal setting and goes on to the struggle to preserve commitment and discipline character—all geared to the effort to achieve what Liu calls a "complete personality."[60]

Apart from formulating a model of moral cultivation for the practical purpose of education, Liu draws some fresh implications from his voluntaristic concept of mind and thus develops the underlying notion of autonomy of self in a new direction. To see the significance of this new departure in his moral thinking, let us begin by recalling that, in the Confucian tradition, autonomy of self is conceived largely in the framework of self-realization. Consequently, it basically means the autonomy of one's moral and spiritual center in relation to the contaminations and bondages of the evil forces arising from one's physical existence: the independence of the higher from the lower self. We may call this kind of autonomy "inner autonomy" to distinguish it from the idea of "outer autonomy" characteristic of the

---

57. 1965, 4: 2306–7.
58. Ibid.: 2306, 2312–13.
59. Ibid.: 2305, 2310.
60. Ibid.: 2310–18.

mainstream of Western liberal tradition.[61] We characterize the latter as "outer autonomy," inasmuch as it stresses the independence of the total self of the individual from external control, either by other individual selves or by the social self. Although it is the idea of inner autonomy which is predominant in the Confucian tradition, this idea also carries certain implications conducive to the development of the notion of outer autonomy. The main reason is that the ideas of self-realization and moral fulfillment, which underlie the conception of inner autonomy, often entail a sense of self-worth and self-respect that have the effect of asserting the independence of the self against the authorities of the state and society. Thus the idea of outer autonomy does have a place, though often in a latent form, in the Confucian tradition.

One branch of the Confucian tradition where the latent idea of outer autonomy often came to the surface was Wang Yang-ming's moral philosophy, which was prominent in Liu's intellectual background. It is significant that the person whom Liu particularly admired among Wang Yang-ming's followers was Wang Ken, the founder of the T'ai-chou School where the idea of outer autonomy was developed further than any other group in the Wang Yang-ming School.[62] In a biography of Wang Ken he composed about the same time that he wrote *Lun-li hsüeh chiao-k'o shu*, he gives special emphasis to Wang Ken's concept of self with its strong overtone of outer autonomy. As he notes, according to Wang Ken, self can embody the *Tao* and thereby become a sage. Therefore, everyone should aim at embodying the *Tao*. When that happens, one becomes the emperor's teacher and thus achieves a status higher than that of the emperor.[63] Elsewhere in his writings, Liu, following this line of thinking, sometimes broadens the concept of self further and sees the self as the potential focus of the heavenly principles (*li*), and, consequently, as a sort of counterweight to the existing structure of sociopolitical authority, which he calls *shih*.[64] In this way, Liu found in Wang Ken's thought, and in the Lu-Wang School as a whole, as much a notion of outer autonomy as that of inner autonomy.

In his *Lun-li hsüeh chiao-k'o shu*, Liu's Confucian heritage was reinforced by his exposure to Western liberal thought, and the result was a tendency to articulate his moral voluntarism not only in terms of the concept of inner autonomy, but also in terms of that of outer autonomy. In fact, in many places in the text, the emphasis of his argument moves toward the latter, for

---

61. This distinction between higher and lower self is implied in the dichotomy of *hsin* [mind-heart] and *t'i* [physical body], which Liu posits throughout his discussions of moral cultivation, e.g., ibid. I am not, of course, saying that there is no notion of inner autonomy in the Western liberal tradition, but its distinguishing characteristic is the emphasis on outer autonomy. For a background discussion, see Berlin (1969: 118–72).
62. Liu Shih-p'ei "Wang Ken chuan" [A biography of Wang Ken] (1965, 3: 2044–46).
63. Ibid.: 2045.
64. *Chung-kuo min-yüeh ching-i* (1965, 1: 701).

example, in his commentary on the Confucian ideal of *i* (righteousness). Liu's point of departure is the Confucian definition of *i* in the context of two parallel dichotomies: namely, *i* versus *li* (personal interest) and *kung* (the sense of the social whole) versus *ssu* (selfishness).[65] In the first dichotomy, *i* is conceived as a sense of righteousness incompatible with any consideration of personal interest. In the second, *i* is further identified with the perspective of the social whole, as opposed to any partial interest of the individual self. Understood in terms of the Confucian context of self-realization, *i* then refers to the virtue of transcending the partial, interested viewpoint of the empirical self to assume the disinterested perspective of one's higher moral self, which is identical with the social whole. Clearly, this concept implies a concept of inner autonomy, that is, the autonomy of a higher, moral self from the lower, partial interests of the individual empirical self. From this traditional concept, Liu however moves on to another concept of *i*, which he defines as "to curb the autonomy of one's self so as to avoid encroaching on the autonomy of other selves."[66] This is quite a shift of ground, because the issue he now addresses is no longer that of inner autonomy, but that of defining the limits of the autonomy of the individual self in its relationship with other selves, clearly a variant of the issue of outer autonomy.

This shift of ground signifies that Liu has moved his emphasis from the concept of inner autonomy to outer. He has thereby articulated a dimension to the notion of moral cultivation, which is largely muted in the Confucian tradition. In this articulation, he understands *i* in terms of a balance between an individual's rights and his obligations. In this way, Western liberal concepts, such as freedom (*tzu-yu*) and rights (*ch'üan-li*), also begin to assume importance in his moral thought.[67]

So far, we have seen how Liu's moral voluntarism, inherited from the Confucian concept of self-cultivation, developed beyond the traditional concept of autonomy of self and blended into the Western liberal conception of individual liberty and rights. We have also seen that all this shifting of grounds and viewpoints, significant as it is, still takes place within the moral perspective of the concern with what he calls the "perfection of the individual." Liu is well aware that, though he was maintaining the same moral perspective throughout all the changes he made, he has drawn some implications that have never been drawn before in the tradition. To him, these implications are not incongruous with the Confucian moral perspective. True, he admits at one point in his book that the tradition of Wang Yang-ming and Mencius goes only to the point of speaking of Heaven-endowed moral sense and dignity, but not of Heaven-endowed rights.[68] However,

---

65. 1965, 4: 2314, 2337.
66. Ibid.
67. Ibid.: 2303.
68. Ibid.: 2312.

from his standpoint, once the former idea has been accepted, the latter follows as a natural corollary. To him it is certainly as natural a corollary as the idea of inner autonomy, which had always been central to the Confucian belief in self-cultivation. Seen in this light, his enthusiastic response to Western liberal ideas, such as rights and freedom, is also a logical evolvement of certain latent, submerged strains in the Confucian concern with self-cultivation.

Although Liu came to embrace Western liberal ideas from the Confucian moral perspective, his acceptance of these ideas also enables him to see some blind spots and dark corners in that perspective. In his *Li-hsüeh tzu-i t'ung shih*, Liu launches a critique of what he considers the inhibitory outlook of orthodox neo-Confucianism toward the natural self. In his *Lun-li hsüeh chiao-k'o shu*, he continues this line of critique, perceiving the whole neo-Confucian concept of man to be negative, in the sense of overly repressing the needs and rights of the individual self. He sees too great an orientation in neo-Confucianism toward what he calls "conquering the self and rooting out selfishness" (*k'o-chi tuan-ssu*).[69] More important, his concern for the integrity of the individual self leads him to question the traditional social norms as embodied in the doctrine of three bonds (*san-kang*). Confucian family ethics naturally became a major target for his attack. He points out that the three basic family relationships as prescribed in the doctrine of three bonds—father-son, elder brother–younger brother, and husband-wife—are all based on the principle of hierarchical domination and therefore run counter to the values of individual independence and equality that he cherishes. For the same reason, he also challenges the Confucian concept of the ruler-subject relationship. Here, however, his iconoclasm, which stems from his quest for the complete man, converges with the other moral concern of his writings—the search for the complete society.[70]

In *Lun-li hsüeh chiao-k'o shu*, Liu's discussion of individual ethics is followed by a discussion of topics that might be grouped under the general rubric of "social ethics." Social ethics is just as essential as individual ethics to the formulation of his new ethical philosophy. This is because he consciously took the *Ta-hsüeh* as his model in writing this book. If the Confucian classic had shown him the priority of self-cultivation in starting a moral life, it had also demonstrated the centrality of social participation to moral fulfillment. More significantly, however, his social ethics is as affected by moral radicalism as his individual ethics. To him, the doctrine of the three bonds is as unacceptable from the standpoint of individual ethics as from that of social ethics.[71]

One manifestation of his moral radicalism in this regard is his attack on

---

69. Ibid.: 2314.
70. Ibid.: 2325–27, 2328–29, 2329–31, 2335–36, 2349.
71. Ibid.: 2336–50.

Confucian family ethics. We have seen how he came to question the moral legitimacy of family ethics from the standpoint of his views on individual ethics. For him, however, Confucian family ethics is no less questionable from the standpoint of the formation of a moral community. He observes that the Chinese heritage has no lack of ideals of universal community, such as the Mohist ideal of universal love and the Confucian ideals of humanity (*jen*) and universal brotherhood (*min-pao wu-yü*), but these ideals have little effect on the moral thinking and conduct of the average Chinese. One basic reason for this is the social dominance of Chinese family ethics, which centers around the Confucian virtue of filial piety. Liu does not deny that filial piety is a meaningful virtue, but he points out that an overemphasis on this virtue, just like an overemphasis on the Confucian doctrine of the three bonds, serves to inhibit the development of broader moral and social commitments and identifications.[72]

What are these broader commitments and identifications? What does Liu mean by social ethics? Again we are struck by the absence of nationalistic language in Liu's discussion of these problems in his *Lun-li hsüeh chiao-k'o shu* and by a moral discourse that still reflects the overriding influence of such universalistic Confucian social virtues as *jen-ai* (humanity and love), *hui-shu* (charity and sympathetic understanding), and *cheng-i* (justice and righteousness).[73] The nature of his moral discourse is hardly surprising; he explicitly sets forth the goal of his writing on social ethics as the realization of what he calls the complete society (*wan-ch'üan ti she-hui*). Just as he drew heavily on the Confucian ethics of self-cultivation in developing his ideal of the complete individual, he also drew heavily on Confucian social ideals in formulating his ideal of the complete society.

Liu gives special priority on his scale of social values to the ideal of *kung*, which may be roughly translated as public-mindedness. *Kung* has always been a pivotal element in neo-Confucian social ethics. In the background of the ideal of *kung*, as Chu Hsi observes, was the ideal of *jen*.[74] *Jen*, of course, was a protean concept. What *kung* represents is one specific dimension of *jen* that evokes a sense of the social whole. As such, it is diametrically opposed to what neo-Confucians call *ssu*, that is, the partial and the private. Put in the framework of neo-Confucian thought, therefore, *kung* may be defined as a moral commitment to the social whole and the common good.[75]

It was from the standpoint of *kung* that Liu came to question the Confucian family ethics. From the same standpoint, he also came to challenge traditional political ethics. At the core of the latter, he discerned a distortion of the meaning of the ideal of *kung*. In his view, the Chinese

---

72. Ibid.: 2335–37.
73. Ibid.: 2338–41.
74. Ch'ien Mu (1971, 2: 68–69).
75. Ibid.: see also Liu (1965, 4: 2336–37).

political tradition had distorted the concept long ago to serve the interest of the imperial rulers. It had been twisted so that it meant a devotion to an individual dynastic ruler or to a specific dynastic regime rather than to the public interest, to the whole people in a society. In consequence, the Chinese popular consciousness was marked by a heightened sense of loyalty to political authority but a deficiency in dedication to the common good and the public interest, which Liu believes to be at the heart of a developed social ethics.[76]

In his indictment of Chinese political tradition, Liu implies that *kung* has a different meaning in Confucian political ethics, when properly understood. Although in *Lun-li hsüeh chiao-k'o shu*, Liu points to the centrality of the ideal of *kung* in his understanding of Confucian political ethics, he leaves the idea largely unexplored. However, we gain a clearer sense of his concept of *kung* from a book he wrote two years earlier, entitled *Chung-kuo min yüeh ching-i* (The essential meaning of Chinese doctrines of social contract).[77]

In this work, Liu views *kung* as a governing political ideal that symbolizes, as it does in neo-Confucianism, the commitment to the social whole but it is also often understood together with two other Confucian ideas that figure prominently in the book. One is the ancient Confucian idea that the will of the people (*min*) serves as a sort of terrestrial surrogate for Heaven's will and thereby constitutes the penultimate source of earthly authority.[78] Another is the Confucian belief that people are all blessed with the same potential for moral fulfillment, a belief in what Donald Munro calls "natural equality." [79] To Liu, these three ideas reinforce each other to form a sort of Confucian populism. The fact that this Confucian populism bulks large in Liu's thought does not necessarily mean that it exists as an integrated, unencumbered strain in the Confucian tradition. In fact, almost from the beginning it was intertwined with another idea that is no less deeply rooted in the Confucian tradition, namely, the idea that, to stay in harmony with the cosmic order, the human order on earth requires the office of kingship. Tension exists between the authoritarian pattern of cosmological kingship and the strains of populism in Confucianism, but this tension is largely contained by the presence of other Confucian concepts of man and society.

Most important is the Confucian notion of the organization of a political community. Even though the presence of populistic strains in Confucianism doubtless feeds the notion of the people or the social whole as an essential source of political legitimation, these strains do not determine the issue of

---

76. Liu (1965, 4: 2336–37).
77. *Chung-kuo min-yüeh ching-i* (1965, 1) is generally regarded as a companion piece to his *Jang shu*. While *Jang shu* is meant as a follow-up to Wang Fu-chih's *Huang shu*, the former is Liu's further development of Huang Tsung-hsi's *Ming-i tai-fang lu*; see preface by Ch'ien Hsüan-t'ung in Liu (ibid.: 34).
78. 1965, 1: 677–78, 682–83.
79. 1969: 11–16.

how the people's will and the interest of the social whole could best be expressed. The Confucian answers to this issue, varied as they are, in general settle on a "qualitative" solution, that is, the will of people can best be expressed by men who have proved to have the necessary moral-spiritual qualities. This principle of "quality" is coupled with a strain of realism that was present almost from the beginning in Confucianism to qualify the belief in natural equality: although all people are assumed to have the potential for moral fulfillment, only an exceptional minority can actually achieve such a fulfillment on their own. These were the ideas that lie behind the Confucian ideal of the sage-king—the notion that power and authority should go to the men of virtue—the moral vanguard. These ideas also make possible the coexistence and articulation of both the populist strain and the idea of cosmological kingship in Confucianism.

Such articulation dissolves in Liu Shih-p'ei's thought. For him, the very ideal of the social whole and the people's will is at odds with the principle of kingship. In Liu's mind, Confucian populism takes on new connotations that derive from the Western ideal of democracy, especially from Rousseau's theory of social contract.

Given the moral perspective that Liu inherited from his Confucianism, it is not surprising that he found Rousseau's notion of democracy congenial. Underlying Rousseau's thought was a moral quest—the same quest for a good society that also animates Liu's social thought. Further, Liu discerns in Rousseau's moral quest a conviction similar to his own that a good society can be formed by expressing the goodness inherent in human nature. If his Confucian background predisposes him in certain broad ways to see the attractiveness of Rousseau's thinking, the study of Rousseau also leads him to develop a new understanding of Confucian populism and, by the same token, to criticize Confucian political thought.[80]

A major target of Liu's criticism is the traditional view that Heaven was the ultimate source of political legitimation. This view, Liu notes, was originally intended to have the function of containing the ruler's political power, because the people could invoke the supernatural authority of Heaven to serve as an ideological deterrent to despotism. However, in later ages it often had just the opposite consequence, because political rulers could just as plausibly claim the divine sanction of Heaven for their exercise of power. The result was a political system where, as Liu characterizes it, "the unity of religious and political authority" (*cheng-chiao ho-i*) inevitably had the effect of augmenting the autocratic power of the traditional monarch, as seen, for example, in the sacred aura that the title of "Son of Heaven" imparted to the throne.[81]

---

80. 1965, 1: 677–78, 682–83.
81. Ibid.: 678, 693–94.

Liu is here using Rousseau's ideal of democracy to challenge a predominant traditional view of political legitimation. For him this traditional view was woefully mistaken, because it looked on the people's will as the penultimate, rather than ultimate, source of political authority. Liu is aware of the strains of thought within the Confucian tradition that come close to Rousseau's idea of democratic legitimacy, but for him these native strains of thought are inadequate as ideological counterweight to despotism in the light of Rousseau's idea of general will. Liu takes the example of the dichotomy between reason (*li*) and authority (*shih*), an idea prominent in the thought of the Ming philosopher Lü K'un. Lü K'un viewed authority as the prerogative of political rulers, whereas reason belonged to the sages. Although Lü K'un considers reason to be superior to authority, he nevertheless looks on them as two mutually independent political forces.[82]

For Liu, this dichotomy suggests a parallel with Rousseau's concept of democracy. The idea of reason reminds him of Rousseau's "general will," and the idea of authority, of Rousseau's concept of political power. But, as Liu hastens to point out, this parallelism can be pushed only so far, because a critical difference between Lü K'un and Rousseau remains. In the framework of Rousseau's thought, political power must follow the direction of the general will. Rousseau regards reason as the "mother of authority," in Liu's words, rather than as an independent and counterbalancing force, as Lü K'un conceived it to be. For Liu, then, Lü K'un's dichotomy is inadequate from the standpoint of Rousseau's democratic ideal. Though conceived in the spirit of containing political power, it nevertheless falls short of the democratic ideal that the general will must serve as the legitimizing source and ultimate determinant of political power.[83]

Liu's principal target is the authoritarian, hierarchical pattern of the sociopolitical order as epitomized by the institution of kingship. In the past, this authoritarian and hierarchical pattern was made compatible with the Confucian "populism" through the principle of "quality." The principle of quality is absent in Liu's political writing, thanks mostly to his acceptance of the ideal of political equality. Liu now finds the whole traditional political order unacceptable from the perspective of Confucian populism. This also accounts for the vehemence of Liu's attack on the traditional ideal of political paternalism, which he finds so much in evidence in the Confucian classics. For Liu, a good example of paternalism occurs in a famous passage in the classic *Kuo-yü*, where political rulers are urged to encourage and guide the people to speak their minds so that the government could know their needs and interests. This idea of encouraging "communication from below" (*t'ung hsia-ch'ing*) has been echoed down through the centuries and has

---

82. Ibid.: 701.
83. Ibid.

become almost a fixture of the Chinese antidespotist tradition. Underlying this idea and the whole tradition of paternalism is the assumption that a ruler has the moral obligation to be both conscientious in running the government and dedicated to serving the interest of the people. Liu admits that the idea of encouraging communication from below has had some mitigating effect on despotism in the past, but he contends that it rests on the wrong assumption—that power and authority are the sole prerogative of the ruler.[84]

Liu's critique of the Chinese intellectual tradition from this particular standpoint is a persistent note in his writings, but his commentaries on Wang Fu-chih's thought are especially significant. Wang's ethnic nationalism had greatly influenced his political outlook from his early youth on, and Wang was something of a culture hero for the Chinese intellectuals of Liu's generation. Liu was well aware that a major reason why Wang Fu-chih was so widely admired was the importance of antidespotism in his thought, but it is exactly this antidespotism of which Liu now disapproves. The idea of communication with the people and sympathy for their suffering, central as it was to Wang's thought, was still premised on the rigid hierarchical organization of society. For Wang, the status distinction between high and low, between prince and subject, must be strictly preserved; this status distinction must serve as the sole basis for the distribution of power and authority in the society. As Liu points out, this idea of maintaining strict status distinction constitutes the core of what he called the ideology of "names and distinctions" (*ming-fen*) or "names and positions" (*ming-wei*). This ideology had a primacy not only in Wang Fu-chih's thought, but also in the writings of many other eminent Chinese antidespotists.[85] By finding it unacceptable, Liu is attacking not just political paternalism but the whole hierarchical order of Chinese society. In this way, he came to see the incompatibility of Confucian populism with the Confucian doctrine of the three bonds.[86]

Thus, Liu's quest for the ideal of a complete man and a complete society led him to accept certain Western liberal ideas and to challenge the ideological foundation of the traditional order. Both quests were fueled by a moral perspective largely rooted in the Confucian tradition, but, side by side with this moral perspective in Liu's mind, was another perspective, one attuned even more to the voices of his own tradition.

CONCEPTS OF SELF AND WORLD IN LIU SHIH-P'EI'S POEMS

A prolific writer, Liu published philosophical and political essays in the midst of carrying on extremely productive scholarly work. He also wrote

---
84. Ibid.: 679, 679–80, 681.
85. Ibid.: 705–6.
86. Ibid.: 710.

many poems. When we turn from his essays to his poetry, we step from a world of broad daylight into a gray, cloudy world of shadows. This change of mental scenery is partly explained by the fact that many of his poems were written to express the all-too-human feeling of nostalgia, and this feeling imparts a certain wistfulness to his writings that does not necessarily reflect any lasting outlook on life on his part.[87]

More important than the nostalgia, however, is a sense of melancholy and loneliness that comes through in some of his poems. In one poem, he pinpoints the source of these feelings in an existential predicament, an unavoidable choice between pursuing a conventional career—which he symbolizes by the image of a fish caught in a fisherman's net—and venturing forth into the world, like a bird flying into the woods. He chooses the latter. But once in the woods, he is also aware of the loneliness of the wandering bird, and the isolation that attends a bird that is able to fly far and high but is little appreciated by birds in the woods who lack this ability.[88] In another poignant poem, he sees himself in the desolate image of a wild swan flying every year far and wide, without company and without a place to rest. Isolation and loneliness are the fate of the wild swan.[89]

Above all, his poems express a sense of the flux and emptiness of human life. In several poems, this sense of flux is evoked by descriptions of visits to historical monuments, such as ancient palaces, where he is struck by the contrast between past glories and present desolation.[90] In others, a wistfulness about the passage of time is expressed through depictions of scenic points, the permanence of the natural scenery throwing into relief the fragility and transience of human events.[91]

This sense of flux in the human world is conveyed with particular vividness in one poem where the initial image is of a beautiful woman weaving a white silk garment. The embroidered garment is hardly completed before it becomes filthy and dark. The initial image is reinforced in the rest of the poem by other images—the water of a river flowing irreversibly away, flower petals falling from trees, and the inevitable fading of a woman's beauty. All these images point to a moral: "The bygone is irretrievable, and the future is unknown." Thus, the present is all the more precious. The precious present will not last, but this is life. The sense of flux thus yields to a sense of emptiness.[92]

Against the background of this gray, heavy mood, it is not surprising to see Liu turning to philosophical Taoism and Mahayana Buddhism for solace

---

87. See three collections of his poems (1965, 4): *Fei-feng chi*, pp. 2159–63; *Tso-an shih*, pp. 2165–69; *Tso-an shih pieh-lu*, pp. 2185–91.
88. *Fei-feng chi*, p. 2a.
89. Ibid.: 1a.
90. Ibid.: 2b–3a; *Tso-an shih*, p. 3a.
91. *Tso-an shih pieh-lu*, p. 4a.
92. *Fei-feng chi*, pp. 1b–2a.

and guidance. The influence of Chuang Tzu stands out in many of Liu's poems.[93] One poem that was directly inspired by Chuang Tzu's idea of "free and easy wandering" (*hsiao-yao yu*) focuses on the fable of the gigantic roc and the small quail. Through the contrast between the vast vista commanded by the vision of a high-flying roc and the limited vision of the quail jumping among the trees, the poem reflects a strong yearning for transcendence from ordinary life.[94]

In another poem, Liu's imagination is captured by another idea of Chuang Tzu's: to detach oneself from one's own life and see it as part and parcel of the cosmic process, the coming-to-be and passing-away that characterizes the whole universe. Seen in this panorama of ceaseless universal flux, the distinction between self and other, life and death, no longer makes sense. This cosmic perspective on life lifts one above the fears and worries that normally bedevil human existence, providing an otherwise unattainable feeling of equanimity and serenity.[95]

If the Taoist ideal of self-transcendence is implicit in the previous two poems, it is explicit in another poem of Liu's. He begins by evoking an image of undifferentiated oneness as the primordial reality of the universe. This undifferentiated oneness is broken when human beings come into existence. With the birth of human beings, a fundamental but fateful distinction emerges between self and the world, giving rise to the problems and troubles that burden human existence. The moral of the poem is to transcend the dichotomy of self and world and return to the blissful innocence of primordial oneness.[96]

Similar themes in Liu's poems are sometimes expressed in Buddhist language. In one poem, for example, he creates an image of a vast, boundless universe made up of an endless flow of life, only to expose it as nothing but an illusion. In this way, he endeavors to drive home the transcendental thrust of Mahayana Buddhism. The individual self is as much a projection of our minds as the external world. Ultimately, nothing exists except in Buddha's mind.[97]

This poem is by no means an isolated example. There are echoes of Buddhist language again and again in his poems. In a poem written specifically for Yang Wen-hui, the leading Buddhist scholar of his time, Liu pays special tribute to Yang's dedicated promotion of Mahayana Buddhism as a mission badly needed in a world that has grown increasingly commercial and materialistic. Here again, the Buddhist idea of transcendence is put forward to make sense of life and the world.[98] In these Buddhist-inspired

93. Ibid.: 1b, 3b, 5b, 7a, 7b.
94. Ibid.: 7b.
95. Ibid.
96. Ibid.: 1b.
97. Ibid.: 8b.
98. Ibid.

poems, as in the Taoist-tinged ones, the individual self is presented in strongly negative terms, as something that must be transcended in order to achieve spiritual liberation. In both kinds of poems, Liu's negative view of self is accompanied by a sense of an ineffable spiritual reality where an undifferentiated oneness allows no trace of individuation.

THE ANARCHIST VISION

We have seen that ethnic nationalism was but one aspect of Liu's radical writings. In the large corpus of his nonnationalistic writings, two strains of thought stand out. One is his moral quest for the good man and the good society; the other, the spiritual, "existential" strain that moves in the direction of the Buddhist-Taoist ideal of self-transcendence and mystical oneness. Soon after Liu went to Japan in 1907, these two divergent strains would, under some new influences from abroad, merge into a single vision of a moral society.

Liu arrived in Japan with a name already well-known among the Chinese intelligentsia. There he quickly established contact with *Min pao*, the magazine of the revolutionist group in Tokyo whose editor at the time was Liu's friend, Chang Ping-lin.[99] Soon Liu began to publish articles in the magazine that continued his blasts against the foreign powers and the Manchus. But before long his nationalism was overshadowed by some fresh notes in his radicalism.[100] He sounds the most striking note in poems that describe the sufferings of the common people in graphic language and strong emotional tone, clearly bespeaking his sympathy for the poor and his resentment against the society that allows these sufferings to happen.[101] The theme of impassioned social protest is spelled out more explicitly in a long article, "Pei tien p'ien" (The sorrows of peasant tenants), which appeared in *Min pao*.[102] The article consists mainly of a historical survey of various forms of predatory landlordism in China's past. It is a moral indictment of the oppressive and exploitative nature of the traditional land system and social structure. It ends with a call for a peasant uprising to smash landlordism and bring about equal distribution of land through public ownership. Thus, Liu joins a minority of intellectuals within the revolutionist group in calling for a social revolution in China.[103]

The call for social revolution was no accidental, momentary cry of

---

99. T'ang Chih-chün (1979, chüan 3: 240–58).
100. Preface by Chang Chi in Liu (1965, 1: 32). See also Liu's "P'u-kao han-jen" [A general announcement to the Han people] (ibid., 3, chüan 14: 1917–24).
101. See some of the poems he published in *Tso-an shih pieh-lu* (1965, 4: 12b–14a). These poems were originally published in *Tien Yee* (*T'ien-i pao*).
102. 1965, 3: 1930–35.
103. Ibid. Toward the end of the article, Liu raises a specific call for a "peasant revolution" (*nung-jen ko-ming*).

protest. It grew out of a new vision of a future society, which was missing in Liu's previous writings. What were the sources of his new social faith? In large part, it was a further development of the moral quest that he had long pursued before going to Japan. But the tone of his writings became more intense and took on a novel stridency. As he looked at the intellectual scene of the mid-1900s, he worried that the Chinese intellectuals' moral concern—indeed, the very idea of moral commitment—would be undermined by the rising tide of utilitarianism. Although he traced utilitarianism in part to the Chinese tradition, he felt that its contemporary popularity was mainly due to the importation of the Benthamite doctrine from the West, largely through Yen Fu's writings.[104] In one published article, therefore, he blasts the popular ideal of wealth and power, calling it a crass, collectivistic expression of utilitarianism that stood in the way of achieving peace and harmony on earth.[105]

In other writings, he is even more concerned with the vogue of utilitarian individualism, which, stripped to its essentials, is nothing but an expression of human selfishness.[106] As such, the idea of self-interest was not only a major source of demoralization among his fellow intellectuals. He also believed it to be the root of all kinds of repressions and dominations in human societies—of a ruler over his people, of the wealthy class over the poor, of strong nations over the weak. If, in the future, men were to have any hope of living in a just society without domination, he asserts, the motive of self-interest must be rooted out.[107] We are reminded here of the Confucian denunciation of selfishness and insistence on purification of motives. In fact, in an important essay, "Li-hai p'ing-teng lun" (On the equality of advantages and disadvantages) published in *Min pao* in 1907, Liu explicitly invokes Tung Chung-shu's emphasis on the relentless disregard of self-interest and any other utilitarian motives for human endeavors and calls attention as well to Wang Yang-ming's ideal of appealing to innate conscience in pursuit of moral goals.[108] Obviously, he was still much influenced by the Confucian "ethics of ultimate ends," which allows no place for the utilitarian mentality.

Liu's attack on utilitarian individualism is not made entirely on moral grounds. Calculation of self-interest, aside from being immoral, is also cited as an exercise in futility, because all calculations depend on the individual, mortal mind, which Liu believes to be filled with illusions.[109] This negative view of self is not a new development in Liu's thought; it had long been an undercurrent in his thinking and is reflected in the poems that he wrote

104. "Li-hai p'ing-teng lun" [On the equality of advantages and disadvantages] (1965, 3: 1924–29).
105. 1963a: 900–6.
106. 1965, 3: 1924.
107. 1963a: 900–4.
108. 1965, 3: 1924, 1929.
109. Ibid.: 1925, 1926–28.

before going to Japan. In these poems, the yearning for self-transcendence and mystic oneness is strongly expressed in both Buddhist and Taoist terms. However, in his essay, "Li-hai p'ing-teng lun," the Buddhist-Taoist idea of mystic selflessness comes to the forefront of his social consciousness and is further accompanied by mystic notions of self-transcendence that stem from the Confucian world view of the "unity of heaven and self."[110] Thus, side by side with the Confucian moral denunciation of the ideals of utility and self-interest are strains of indigenous spirituality that converge in a negative view of the individual self and at the same time elevate the vision of a selfless whole.[111] These tradition-inspired ideals of the selfless whole inevitably had the effect of dampening his enthusiasm for the ideal of individual liberty, which helps to explain why Liu eventually came to attach a greater weight to equality than to liberty in his vision of the future society.

The background to his newly acquired ideals about the future society consists of long-held ethical aspirations and spiritual yearnings that account for the moral zeal and idealistic tone of his sociopolitical writings. But did this background also supply the content of these ideals? A clue to the content of his new social vision can be found in a 1907 article that he wrote about the fourth-century Taoist philosopher Pao Ching-yen. Liu depicts the Taoist glorification of naturalness as central to Pao's thought.[112] He expresses enthusiasm for the idea of naturalness insofar as it asserts the integrity of human nature against the restraints and interferences of the sociopolitical environment. But, typical of philosophical Taoism, the idea of naturalness as Liu presents it also involves a strain of primitivism that idealizes the simplicity and innocence of the village settlements that were believed to exist before the rise of civilization.[113] Did Liu believe that this Taoist primitivism indeed portrayed the ideal order of the future?

It is significant that Liu never pursues the idea of primitivism at length in any of his other sociopolitical writings. True, the idea sometimes turns up in his poetry but serves more to express an occasional mood of weariness with the complications of life than any serious reflection about the society of the future. Thus, to the extent that Taoist primitivism has any place in his sociopolitical writings, it is more as a symbol of protest against the existing society than as a signpost to his vision of the future.[114]

The main reason why he could not embrace the Taoist philosophy in toto is that he was at that time being subjected to the powerful pull of a new intellectual trend that was spreading around him—Western anarchism.

---

110. Ibid.: 1928–29.
111. Ibid.: 1924–29.
112. "Pao-sheng hsüeh-shu fa-wei" [An interpretation of Pao Ching-yen's scholarship] (1965, 3: 1766–68).
113. Ibid.: 1766–67.
114. Ibid.: 1766–68.

Anarchism was not entirely new to Liu by the time he went to Japan. A philosophical tract that he wrote in 1903 shows that he was already aware of some of the basic notions of anarchism as well as socialism. To him they both vaguely seemed to represent variations on the ideal of democracy that sprang from Rousseau.[115] However, Liu did not become a fervent advocate of anarchism until he arrived in Japan. There, largely through his acquaintance with Chang Chi, a member of the revolutionist intelligentsia who had close ties with Japanese anarchists, he quickly became converted to anarcho-socialism and soon began actively propagating his new social faith.[116] He and Chang Chi organized the *She-hui chu-i chiang-hsi-hui* (Institute for the Study of Socialism).[117] At about the same time, Liu also started to publish writings about anarchism: first in a magazine entitled *Tien Yee* (The principles of nature), which he and his wife coedited, and then in the short-lived magazine, *Heng pao*, founded after *Tien Yee* ceased publication.[118] Liu was in Japan barely two years, but, because of his enthusiastic involvement in the propagation of anarchism, his short stay there proved to be the high point of his radical career.

For Liu, anarchism represents the ideals of freedom and equality carried through to their logical conclusion. From the beginning, Liu's notions of freedom and equality betrayed significant differences from those that prevailed among the early Chinese intelligentsia. Whereas the majority of intellectuals understood democratic ideals in terms of nationalism, Liu views them largely from the moral perspective of the quest for a "complete individual" and a "complete society." Espousing anarchism now allows him to pursue more or less the same moral perspective, while considerably broadening his understanding of democratic ideals. His study of the anarchist Max Stirner is a case in point. Paraphrasing Stirner, Liu presents the view that human history is the development of freedom through three stages. The first stage saw the emancipation of human beings from enslavement by despotic rulers and feudal lords. This initial stage of "political freedom" would then be followed by a stage of "social freedom" in which poor people were freed from economic exploitation by the wealthy. In the final stage, individual human beings would attain complete freedom, in the sense of eliminating the mental bondage imposed by all kinds of selfish thought. What Liu finds exhilarating in this view is its moral vision: The development of human history would consummate in the emergence of individual persons, freed not only from external bondages imposed by society, but also from internal bondages created by human selfishness.[119]

---

115. 1965, 1: 688–89.
116. Preface by Ts'ai Yüan-p'ei (1965, 3: 23). See Bernal (1976: 219–22).
117. Bernal (1976: 219).
118. Preface by Ts'ai Yüan-p'ei (1965, 3).
119. *Tien Yee* (1966, nos. 8/9/10: 239–44).

For Liu, however, Max Stirner's thought represents only one type of anarchism—the individualistic type, which puts stress on individual freedom, as distinguished from the collectivistic type, which places a premium on equality.[120] Sympathetic as Liu is with individualistic anarchism, it is the collectivistic type that captured his heart and imagination. In other words, equality has a higher priority than freedom on Liu's scale of values. He points out that freedom, when developed to the fullest extent among some people, would inevitably cut into the freedom of others.[121] Liu never fully clarifies this point. Presumably, he means that, under a socioeconomic system like capitalism, the freedom of the wealthy is often expanded at the expense of the rest of the society. Consequently, in his view, freedom, unlike equality, is not an unmixed blessing.[122] Apart from reflecting a greater appreciation of equality as a social value, his preference for collectivistic anarchism may also reflect his skepticism about the value of the individual self, which stemmed from his mystic notions of selfless oneness.

Thus, equality, more than freedom, constitutes the guiding ideal of Liu's collectivistic anarchism. Dominated by his new social vision, he became a radical critic, condemning the existing institutions of human societies across the board. His arguments for this condemnation provide ample clues to his vision of a new society.

Not surprisingly, the premise for his radical critique of human society is the observation that inequality is an oppressive reality everywhere. He traces this ubiquitous evil to several sources. One major source is the institution of government, which, in whatever form, invariably degenerates into an instrument of oppression by the ruler over the ruled.[123] To him, representative government is no exception. In fact, in view of the popularity of the Western ideal of parliamentary democracy, Liu warns in particular against representative government, calling it a breeding ground for inequality. Liu points out that inequality frequently accompanies parliamentary democracy, because it operates on the principle of decision by majority. This practice can, and often does, mean the tyranny of majority over minority.[124]

More important, Liu charges that a parliamentary government cannot perform its most important function, namely, to express the will of the majority of the people. Surveying the democratic countries of his day, he argues that most elections, being saddled with property qualifications and riddled with all kinds of abuses, turn representative government into an instrument used by the wealthy to exploit and lord over the poor. Thus,

---

120. Ibid., no. 6, pp. 145–48.
121. 1963b: 918–19.
122. Ibid.: 918–32.
123. Ibid.: 925–26. See also "Cheng-fu che wan-o chih yüan yeh" [Government, the source of all evils!] (ibid.: 914–15).
124. Ibid.: 925–26; see also Liu's "Hsüan-chü tsui-o shih" [A history of the evils attending elections], *Tien Yee* (1966, nos. 16/17/18/19: 637–44).

parliamentary government is democracy in name but plutocracy in reality.[125] Liu attaches great significance to this weakness in the democratic government. The attack on this weakness, in fact, is a main theme in *Tien Yee*. In his view, it not only proves the inherent flaw of democratic government but also points to another major source of inequality in society, that is, that the institution of private property polarizes society into a wealthy minority and a poor majority.[126]

Liu's perception of this social inequality was strongly colored by the socialist-anarchist publications that he read in Japan. An overriding theme in *Tien Yee* is that class division between the rich and poor has been a fundamental reality of society throughout history.[127] Significantly, he sees class division in terms of conflict between capitalists and laborers, but he also bases his view on his own understanding of agrarian society in China. Indeed, reports and analyses of the oppression of peasant tenants by landlords are a recurrent feature of Liu's *Tien Yee*. Thus, in contrast to fellow intellectuals like Chang Ping-lin and Liang Ch'i-ch'ao, who often idealized traditional Chinese society as being blessed with a lack of class division, Liu's writings reveal a deep awareness of the long-standing social inequality that attended landlordism in Chinese history.[128]

Liu's remedy is a peasant revolution (*nung-jen ko-ming*) to redistribute land.[129] Lying behind the idea of land redistribution is his overall solution to the universal problem of social inequality, namely, an outright abolition of private property.[130] Liu makes it clear that he owes the idea to Western socialism and anarchism; and he commends both.[131] However, when it comes to the issue of designing a new socioeconomic order to replace the system based on private property, his preference is clearly for anarchism over socialism, because he notes that anarchism envisages a new society of equality without government, but socialism still emphasizes the need for a strong government, at least until the advent of the final communist society. In Liu's eyes, the socialist program of nationalization of private property raises the

---

125. Liu (1963b: 914–15).
126. For Liu's criticisms of representative government, see "She-hui chu-i yü kuo-hui cheng-ts'e" [Socialism and parliamentary policies] (*Tien Yee* 1966, no. 15: 451–60); "O-kuo ko-ming chih chu-chih" [The meaning of the Russian Revolution] (ibid., nos. 16/17/18/19: 573–74); "Chih Chung-kuo-jen shu" [A translation of Tolstoy's letter to the Chinese] (ibid.); and "Hsüan-chü tsui-o shih" (ibid.: 637–44).
127. This theme is spelled out most clearly in Liu's article (1963b).
128. E.g., in one issue of *Tien Yee* (1966, nos. 8/9/10), there were two articles discussing the problems of peasants in China and two factual reports about actual rural conditions.
129. 1963, 3: 1935.
130. The abolition of private property was, in fact, one of the five declared goals of *Tien Yee* (1966, nos. 8/9/10: 174, 266).
131. "Ou-chou she-hui chu-i yü wu cheng-fu chu-i i-t'ung k'ao" [A study of the differences and similarities between socialism and anarchism in Europe], in *Tien yee* (1966, no. 6: 147–48).

specter of a powerful government running roughshod over the liberties and rights of people.[132]

However, society without government does not mean a lack of cohesion and unity, according to Liu. This may appear incongruous in an era dominated by the Darwinian picture of struggle and conflict inherent in life. However, it is hardly surprising in light of Liu's intellectual background. He was brought up on the Confucian doctrine that love and sympathy are the natural feelings of human beings. Later, this optimistic concept of human nature was reinforced by his exposure to the ethical naturalism that underlies Rousseau's liberal thought.[133] Then in Japan he gives prominent place in *Tien Yee* to the ethical doctrine of anarchism, especially to Kropotkin's anti-Darwinian view that cooperation is as important a phenomenon in nature and society as the struggle for survival.[134] Liu's sympathy with all these socioethical theories naturally make it easier for him to accept the anarchist belief that harmonious, organized society can be formed on the basis of free association.

Inspired by the social philosophy of anarchism, Liu published an article in *Tien Yee* in July 1907 in which he sets forth his own vision of a unified society without government.[135] According to this vision, human beings on earth would be organized into numerous small "free associations" (*hsiang*). Each free association would comprise a thousand people.[136] Although he does not explicitly specify it, it is taken for granted that, in these small associations, private property would be abolished and replaced by public ownership. In each of these small communities, there would be public nursing homes for both young and old. Each person, from the date of his or her birth until 20, would be placed in the care of such a home. After reaching the age of 50, both men and women would reenter a home for retirement.[137] Retirement from active public life, however, carries with it an important social function: the old are now given the responsibility of educating the young. The education of the young would start at age 6. For the first five years, they would be taught a simplified language that could be used anywhere in the world. From age 10 to 20, the emphasis of education would gradually be shifted from language to substantive knowledge. Students' time would be equally divided every day between courses dealing with general knowledge, such as geography, history, mathematics, and natural sci-

---

132. 1963b: 930–31.
133. See Liu's discussion of the thought of Mencius and Wang Yang-ming as compared with Rousseau's (1965, 1: 701–2).
134. As in the case of another important forum for the Chinese anarchists, *Hsin shih-chi*, in Paris, Kropotkin's anarchism had a more prominent place than any other brand of Western anarchism in *Tien Yee* (1966, no. 3: 43–50; nos. 11/12: 383–88; no. 15: 475–80; nos. 16/17/18/19: 547–61, 563–72).
135. Ibid., no. 3: 24–36.
136. Ibid.: 27.
137. Ibid.: 25–27.

ences, and specialized courses teaching knowledge and skills of a practical nature.[138]

After reaching 20, a young person would assume the adult function of working for the society.[139] Liu observes that "today those who espouse communism want to do away with power, abolish government, turn land into something public-owned and capital into the common property of society, [so as to] make everyone work and labor."[140] However, the principle that everyone is to have work does not necessarily mean equality. There are all kinds of work, he points out; some are easy and some difficult, and some involve hardship and some give pleasure. Thus, the division of labor means different lives for different people and thereby gives rise to social inequality. The natural corollary of the division of labor and occupational specialization is the Mencian idea that those who labor with the mind should rule over those who labor with muscle.[141]

However, Liu contends that, from the standpoint of equality, the ancient philosopher Hsü Hsing, who took exception to this Mencian idea, made better sense but did not go far enough. Liu agrees with Hsü Hsing's idea of abolishing the distinction between mental work and physical labor and his attack on government's exploitation of people, which implies that he advocated a classless society. But Liu balks at the fact that Hsü Hsing still saw the necessity for some division of work between peasants on the one side and artisans and merchants on the other. Liu makes it clear that he has no objection to the division of work or to occupational specialization per se. In fact, he still finds them essential and emphatically rebukes those who oppose them. What he does reject is the division of labor without institutional safeguards to prevent such a division from leading to social inequality.[142]

Liu's own answer to the problem of combining occupational specialization and equality is to design a new educational system for the new society. His educational ideal was to give young people all-around training in general knowledge as well as practical knowledge and skills. This kind of educational training would then enable people to take up different work at different ages, after becoming working adults. The idea was to prevent an individual from holding any particular job for too long. Thus, neither the advantages nor the disadvantages that necessarily go with any particular work would determine the person's position in society. In this way, Liu believes, social equality could be preserved, while also maintaining the division of labor.[143]

Although the role of family is not explicitly discussed in Liu's blueprint

---

138. Ibid.
139. Ibid.: 27–28.
140. Ibid.: 25–26.
141. Ibid.: 26.
142. Ibid.: 34–35.
143. Ibid.: 26–30.

for the future anarchist society, his idea that children from birth on would be raised and educated under public care certainly implied a drastic change for the family as an institution. This implication is in fact amply borne out in many articles in *Tien Yee*. Because Liu's wife, Ho Chen, a dedicated feminist, was a coeditor of *Tien Yee*, the journal championed women's liberation as one of its principal causes. It featured many articles calling for sexual equality and blasting the traditional moral order for the subservient role it assigns to women.[144] The traditional male chauvinism that regards women as nothing more than instruments or playthings is described in the journal as a complete betrayal of the twin moral ideals of equality and liberty. The protest went so far that not only is Confucius condemned for his alleged bias against women, but a call is even sounded for family revolution (*chia-t'ing ko-ming*), foreshadowing, perhaps, the social radicalism of the May Fourth era. All this obviously had the full support and sympathy of Liu Shih-p'ei, who envisages absolute equality between man and woman as a defining ideal for the anarchist society of the future.[145]

In addition to government, private property, and male domination, another source of inequality that Liu wanted to see eliminated is the boundary people draw between countries and between races. Thus, the ideal society envisioned by Liu is a universal community made up of small free associations and devoid of conflict of any kind—national, class, ethnic, or sexual.[146] To promote the emergence of this universal community in the future, Liu became a fervent advocate of Esperanto. In his view, a common language like Esperanto, adopted throughout the world, would be a great step toward reducing emotional animosity, which, together with the unequal distribution of wealth, constitutes the two main sources of conflict among nations and among races.[147]

Liu's universalistic vision also explains the significant changes in his concept of imperialism and his attitude toward nationalism. After his arrival in Japan, anti-imperialism continued to figure prominently in Liu's thought. However, he emphasizes that anti-imperialism for him did not represent racial hatred against white people; rather, it was an expression of moral indignation against the aggressions and exploitations that stronger nations inflicted on weaker.[148] He opposed the Manchu regime on more or less

---

144. Equality of the sexes is one of the four goals spelled out in the preamble, published on the first page of every issue.

145. *Tien Yee* (1966, nos. 11/12: 425–30); see also "Nü-tzu fu-ch'ou lun" [Retaliation on behalf of women] (ibid., no. 3: 7).

146. The first of the four guiding goals for *Tien Yee* was "to break down any national and social boundary and to put into practice globalism (*shih-chieh chu-i*)."

147. "Esperanto tz'u-li t'ung-shih tsung-hsü" [A preface to a general explanation of Esperanto] (ibid., nos. 16/17/18/19: 655).

148. "Ya-chou hsien-shih lun" [On the current situation in Asia] (ibid., nos. 11/12: 345–64).

similar grounds. He says that his opposition was raised not so much because the Manchu regime represented an alien ethnic group as because the Manchus were a ruling elite tyrannizing the common people. Thus, in his anarchist framework, anti-Manchuism had completely lost its ethnic coloration and become incorporated into the cause of moral revolt against political tyranny.[149] At first, nationalism signified both anti-imperialism and anti-Manchuism to Liu. Now that the meaning of both concepts had undergone a significant change, nationalism no longer made any sense to him. It is thus no surprise that, soon after *Tien Yee* commenced publication, Liu criticizes the ideal of racial revolution (*chung-tsu ko-ming*) that was advocated in the revolutionists' *Min pao*.[150] In a long article published in *Tien Yee*, he suggests to his fellow revolutionists that they replace their ideal of racial revolution with that of anarchist revolution.[151] This suggestion is a clear indication that the ethnic nationalism that had hitherto been a prominent strain of Liu's thought was now being eclipsed by the universalistic ideals of anarchism. In these anarchist ideals, he finally found what he calls the "complete society."

Liu's vision of a complete society in the future is reminiscent of K'ang Yu-wei's futuristic utopianism; in fact, Liu sometimes used the very expression "grand unity" (*ta-t'ung*) to name his ideal society.[152] However, significant differences separated Liu's utopianism from K'ang's. K'ang looked forward to the advent of the so-called age of the grand unity in the distant future, but Liu sees the possibility of its imminent arrival. K'ang Yu-wei envisaged the age of grand unity as the culmination of an inevitable process of history, but Liu looks on his ideal society as a creation of deliberate human action—a social revolution. K'ang looked forward to a universal community in the future presided over by a world government, but Liu's vision of the future society takes the form of anarchism. Differences between the two versions of utopianism, however, should not be allowed to obscure the significant parallels between them. Both utopianisms are premised on a total negation of the existing institutional structures of society. Both are informed by moral impulses that stem from a lifelong moral quest. Finally, both take on moral colorations, which, however different from each other, owe as much to indigenous influences from Chinese tradition as to external influences from the West.

---

149. "Lun chung-tsu ko-ming yü cheng-fu ko-ming chih teh-shih" [On the advantages and disadvantages of the racial and political revolution] (ibid., no. 6: 135–44).
150. Ibid.: 140–44.
151. Ibid.: 144. See also the speech Liu made at the opening session of the She-hui chu-i chiang-hsi hui (Institute for the Study of Socialism) (ibid.: 151–54).
152. Ibid., nos. 11/12: 353–54. See also "*Heng pao* fa-k'an tz'u" [The statement for the opening issue of *Heng pao*] (1965, 3: 1935).

6

Conclusion

IN THIS book, I have examined the thought of four intellectuals of the transitional generation. In each case, a world view stands out that addresses itself equally to the problems that a Chinese intellectual self-consciously faced as a member of a particular national and cultural community and to the issues he encountered as a human being, and thus to the human condition as such. These world views enabled the four minds to evolve beyond the sort of nationalism that prevailed in the reformist and revolutionist cricles of the Chinese intelligentsia.

These world views, though differing in many ways, were all characterized by a fusion of moral and spiritual strains of thought. In the cases of K'ang Yu-wei and Liu Shih-p'ei, the moral strain dominated their world views; for T'an Ssu-t'ung and Chang Ping-lin, it was the spiritual strain.

The dominance of the moral strain in the thought of K'ang and Liu was expressed in a theme that lay at the core of their world views—a theme of viewing life as a *consummatory process of quest for moral perfection*. This theme can be seen in their concept of the human individual as engaged in the process of striving to fulfill certain moral ends preordained by human nature or by cosmic reality or by both. It can also be seen in their concept that the collective life of a society (indeed, of history) is a process of fulfilling itself in an ideal order in the future. K'ang's concept in this regard was explicitly spelled out as a three-staged, developmental view of history. Liu's concept was different, but nevertheless in his view the anarchist society of the future is no less a fulfillment of his envisaged moral ends than is his ideal of the complete man. In short, we see in the writings of K'ang and Liu two different articulations of the same idea of quest for the paradigmatic self and society.

The dominance of the spiritual strain was manifested in a theme of *immersion into a primordial oneness*: a theme that stands out in T'an Ssu-t'ung's *Jen-hsüeh* and Chang Ping-lin's Buddhist world view. True, the language in which the theme was articulated in their writings varied. T'an's writings expressed it in a language charged with the feeling of love and the yearning to lose oneself in the embrace of the all-encompassing whole. In Chang's Buddhist writings, it was couched in a cool, philosophical language that lays bare the emptiness of the self and drives home the need for transcendence into the mystic oneness. T'an's world view projected a vision of feeling; Chang's world view projected a vision of intellect. But, despite their different styles of expression, we must not lose sight of the virtually identical theme of selfless oneness that lay at the root of their respective world views.

Both the moral theme and the spiritual reflect the kinds of situations in their milieu to which our four subjects were responding. One situation that these themes brought out is what I refer to in the introduction as the "existential situation," which is reflected most clearly in T'an Ssu-t'ung's thought. T'an's quest for a philosophy of selfless oneness had much to do with his struggle to make sense of the tragedies he encountered in his early life. In the case of K'ang Yu-wei, too, his sensitivity to the existential situations of his early life was also partly responsible for launching him on a moral-spiritual quest for fulfillment. The paucity of biographical material for Chang Ping-lin and Liu Shih-p'ei does not allow us to see their responses in this regard clearly. But it is by no means accidental that Chang became deeply interested in studying Mahayana Buddhism at one of the darkest moments of his life, while imprisoned and witnessing a close friend languishing to death. Liu's early life did not have such dramatic moments, but many of his poems clearly show his sensitivity to the tensions, shadows, and puzzlements of human existence. Consequently, to a great extent the world views of these four intellectuals can be seen as what Suzanne Langer calls "symbols of *Weltanschauung* and *Lebensanschauung*" formed in response to the different existential situations that each faced.[1]

The symbols of *Weltanschauung* and *Lebensanschauung* in their writings can be seen only partly in this light, however, because their work was also a response to the crisis of order that was emerging toward the end of the nineteenth century. For many Chinese intellectuals, the crisis of order was not just the disintegration of the sociopolitical order as a result of Western expansion, but also a disruption of the traditional universe of meanings, to the extent that the basic Chinese orientational symbolism was being questioned and challenged. As the crisis deepened, sensitive minds naturally felt the need to devise world views that would restore cognitive and moral coherence around them to put the world back in order for themselves, so

---

1. 1951: 241–42.

to speak. This need was much in the minds of our four subjects as they attempted to see life and world in the broadest possible terms.

Thus, the symbols of *Weltanschauung* and *Lebensanschauung* in the writings of the four were responses to both their own existential situations and the crisis of order they faced. Seen in this light, these symbols bespeak a struggle for meaning, that is, an attempt to make sense of life and the world in an integral way. In their respective world views, this struggle took two forms.

The theme of consummatory process may be seen as a struggle for meaning with a moral thrust. This is quite obvious inasmuch as at the heart of the world views of both K'ang Yu-wei and Liu Shih-p'ei lay a moral vision of self and society that served as a value center for both. But this moral thrust must not be allowed to obscure some other trans-moral, spiritual imports that their world views had for K'ang and Liu themselves. A comprehensive world view that saw life in the context of history moving toward an ideal society in the future was able to provide them with a "cognitive map" to place and orient themselves cosmically. It also served to anchor their aspirations and passions and allay the anxieties and tensions inherent in life.

On the other hand, the theme of selfless oneness may be seen as a struggle for meaning with a spiritual thrust. Just as the moral thrust of the theme of consummatory process must not be allowed to obscure the spiritual imports it also had for K'ang and Liu, the spiritual thrust of the theme of the selfless whole must not be allowed to hide the moral significance that it also had for T'an Ssu-t'ung and Chang Ping-lin. In both men's thought, one is struck by a "metaphysical" struggle for a vision of the real and the whole and by the effort to make sense of life and world in terms of that vision. But, for both, this vision also constituted a value center by dint of which they formed value judgments and made moral choices in life.

Both styles of quest for meaning owed heavily to the Chinese tradition. The symbols of *Weltanschauung* and *Lebensanschauung* that stand out so strikingly in their writings stemmed mostly from such high traditions as Confucianism, Taoism, and Buddhism. In two aspects in particular, these traditions left a strong imprint on the main themes of the world views of all four men. One is what I call the universalistic perspective, which was imbedded in the various indigenous developments of thought in the late nineteenth century. Most of these developments grew out of high traditions that had their origins in the intellectual transformations that took place in ancient China and India in the so-called "axial age." A major consequence of these axial transformations was the emergence of a universalistic perspective, that is, a perspective that allows an individual person to see beyond his particular identifications and attachments and thereby to envision all human beings as belonging to one universal community. From this perspective stemmed a tendency to define an individual not in terms of the ethnic group or social class he comes from or of the particular deities he worships, but in terms of certain general moral-spiritual qualities that he as a human being is capable of developing and embodying in his life.

Out of this perspective also grew a reflective thinking addressed to the human condition as such, in which human life was seen as a single structure of universal and perennial problems. From the beginning, Buddhism, Confucianism, Taoism, and certain other classical Chinese philosophies, such as Mohism, carried this universalistic perspective in their thought. Because all four of our subjects were deeply involved in the revival of these indigenous traditions in the late Ch'ing, they too in one way or another inherited this perspective. For them, this perspective did not necessarily preclude a concept of national community. In fact, in varying degrees, they did have some commitment to the ideal of a national community, but they did not see nationalism as an end in itself. A nation-state for them was not a terminal community but only a way station to the universal order that was the focus of their world view.

The other aspect of the themes that reflected indigenous influences refers to some deeply ingrained images of life. The theme of consummatory process bespeaks an image, rooted largely in the Confucian tradition, that viewed life as an ineluctable drive to fulfill a primordial paradigm or a preordained end inherent in universal human nature or in the reality of the world. Seen in this light, life appears as a unitary, consummatory process, a moral drama of commitment, struggle, and fulfillment. Meanwhile, the theme of selfless oneness also bespeaks archetypal images inherent in the Chinese tradition, especially in the mystic strains of the tradition. In these images, life appears as a drama of separation and return. The backdrop for this drama is the vision of reality as a primordial oneness. In the process of individuation that follows the birth of a person, a self-ego inevitably appears that separates the individual from the whole. Against this backdrop, life's paramount task is to overcome and dissolve the self-ego so as to return to the primordial oneness from which one originally comes. This archetypal image of separation and return, as well as the theme of consummatory process, constitutes another source of traditional influences, one just as significant as the universalistic perspective.

Given such striking continuities with tradition in the thought of these four individuals, what can we make of the role of Western influences? Metzger, in his *Escape From Predicament*, considers their role to be very limited in the intellectual scene of modern China as a whole.[2] In his view, Chinese intellectuals accepted Western thought only to the extent that they saw it as instrumental in fulfilling the basic goals and values that they inherited from tradition. Consequently, intellectual changes in modern China were largely a matter of traditional tensions finding new releases. My study, though

---

2. 1977: 191–235.

leading me to appreciate Metzger's insight in this regard, nonetheless reveals a more complex picture of the role of Western influences.

To understand the world views of our four subjects, it is just as important to envisage the situations they were responding to as to see the influences that shaped and conditioned their responses. All four were to varying extents responding to a crisis of orientational order that was largely brought on by China's encounter with the West. Would the world views of these four men have taken the same forms as they did, if the Western impact had not been present? The answer is no, for the conscious and deliberate conceptualizations that went into their efforts to draw on traditional moral-spiritual beliefs and world views were at variance with the premises and assumptions that these same beliefs and world views usually constituted in traditional minds.

Further, the striking continuities of their world views with the past must not blind us to certain significant discontinuities. To see these discontinuities, we must make a distinction between the contents of their world views and the original motivating sources for the crystallization of these world views. In each case, the world view, in its theme and gestalt, owed its initial impetus mainly to the Chinese tradition, but, in each case, in terms of content, we see novel colorations that reflected Western influences. The extent of this novel coloration varies from individual to individual. In the case of Chang Ping-lin, the contribution of Western influences, though significant in his early thought, was largely marginal to his world view, which basically stemmed from Mahayana Buddhism and philosophical Taoism. The imprint of Western influences is stronger in T'an Ssu-t'ung's thought, inasmuch as it featured strains of dynamism and universalism that owe much to Western secular culture and Christian ideals. However significantly the world views of Chang and T'an were affected by Western influences, in neither case did these influences result in any alteration of the spiritual theme of selfless oneness that marks both their world views.

When we turn to the world views of K'ang and Liu, which featured the theme of consummatory process, however, Western influences play a greater role. In the world views of K'ang Yu-wei and Liu Shih-p'ei, the elements that derive from Western sources have such a large place that they help to determine the very shape and coloration of their moral themes. This is demonstrated by the centrality of futuristic utopianism to each. Although this utopianism certainly has its roots in the Confucian concern with the paradigmatic society, its heightened futuristic orientation is mostly attributable to the impact of Western historical consciousness. Thus, the striking continuities of the four intellectuals' minds with the past are coupled with significant Western-induced discontinuities.

The role of Western influence can be further clarified by taking into account another key aspect of the four men's world views, which were all colored by a universalism that sprang mainly from the Chinese tradition.

It must be noted that in this tradition, universalism was almost invariably intertwined with a cosmological myth that had deep roots in China's cultural past. By cosmological myth, I refer to the view embodied in the Confucian doctrine of "three bonds," namely, that the central institutions of the Chinese socio-political order, kingship and the family, are imbedded in the sacred cosmos and constitute the core of a universal order on earth that revolves around China as its center. It is significant that the tradition-induced universalism found in the thought of all four men was marked by a clear break with this cosmological myth.

This break was nowhere more clearly seen than in the challenge each mind posed to the doctrine of three bonds. In the writings of T'an Ssu-t'ung and Liu Shih-p'ei, the challenge was frontal and unqualified. In the works of K'ang Yu-wei and Chang Ping-lin, it was largely implicit or indirect. Although the doctrine has been challenged at times in China's long history, these isolated challenges rarely went as far as those of our four protagonists. Further, the latter challenges took place in the context of massive and sustained intellectual changes that culminated in the radical iconoclasm of the May Fourth period. Seen in this context, the four might be viewed as the spearhead of a growing intellectual drive that would result in dissolving the ideological foundation of the traditional order.

The important fact is that the West played an indispensable role in making possible the challenge to the doctrine of three bonds and, thereby, the break of the four universalistic world views with the cosmological myth. For one thing, it confronted the Chinese intellectuals with an alternative order that forced them to see the contingency and even defectiveness of the basic institutions of their own order. This awareness of an alternative order no doubt played a part in all four cases in undermining their confidence in the legitimacy of their own order as hitherto enshrined in the doctrine of three bonds. But this direct cultural influence of the West must not lead us to overlook a more subtle, indirect, but no less significant, role the West played in bringing about the break between the universalism of the four world views and the cosmological myth. In short, I am arguing here that the contact with the West not only injected new ideas and values into the Chinese consciousness, but also had the catalytic effect of intensifying the internal tensions within the Chinese tradition to the point of making its elements of universalism incompatible with the "particularism" of its cosmological myth. To see this indirect, catalytic role of the West, we need to put the four world views in a historical perspective.

Each of these four world views featured a theme that was shaped by some universalistic ideas and perspectives from China's high tradition. These ideas and perspectives inevitably generate tensions with the particularistic orientation of the central values and institutions of the existing order. As Ernst Nolte puts it so aptly: "In all great societies throughout history, a universal doctrine and a particular reality have always lived in a precarious symbiosis."³ But the ideas and perspectives that make up the universal doctrine, typical of moral-spiritual symbolism in general, are multivalent. They can be understood and interpreted in different ways and hence carry different connotations and implications in them. As far as the tensions that these ideas and perspectives generated with the existing order are concerned, we can distinguish two kinds: (1) radical tensions generated by the connotations and implications that are incompatible with the central values and institutions and thereby tend to challenge and transcend them; and (2) the accommodative tensions generated by those connotations and implications that are reconcilable with central values and institutions. In this sense, both radical and accommodative tensions are inherent in these ideas and perspectives. True, over the centuries it is largely the accommodative tensions that have come to the fore. But, deep in the multivalent structure of these symbols and ideas, the radical tensions are still latent and occasionally have broken through to the surface. A brief look at the historical background of the three major indigenous developments of the late Ch'ing thought will clarify my point.

In the realm of noncanonical classical thought, philosophical Taoism stands out as the intellectual trend pregnant with universalistic and transcendental symbolism. Although Taoism's radical tension with the existing order was muted for most of its development, it did occasionally surface, as seen, for instance, in the sociopolitical anarchism of such Taoist intellectuals as Pao Ching-yen and Yuan Chi of the Age of Disunity and Wu-neng Tzu of the late T'ang.⁴ The dominance of the accommodative tensions in the spiritual symbolism of Taoism must not lead us to overlook the submerged potential for radical tensions in its multivalent structure.

The development of Mahayana Buddhism in China also generated a tension that was twofold in character. Mahayana Buddhism, with its radical other-worldliness, carried a relentless logic of negation that inevitably subjected any human institution to criticism and indictment. Consequently, it is little surprise that, after the introduction of Buddhism to China, the issue of whether Buddhist clerics should bow to the political and social authorities was long a focus of heated dispute. Although the issue was eventually resolved in a way that allowed accommodative orientations to predominate in Chinese Buddhism, the persistence of this dispute for an extended period of time clearly reflects the potential of radical tensions in the Buddhist tradition.⁵

In Confucianism, too, there exists a dual tension that can be seen in some key components of its "ethics of spiritual aspirations." One such component,

---
3. 1969: 531.
4. Hsiao Kung-chuan (1961, 3: 370–74, 426–32).
5. Ch'en (1973: 14–124).

for instance, is the Confucian ideal of *jen*. A basic issue involved in the development of this ideal is whether the ideal of a universal community could accommodate the Confucian emphasis on the family values. The answer of mainstream Confucianism, was, of course, the Mencian idea of graded love, signifying the indispensability of family values to the formation of a universal community. But this does not mean that its alternative—the idea of undifferentiated love—was excluded completely from the Confucian universe of meanings. It only means that the idea of undifferentiated love became the latent component, whereas the idea of graded love was predominant. Occasionally, however, the idea of undifferentiated love still manifested itself as an alternative, especially in neo-Confucian definitions of love, such as Chang Tsai's, which featured a strong mystical strain.[6] The presence of this alternative certainly meant a latent impulse in Confucianism to negate familism and other particularistic institutions of the existing social order.

Another example provided by the Confucian ethics of spiritual aspirations was the belief that every human being has the potential for moral fulfillment. Logically, this belief in the moral autonomy of the individual self can have libertarian and egalitarian implications. However, in mainstream neo-Confucianism, these radical implications remained largely submerged, and the idea was generally understood in a way that accommodated, rather than challenged, the existing order. Still, outside of mainstream Confucianism, radical implications are sometimes drawn, as can be seen, for example, in some of the developments in the so-called left-wing school of Wang Yang-ming in the late Ming.[7] This instance again reminds us of the twofold tensions inherent in Confucian moral thought.

In all three indigenous realms of meaning, both accommodative and radical tensions are inherent in their moral-spiritual symbolism. Although the accommodative tensions predominated in these indigenous traditions, the radical tensions were the latent strain. From this perspective, the significant fact apropos of the four intellectuals I study here is that the radical tensions now have come to the fore and become the dominant strain. The inevitable question is: Why this change now in the transitional generation? The answer must be sought in the effects of Western influences mentioned above.

A close examination of the four minds shows that their contacts with the West sometimes played the role of an ideological switchman that redirected their selective attention and sensitivity and focused their minds on certain radical implications of traditional ideas. In this way, Western ideas and values acted as a sort of cultural catalyst, reinforcing certain radical tensions

---

6. Ch'ien Mu (1978: 85–112).
7. de Bary (1970: 145–247).

inherent in the indigenous thought and thereby tipping the traditional balance to let the strains of radical tensions emerge as dominant. Taking account of this indirect, catalytic role, we begin to see that the combination of traditional thought and Western influences in certain novel ways partly accounts for the ideological challenges that the four world views posed to the foundation of traditional order. Although the Chinese tradition supplied the critical impulses from its inherent radical tensions, the West too played certain indirect, but nonetheless essential, roles in helping to release the radical tensions latent in the Chinese tradition. Consequently, the emphasis on the role of Chinese tradition in shaping the four minds must be accompanied by an equal stress on sensitivity to the various complex and subtle ways in which the West exerted its important impact.

What is the historical significance of the four world views as seen from the perspective of twentieth-century Chinese thought? To assess this significance, we have to make a distinction between the problems these minds grappled with and the answers they provided. As argued in this book, their world views were addressed to problems that stemmed largely from the crises of order in both political and orientational senses. These problems, however, were not unique for the transitional generation but a part of the cultural crisis that continued to face the intelligentsia of later generations. The quest for meaning and order, first exhibited in the development of four minds, can be found to lie behind much of the feverish interest shown by the twentieth-century Chinese intelligentsia in the modern ideologies and traditional thought. More important, this quest also had a lot to do with the tremendous appeal of such "political religions" as Communism and nationalism. In recent decades, these "political religions" seem to have lost much of their previous hold. The "crisis of faith" that has been going on in mainland China since the end of the Cultural Revolution is an eloquent testimony to this decline of political religions. In non-Communist China, this decline is also evident in the general indifference people have shown toward nationalism and the "Three Principles of the People." Inasmuch as political religions provide shelter from the crisis of meaning and order, their decline implies that the crisis probably exists in a form more acute than ever since the transitional generation.

Turning to the four world views as answers to the intellectual crises they faced, we find that the echoes among the later generations of Chinese intelligentsia are not as clear and strong. Nevertheless, the two moral-spiritual themes that stand out in these world views are symptomatic of twentieth-century Chinese thought in some significant ways. As mentioned before, the moral theme of consummatory process was expressed on two levels in the thought of the transitional generation. On the level of conceptions of man, the theme took the form of seeing life as a moral drama of fulfilling certain inherent ends and meanings of human existence. The specific Confucian concept of the moral end of the individual life—the idea of sagehood as the embodiment of moral perfection—still played a key role in the images of man held by K'ang Yu-wei and Liu Shih-p'ei. It is doubtful that this ideal of sagehood still had the same hold over Chinese intellectuals of the May Fourth generation, not to mention the post–May Fourth generations, except perhaps among small circles of neo-traditionalists.

However, some other aspects of the moral theme continued to be influential among Chinese intellectuals of later generations to a greater degree than the specific Confucian concept of the moral goal. In the first place, there is the very idea of life as a dramatic, consummatory process of commitment, striving, and fulfillment. Another closely related aspect is the view of moral fulfillment as an arduous process that requires cultivation of some special techniques and approaches to the discipline of mind and character. A third aspect is the belief that the moral cultivation of mind is the first prerequisite to social action in the world. Whatever social action may involve in the process, it must always start with moral cultivation. Because both K'ang and Liu still more or less accepted the Confucian belief that moral cultivation in the first instance means cultivation of mind, their belief in the primacy of moral cultivation implies belief in the primacy of consciousness or of the subjective force in shaping social and political actions.

Although the theme of consummatory process rarely appeared in its entirety in later developments in twentieth-century thought, the three aspects of it mentioned above, separately or together, found widespread resonance among Chinese intellectuals and politicians of all stripes. Many of them may not have been attracted by the specific Confucian goal of life that K'ang or Liu more or less accepted, but most still accepted the ideas associated with it. This was in fact the case, for instance, with both conservatives like Chiang Kai-shek and Yen Hsi-shan and radicals like Mao Tse-tung and Liu Shao-ch'i.[8]

What is the role of the theme of consummatory process in the twentieth-century Chinese concepts of society? As shown above, in the social thinking of both K'ang Yu-wei and Liu Shih-p'ei, this theme gave rise to a futuristic utopianism. Underlying their utopianism is a vision of a future universal society as the denouement of a moral drama playing out in history. However, each conceived the process of history differently. K'ang saw history as an inexorable march through determinate stages of a long process toward a predetermined end; Liu's fervent espousal of anarchism implied a view of history as a cataclysmic leap to a radically new future through revolutionary action. In the thought of K'ang and Liu, as in that of the transitional era as a whole, these two views of history are, by and large, kept separate from each

---

8. Lin Ta-chuang (1976: 6–9, 225–395); Yen Hsi-shan and Chao Tai-wen (1967: 1–108, 417–61); Li Jui (1979: 33–51); Liu Shao-ch'i (1969: 151–281).

other. In the subsequent decades, however, the two views tend to be fused into one of the most powerful ideological perspectives in modern China: millenarianism.

As for the theme of selfless oneness, a distinction needs to be made between the two forms—integral and limited—in which it existed in the minds of Chinese intellectuals. In its integral form, the theme featured a transcendentalism that ran afoul of the basically this-worldly temper of contemporary Chinese consciousness. Hence, it appeared only in some restricted circles, such as neo-Buddhism. In its limited form, the theme was expressed as an urge to dissolve the self into a larger whole, and it appeared widely among Chinese intellectuals of all persuasions. The group to whom the theme had its broadest appeal was the neo-traditionalists, as evidenced clearly in the writings of such representative figures as Hsiung Shih-li, Ma I-fu, and Liang Shu-ming.[9]

Even among radicals and liberals, it has found some echo. We now know that the two people who exerted the greatest influence on the early mind of Mao Tse-tung—Yang Ch'ang-chi and Li Ta-chao—were both admirers of T'an Ssu-t'ung.[10] In view of this, it is quite possible that the radical collectivism of Mao's thought may have owed something to the traditional ideal of immersion into a selfless whole. Even liberals, such as Ting Wen-chiang and Hu Shih, provide some evidence in their writings of resonance with the theme. In an essay published in *Tu-li p'ing-lun* (Independent critic) discussing his personal faith, Ting showed himself very much under the thrall of the ideal of a selfless whole.[11] Hu Shih, too, his individualism notwithstanding, felt no qualms about espousing an ideal that he called social immortality. In his view, a human individual that he called small self (*hsiao-wo*) can only fulfill himself by identifying with the larger self (*ta-wo*), the social whole.[12]

In these various ways, then, the two themes found echoes in the intellectual world of twentieth-century China. These echoes by no means signify simple and straight continuities with the world views that they represented. But they do mean that an examination of these four thinkers' world views can shed considerable light on some enduring characteristics of twentieth-century Chinese thought.

---

9. For a concise characterization of Hsiung Shih-li's thought in this regard, see Hsiung (1962, 3: 22a–23b, 46a–53a). For a brief discussion of Ma I-fu's thought, see Ho Ling (1947: 16–19). For this aspect of Liang Shu-ming's thought, see Liang Shu-ming (1963: 133–39).
10. Li Jui (1979: 33–51).
11. Hu Shih (1956: 55–59).
12. Hu Shih (1953, 1, chüan 4: 692–702).

Appendix

An Elegy by T'an Ssu-t'ung

Although we know that this life can last barely a hundred years, still we dream of living forever.
Although we shall die, we cannot give up this longing.
When autumn comes, the living leaves will wither; when the frost falls, the blossoms will wilt.
Who can believe that the young man in his health will depart from us forever?
How it breaks the parents' hearts to lose a son like this!

In the dark of the night, we listen for the village roosters to crow, and in the morning we watch for flooding on the roads.
The bier rolls to take you into the mountains.
This road does not lead to faraway places, nor are the mountains steep and craggy.
Then how can it be that, with a single wave of the hand, your voices and faces forever disappear?
The willow on the riverbank moves with remembering, and the grasses of the fields seem melancholy.
These are our most familiar places, yet it frightens me to visit them.
Why do they still frighten me, for the palace of the dead has already shut itself tight, already separated itself from our human world?

Now we feel the most painful grief at the death of a stranger whom we met on the road.
Just as the north wind withers the red flower, this tragedy of human death has grasped a single household!
What were once this same tree's branches, redolent of cassia and orchids, are now dust and ashes, covered everywhere by grasses, and chilled by frosts and dews.
This steep valley may become a hill, but your face can no longer be seen.

"Hsiang-hen tz'u pa-p'ien" 湘痕詞八篇 (Eight stanzas of the Hsiang-hen poems) 1954: 452–54.

There are also graves in these fields, but I see them only as presences from the other world.

He was once possessed by a heroic spirit and deep compassion for others; why has all this vanished, dissipated into the void?

He once had abundantly flowering talents, but now these gifts are darkly locked in the casket.

Who is it in the coffin?

O, it is the one whom I have loved all my life!

When I was a child, I knew nothing of death, thinking it was only a journey to a far-off land.

Even if it were only such a journey, how can a child feel the sorrow which attends this bitter separation?

The towering clouds disappear into the northwest, and the river water flows always to the southeast.

After flowing away in opposite directions, both clouds and water will never meet again.

Only then do I come to know life as floating clouds and water.

We once lived so closely together that we took our closeness for granted, but when we were about to leave each other, our hearts opened enormously with all our warm love for each other.

Aren't embroidered clothes warm enough for you? Now I long to cover you also with richly embellished fur coats.

And I only fear that you will not ask me for the most wonderful food and soup.

Our reluctance to leave each other must last only a moment, but still I hesitate to shake hands with you.

But, once you pass away, must you be inevitably abandoned, like the fallen pine trees?

The slender branches of the trees are just budding, knowing only that they share the same root.

The vines are entwined together, and they lean on each other as they grow.

But even brothers and sisters who grew together from the same root cannot protect each other, and so much less can they protect their spouses, children!

So we search everywhere and ask who can end this trouble and this wrong.

When we were young and small, we were joyfully together.

You loved me so much, and you expected so much from me too.

Thinking that your expectations were nothing to me, I stopped my ears as if I hated your voice.

But our joyful time together has come to an end, and I can no longer hear your wise voice.

O, we were together all day long; why have you now departed from me forever, as if you would forsake me?

Suddenly the heavy frost fell, and we followed paths which separated, came to live in different worlds.

Now I live in a large house, and you sleep in the wilderness.

When tragedy came to you, I could not substitute myself for you. I have been a brother to you in vain!

An Elegy by T'an Ssu-t'ung

The sunshine casts its rose light over the beautiful land; the birds sing in the depths of the woods; all of creation is exuberantly growing, but only I live with such a sad grief.
Who knows that springtime now turns into a withering fall?
The little girl plays and cries also; her loved ones laugh and adore her.
Although I came to see you every day, each day I also had to leave you.
My beloved one descended to earth in the frame of a body.
But her body no longer lives; let me at least offer a libation in memory of you.
Perhaps from the other side of the world, you will turn to see me now.

We must accept life with patience, not permitting our minds to be moved by what is outside of them.
How can mere things affect the sorrow and joy which we feel in our hearts?
And even these things presented to us from those now dead cannot give us our loved ones' deepest feelings, and their time with us only makes this sorrow linger painfully now.
With a heavy heart, I lived out this endless day, only to hate my life for the burden it has become to me!
I used to dream that I was crying in my chair.
When the morning wind rushed resoundingly through the forest, I woke and felt joy to know that this had been merely a dream.
Now, suddenly, my dream has come to be terribly true.
Now, how do I know that these present tragedies might not also be a bad dream?
But I can believe this only for a moment, for I know there are differences between life awake and life in a dream.
If you want to feel the remorse felt by the dead, watch the cuckoo crying blood from its eyes.
Only listen to the lone swan; then you will know the feelings of one who is still alive.

Glossary

an-hsin li-ming 安心立命
Anhui 安徽

Ch'an 禪
Chang Chih-tung 張之洞
Chang Tsai 張載
Ch'ang-hsing hsüeh-chi 長興學記
Ch'ang-hsing hsüeh-she 長興學舍
Chekiang 浙江
chen-chün 眞君
chen-hsin 眞心
chen-tsai 眞宰
Ch'en Fu-ch'en 陳黻宸
cheng 政
cheng-chiao ho-i 政教合一
cheng-hsin 正心
cheng-i chih fan-k'ang 正義之反抗
Cheng meng 正蒙
Cheng Ssu-hsiao 鄭思肖
ch'eng 誠
Ch'eng Hao 程灝
ch'eng-hsin 成心
ch'eng-i 誠意
Ch'iang-hsüeh hui 強學會

chi-shen ti lun-li	己身的倫理
ch'i	氣
ch'i-shih-chien	器世間
ch'i-wu lun	齊物論
Chia-t'ing ko-ming	家庭革命
chiao	教
Chiao-hsüeh t'ung-i	教學通議
chien-ai	兼愛
chien-min	賤民
chien-wen chih chih	見聞之知
chih-ch'i	知氣
chih-ch'ing	治情
chih-hui	智慧
chih-p'ing	治平
chih-shan	至善
chih-shih	治事
chih-yen	治言
chih-yung	致用
ch'in-shou chih kuo	禽獸之國
ching	靜
ching-i	經義
ching-shih	經世
Ching-shih pao	經世報
ch'ing	情
chiu-min	救民
chiu-shih	救世
Ch'iu shu	訄書
Chou-li	周禮
Chu I-hsin	朱一新
chu-tzu hsüeh	諸子學
Chu-tzu hsüeh lüeh shuo	諸子學略說
Chu-tzu p'ing-i	諸子平議
Chu Tz'u-ch'i	朱次琦
ch'u-shih	處識
chü-jen	舉人
chü-lo	聚落
chü-luan	據亂
chü-sheng wo	俱生我
Ch'üan-hsüeh p'ien	勸學篇

Glossary

ch'üan-li	權力
Chuang Tzu	莊子
chüeh-min	覺民
Ch'un-ch'iu	春秋
ch'ün	群
Ch'ün-ching p'ing-i	群經平議
Chung-kuo min yüeh ching-i	中國民約精義
chung-tsu ko-ming	種族革命
chung-tzu	種子
Fa-hsiang	法相
Fa-tsang	法藏
fen	分
fen-pieh	分別
fen-pieh wo	分別我
feng-chien	封建
Feng Kuei-fen	馮桂芬
fu-ch'iang	富強
fu-ch'ou	復仇
Han-shan Teh-ch'ing	韓山德清
Han-Sung ho liu	漢宋合流
han-yang	涵養
Han Yü	韓愈
hao-jan chih ch'i	浩然之氣
hao-sheng hsin	好勝心
Heng pao	衡報
hsi-li	吸力
Hsi-ming	西銘
hsiang	相
hsiang-fen	相分
hsiang-shih	相識
hsiao-k'ang	小康
hsiao-wo	小我
hsiao-yao yu	逍遙遊
hsien-chüeh	先覺
hsin	心
hsin-li	心力
Hsin-min shuo	新民說

hsin-tang	新黨
hsing	性
hsiu-shen	修身
Hsü Chi-yü	徐繼畬
Hsüeh Fu-ch'eng	薛福成
Hsüeh-hai t'ang	學海堂
Hsün Tzu	荀子
Hua-Hsia chih kuo	華夏之國
Hua-yen	華嚴
huan-hsiang	幻相
Huang I-chou	黃以周
Huang-ti	黃帝
Huang Tsung-hsi	黃宗羲
hui-shu	惠恕
hun-ch'i	魂氣
hun-ling	魂靈
I-cheng	儀徵
i hsin wan-chieh	以心挽劫
i shih wei li	以勢為理
i-t'ai	以太
I-t'ai shuo	以太說
i-ti chih kuo	夷狄之國
i-to hsiang-yung	一多相容
Jang shu	攘書
jen	仁
jen-ai	仁愛
jen-ch'ing chih-k'u	人情之苦
jen-hsin	人心
Jen-hsüeh	仁學
jen hua wu	人化物
jen-i chih shih	仁義之師
jen jen yu tzu-chu chih ch'üan	人人有自主之權
jen-sheng chih k'u	人生之苦
jen-tao chih k'u	人道之苦
jen wu-wo fa wu-wo	人無我法無我
jih-hsin	日新
jou	柔
Ju-shu chen-lun	儒術真論

kai-chih	改制
K'ang-tzu nei-wai p'ien	康子內外篇
Kao Hsüeh-chih	高學治
ko-ming	革命
ko-ming ti tao-teh	革命的道德
ko-wu	格物
k'o-chi tuan-ssu	克己斷私
Ku-ching ching-she	詁經精舍
Ku Yen-wu	顧炎武
k'u	苦
kuang-fu	光復
kung	公
kung-fu	工夫
kung-teh	公德
kung-yang	公羊
kuo-chia	國家
Kuo Sung-t'ao	郭嵩燾
kuo-ts'ui	國粹
Kuo-ts'ui hsüeh-pao	國粹學報
Kuo-yü	國語
li	理
Li	禮
Li chi	禮記
Li-hsüeh tzu-i t'ung-shih	理學字義通釋
li-i chih ming	理義之命
li-i fen-shu	理一分殊
Li-yün	禮運
Li-yün chu	禮運注
ling-hun	靈魂
Ling T'ing-k'an	凌廷堪
liu-ch'u sheng-ch'en	六畜升沉
Liu Shao-ch'i	劉少奇
Liu Wen-ch'i	劉文淇
lo	樂
Lü K'un	呂坤
luan	亂
lun-li	倫理
Lun-li hsüeh chiao-k'o shu	倫理學教科書
Lu-Wang	陸王

Glossary

min	民
Min-pao	民報
min-pao wu-yü	民胞物與
ming	命
ming-fen	名分
ming-shu chih ming	命術之命
ming-teh	明德
ming-wei	名位
mo-shih	末世
Mo Tzu	墨子
Nan-pei shih	南北史
nung-jen ko-ming	農人革命
pa	霸
Pao Ching-yen	鮑敬言
Pao Shih-ch'en	包世臣
Pei tien p'ien	悲佃篇
pen-t'i	本體
pen-yu chung-tzu	本有種子
P'eng Shao-sheng	彭紹升
pien-fa	變法
p'o-chih	魄質
pu-tung hsin	不動心
san-chiao ho-i	三教合一
san-kang	三綱
san-kang wu-ch'ang	三綱五常
san-shih i-shih	三世一時
sang-wo	喪我
shang-chan	商戰
Shang Yang	商鞅
she	奢
she-hui chu-i chiang-hsi-hui	社會主義講習會
shen-ch'i	神氣
shen-ming	神明
shen-nung	神農
shen-tu	慎獨
Sheng-ch'ao hsün-yang lu	勝朝殉揚錄
sheng-jen	聖人

sheng-p'ing	升平
sheng sheng pu-i	生生不已
sheng-yüan	生員
shih	實
shih-ch'i chung-tzu	始起種子
shih-hsüeh	實學
Shih K'o-fa	史可法
Shih-li kung-fa	實理公法
shih-shih	時識
shih-t'ien	事天
Shih-wu pao	時務報
shou-lien	收斂
shu-shih	數識
ssu	私
Sun Ch'iang-ming	孫鏘鳴
Sun I-jang	孫詒讓
Sun I-yen	孫衣言
Sung	宋
ta-t'ung	大同
ta-wo	大我
Tai Chen	戴震
t'ai-chi	太極
T'ai-chou	泰州
t'ai-p'ing	太平
T'an Hsien	譚獻
tao	道
tao-hsin	道心
tao tao chih shih	道道之世
tao t'ung wei i	道通為一
teh-hsing	德性
teh-hsing chih chih	德性之知
ti-ch'iu chih chih	地球之治
t'i-p'o	體魄
Tien Yee (*T'ien-i pao*)	天義
t'ien	天
t'ien-chih	天志
t'ien-hsia	天下
t'ien-hsia i-chia	天下一家
t'ien-i	天義

T'ien-i pao	天義報
t'ien-jen ho-i	天人合一
t'ien-li	天理
T'ien-lun p'ien	天論篇
t'ien-min	天民
T'ien-t'ai	天台
t'ien-ti wang lai chih ch'i	天地往來之氣
ts'ang-jan chih kan	蒼然之感
tsao-ming	造命
tsao-t'ien	造天
Tseng Kuo-fan	曾國藩
tso-ch'an	坐禪
tsui ch'ing-ching hsin	最清淨心
tsung-fa	宗法
Tu-li p'ing-lun	獨立評論
t'u-hao	土豪
Tung Chung-shu	董仲舒
t'ung	通
T'ung-chih	同治
t'ung hsia-ch'ing	通下情
tzu ch'iang	自強
tzu-jan kuei-tse	自然規則
Tzu Yu	子游
tzu yu	自由
wan-ch'üan chih jen	完全之人
wan-ch'üan ti she-hui	完全的社會
Wan-mu ts'ao-t'ang k'ou-shuo	萬木草堂口說
Wang An-shih	王安石
Wang Chin	汪縉
Wang Chung	汪中
Wang Fu-chih	王夫之
Wang Ken	王艮
Wang Yang-ming	王陽明
Wei Yüan	魏源
wo-man hsin	我慢心
wu-ch'ang	五常
wu-chin yüan-ch'i	無盡緣起
wu-hua	物化

wu-tai	無待
Wu-wu lun	五無論
yang-ch'i	養氣
Yangchou	揚州
Yang-chou shih-jih chi	揚州十日記
yang-hsin	養心
Yang-min ch'üeh-lu lu	揚民却虜錄
Yang Wen-hui	楊文會
yeh-shih	業識
Yen Hsi-shan	閻錫山
Yen Yüan	顏元
yin-kuo shih	因果識
yin-tun	隱遁
yin-yang	陰陽
yu-ch'ing shih-chien	有情世間
yu-tai	有待
Yü-hang	餘杭
Yü Yüeh	余樾
yüan-ch'i	元氣
yüan-su	元素
Yüeh-hsüeh	粵學
Yün-ch'i Chu-hung	雲棲袾宏

Bibliography

WORKS BY K'ANG YU-WEI 康有為

1917. *Ch'un-ch'iu pi-hsüeh ta-i wei-yen k'ao* 春秋筆削大義微言考 [A study of the major principles and hidden meanings in the emended *Annals of Spring and Autumn*]. In *Wan-mu ts'ao-t'ang ts'ung-shu* 萬木草堂叢書 [The collected works of the thatched hut among ten thousand trees].

1947. *K'ang-tzu nei-wai p'ien ch'ao-pen* 康子內外篇抄本 [The handwritten copy of the inner and outer books of the philosopher K'ang]. Hoover Institution Library.

1956. *Ta-t'ung shu* 大同書 [The book on the ideal of grand unity]. Shanghai.

1960. "Ta Chu Jung-sheng hsien-sheng shu" 答朱榕生先生書 [A letter in reply to Mr. Chu I-hsin]. In *Wan-mu ts'ao-t'ang i-kao* 萬木草堂遺稿 [Unpublished works from the thatched hut among ten thousand trees]. Ed. by K'ang T'ung-pi 康同璧. Mimeo, Peking.

1968a. *Chung-yung chu* 中庸注 [The doctrine of the mean annotated]. Taipei.

1968b. *Meng-tzu wei* 孟子微 [Esoteric meanings of the Mencius]. Taipei.

1969. *Ch'un-ch'iu Tung-shih hsüeh* 春秋董氏學 [Tung Chung-shu's study of the *Annals of Spring and Autumn*]. Taipei.

1976a. *Wan-mu ts'ao-t'ang i-kao* 萬木草堂遺稿 [Unpublished works from the thatched hut among ten thousand trees]. Ed. by Chiang Kuei-lin 蔣貴麟. Taipei.

1976b. *Wan-mu ts'ao-t'ang i-kao wai-p'ien* 萬木草堂遺稿外篇 [Additions to the unpublished works from the thatched hut among ten thousand trees]. Ed. by Chiang Kuei-lin 蔣貴麟. 2 vols. Taipei.

1976c. *K'ang Nan-hai hsien-sheng i-chu hui-k'an* 康南海先生遺著彙刊 [The collected works of K'ang Yu-wei]. Ed. by Chiang Kuei-lin 蔣貴麟. Taipei.

WORKS BY T'AN SSU-T'UNG 譚嗣同

1954. *T'an Ssu-t'ung ch'üan-chi* 譚嗣同全集 [The complete collection of T'an Ssu-t'ung's writings]. Peking.

WORKS BY CHANG PING-LIN 章炳麟

1906. "Yen-shuo lu" 演説録 [A speech text]. *Min pao* 民報 (The people), no. 6 (July 23).
1914. *Chang-T'an ho-ch'ao* 章譚合鈔 [A joint collection of writings by Chang Ping-lin and T'an Ssu-t'ung]. Shanghai.
1919. *Chang-shih ts'ung-shu* 章氏叢書 [The collected writings of Chang Ping-lin]. Hangchou, Chekiang Library.
1965. *T'ai-yen hsien-sheng tzu-ting nien-p'u* 太炎先生自訂年譜 [A chronological autobiography of Chang Ping-lin]. Hong Kong.
1968. *Ch'iu shu* 訄書 [Book of raillery]. Taipei. (2nd ed., 1904)
1977. *Chang T'ai-yen cheng-lun hsüan-chi* 章太炎政論選集 [Selected political essays by Chang Ping-lin]. Ed. by T'ang Chih-chün 湯志鈞. Peking.
1978. *Ch'iu shu* 訄書 [Book of raillery]. Taipei. (1st ed., 1900)
1981. *Chang T'ai-yen hsüan-chi* 章太炎選集 [Selected writings of Chang Ping-lin]. Ed. by Chu Wei-cheng and Chiang I-hua. Shanghai.

WORKS BY LIU SHIH-P'EI 劉師培

1963a. "Fei-ping fei-ts'ai lun" 非兵非財論 [On the abolishment of the military and wealth]. In *Hsin-hai ko-ming ch'ien-shih-nien chien shih-lun hsüan-chi* 辛亥革命前十年間時論選集 [A collection of essays on current affairs during the ten years before the Revolution of 1911]. Ed. by Chang Nan 張枬 and Wang Jen-chih 王忍之. Vol. 2, no. 2. Peking.
1963b. "Wu cheng-fu chu-i chih p'ing-teng kuan" 無政府主義之平等觀 [The egalitarian outlook of anarchism]. In *Hsin-hai ko-ming ch'ien-shih-nien chien shih-lun hsüan-chi*.
1965. *Liu Shen-shu hsien-sheng i-shu* 劉申叔先生遺書 [The collected writings of Liu Shih-p'ei]. 4 vols. Taipei.

WORKS BY OTHER AUTHORS

Bellah, Robert N. 1965. "Ienaga Saburo and the Search for Meaning in Modern Japan." In *Changing Japanese Attitudes Toward Modernization*, ed. by Marius B. Jansen. Princeton, N.J.
Bennett, Adrian A., and Kwang-ching Liu. 1974. "Christianity in the Chinese Idiom: Young J. Allen and the Early Chiao-hui hsin-pao, 1868–1870." In *The Missionary Enterprise in China and America*, ed. by John K. Fairbank. Cambridge, Mass.
Berlin, Isaiah. 1969. *Four Essays on Liberty*. Oxford, England.
Berling, Judith A. 1980. *The Syncretic Religion of Lin Chao-en*. New York.
Bernal, Martin. 1976. *Chinese Socialism to 1907*. Ithaca, N.Y.
Chan Wing-tsit. 1963. *A Source Book in Chinese Philosophy*. Princeton, N.J.
Chang Chih-tung 張之洞. 1966. *Ch'üan-hsüeh p'ien* 勸學篇 [Exhortation to study].
Chang Ch'i-chih 張豈之. 1965. "Lun Wang Fu-chih ti *Chang-tzu cheng-meng chu*" 論王夫之的張子正蒙注 [On Wang Fu-chih's commentaries on Chang Tsai's *Correct Teaching for Beginners*]. In *Wang Ch'uan-shan hsüeh-shu t'ao-lun chi*.

Chang Hao. 1971. *Liang Ch'i-ch'ao and Intellectual Transition in China*. Cambridge, Mass.

———. 1974. "On the *ching-shih* Idea in Neo-Confucianism." In *Ch'ing-shih wen-t'i* 3, no. 1 (Nov.).

———. 1980. "Intellectual Change and the Reform Movement, 1890–1898." In *The Cambridge History of China*, vol. 2, *Late Ch'ing, 1800–1911*, pt. 2, ed. by John K. Fairbank and Kwang-ching Liu. Cambridge, England.

Chang P'eng-yuan 張朋園. 1964. *Liang Ch'i-ch'ao yü Ch'ing-chi ko-ming* 梁啟超與清季革命 [Liang Ch'i-ch'ao and the Late Ch'ing Revolution]. Taipei.

Chang Shun-hui 張舜徽. 1962. *Ch'ing-tai Yang-chou hsüeh-chi* 清代揚州學記 [A study of Yang-chou scholarship in the Ch'ing dynasty]. Shanghai.

Chang Teh-chün 張德鈞. 1974. "T'an Ssu-t'ung ssu-hsiang shu-p'ing" 譚嗣同思想述評 [A critical account of T'an Ssu-t'ung's thought]. In *Chung-kuo chin san-pai-nien hsüeh-shu ssu-hsiang lun-chi* 中國近三百年學術思想論集 [A collection of essays on Chinese scholarship and thought in the past three hundred years]. Hong Kong, "chia-chi" 甲集.

Ch'en Chih 陳熾. 1970. *Yung Shu* 庸書. Taipei.

Ch'en Ch'iu 陳虯. 1893. *Chih-p'ing t'ung-i* 治平通議 [A general discussion of setting state and world in order]. Yung-chia.

Ch'en Ch'i-yün. 1962. "Liang Ch'i-ch'ao's 'Missionary Education': A Case Study of Missionary Influence on the Reformers." In *Papers on China* 16: 111–13. Harvard University, East Asian Research Center.

Ch'en, Kenneth K. S. 1973. *The Chinese Transformation of Buddhism*. Princeton, N.J.

Cheng Kuan-ying 鄭觀應. 1896. *Sheng-shih wei-yen* 盛世危言 (Warnings to a prosperous age].

Ch'eng Chung-ying. 1979. "Practical Learning in Yen Yuan, Chu Hsi and Wang Yang-ming." In *Principle and Practicality: Essays in Neo-Confucianism and Practical Learning*, ed. by Wm. Theodore de Bary and Irene Bloom. New York.

Chi Wen-fu 稽文甫. 1962. *Wang Ch'uan-shan hsüeh-shu lun-ts'ung* 王船山學術論叢 [A collection of essays on Wang Fu-chih]. Peking.

Ch'i Ping-feng 亓冰峯. 1964. *Ch'ing-mo ko-ming yü chün-hsien ti lun-cheng* 清末革命與君憲的論爭 [The controversy over revolution and constitutional monarchy toward the end of the Ch'ing dynasty]. Taipei.

Chiang Wei-ch'iao 蔣維喬. 1972. *Chung-kuo chin san-pai-nien che-hsüeh-shih* 中國近三百年哲學史 [A history of Chinese philosophy in the past three hundred years]. Taipei.

Chien Ch'ao-liang 簡朝亮. 1964. "Chu Chiu-chiang hsien-sheng nien-p'u" 朱九江先生年譜 [A chronological biography of Chu Tz'u-ch'i]. In *Chu Chiu-chiang hsien-sheng chi* 朱九江先生集 [A collection of Chu Tz'u-ch'i's writings], ed. by Chien Ch'ao-liang. Taipei.

Ch'ien Mu 錢穆. 1958. "K'ung-tzu yü Ch'un-ch'iu" 孔子與春秋 [Confucius and the *Annals of Spring and Autumn*]. In *Liang-Han ching-hsüeh chin-ku wen p'ing-i* 兩漢經學今古文平議 [Essays on the new text and the ancient text studies of the Confucian canons of both the former and the later Han dynasties]. Hong Kong.

———. 1964. *Chung-kuo chin san-pai-nien hsüeh-shu shih* 中國近三百年學術史 [A history of Chinese scholarship in the past three hundred years]. 2 vols. Taipei.

———. 1966. *Hsüeh-yüeh* 學籥 [The key to scholarship]. Hong Kong.

———. 1971. *Chu-tzu hsin hsüeh-an* 朱子新學案 [A new study of Chu-tzu's scholarship]. 6 vols. Taipei.

———. 1978. "Cheng meng ta-i fa-wei" 正蒙大義發微 [An interpretation of the general meaning of the *Correct Teachings for Beginners*]. In *Chung-kuo hsüeh-shu ssu-hsiang lun-ts'ung* 中國學術思想論叢 [Collection of essays of the history of Chinese scholarship and ideas]. Taipei.

Chih-hsin mien ping fa 治心免病法 [The prevention of illness through the cure of mind]. 1896. Shanghai.

Ching, Julia. 1976. *To Acquire Wisdom: The Way of Wang Yang-ming*. New York.

Ching-chung jih-pao 警鐘日報 [Alarming Bell Daily News]. 1968. Photographic rept. Taiwan.

Ching-shih pao 經世報 [Journal of practical statesmanship]. 1897. Hangchou.

Chou Fu-ch'eng 周輔成. 1962. *Lun Tung Chung-shu ssu-hsiang* 論董仲舒思想 [On Tung Chung-shu's thought]. Shanghai.

Chou Tse-tsung. 1960. "Anti-Confucianism in Early Republican China." In *The Confucian Persuasion*, ed. Arthur F. Wright. Stanford.

Chou Yü-t'ung 周予同. 1926. *Ching chin ku wen hsüeh* 經今古文學 [New text and ancient text scholarship of Confucian canons]. Shanghai.

Chu Hsi 朱熹. 1970. *Chu Tzu yü-lei* 朱子語類 [Classified conversations of Master Chu]. Taipei.

Chuang Tzu. 1968. *The Complete Works of Chuang Tzu*. Trans. by Burton Watson. New York.

Chung-kuo chin san-pai-nien hsüeh-shu ssu-hsiang lun-chi 中國近三百年學術思想論集 [A collection of essays on Chinese scholarship and thought in the past three hundred years] 5, A&B. 1974. Hong Kong.

Chung-kuo chin-tai ssu-hsiang-shih lun-wen chi 中國近代思想史論文集 [A collection of essays on the history of modern Chinese thought]. 1958. Shanghai.

Ch'u Po-ssu 褚柏思. 1973. *Fo-men jen-wu chih* 佛門人物志 [Notes on Buddhist notables]. Taipei.

de Bary, William Theodore. 1970. "Individualism and Humanitarianism in Late Ming Thought." In *Self and Society in Ming Thought*, ed. by de Bary and the Conference on Ming Thought. New York.

———. 1981. *Neo-Confucian Orthodoxy and the Learning of the Mind-and-Heart*. New York.

Eastman, Lloyd E. 1968. "Political Reformism in China before the Sino-Japanese War." *Journal of Asian Studies* 27 (Aug.).

Elman, Benjamin A. 1978. "The Hsüeh-hai T'ang and the Rise of New Text Philology in Canton." Unpublished paper.

———. 1984. *From Philosophy to Philology: Intellectual and Social Aspects of Change in Late Imperial China*. Harvard East Asian Monograph, Cambridge, Mass.

Feng Yu-lan 馮友蘭. 1959. *Chung-kuo ssu-hsiang-shih* 中國思想史 [A history of Chinese philosophy]. Hong Kong.

Gasster, Michael. 1969. *Chinese Intellectuals and the Revolution of 1911: The Birth of Modern Chinese Radicalism*. Seattle.

Geertz, Clifford. 1973. *The Interpretation of Cultures*. New York.

Ho Lin 賀麟. 1947. *Tang tai Chung-kuo che-hsüeh* 當代中國哲學 [The contemporary Chinese philosophies]. Nanking.
Hou Wai-lu 侯外廬. 1958. *Chung-kuo ssu-hsiang t'ung-shih* 中國思想通史 [A general history of Chinese thought]. Peking.
Howard, Richard C. 1962. "K'ang Yu-wei (1858–1927): His Intellectual Background and Early Thought." In *Confucian Personalities*, ed. by Arthur F. Wright and Denis Twitchett. Stanford.
———. 1967. "Japan's Role in the Reform Program of K'ang Yu-wei." In *K'ang Yu-wei: A Biography and a Symposium*, ed. by Lo Jung-pang. Tucson.
Hsiao Chieh-fu 肖箑父. 1965. "Wang Fu-chih ssu-hsiang ch'u-t'an" 王夫之思想初探 [An initial exploration of Wang Fu-chih's thought]. In *Wang Ch'uan-shan hsüeh-shu t'ao-lun chi*.
Hsiao Kung-chuan. 1961. *Chung-kuo cheng-chih ssu-hsiang-shih* 中國政治思想史 [A history of Chinese political thought]. 6 vols. Taipei.
———. 1967. "K'ang Yu-wei's Excursion into Science: Lectures on the Heavens." In *K'ang Yu-wei*, ed. by Lo Jung-pang.
———. 1975. *A Modern China and a New World: K'ang Yu-wei, Reformer and Utopian 1858–1927*. Seattle.
Hsin-hai ko-ming ch'ien-shih-nien chien shih-lun hsüan-chi 辛亥革命前十年間時論選集 [A collection of essays on current affairs during the ten years before the Revolution of 1911]. 1963. Ed. by Chang Nan 張枬 and Wang Jen-chih 王忍之. Peking.
Hsiung Shih-li 熊十力. 1962. *Shih-li yü-yao* 十力語要 [The essential sayings of Hsiung Shih-li]. Taipei.
Hummel, Arthur W. 1943. *Eminent Chinese of the Ch'ing Period*. Washington.
Hu Shih 胡適. 1953. "Pu-hsiu, wo ti tsung-chiao" 不朽, 我的宗教 (Immortality, my religion]. In *Hu Shih wen-ts'un* 胡適文存 [Collected essays of Hu Shih], I, chüan 4: 693–702. Taipei.
———. 1956. *Ting Wen-chiang ti chuan chi* 丁文江的傳記 [A biography of Ting Wen-chiang]. Taipei, Academia Sinica.
Ku Chieh-kang 顧頡剛. 1957. *Ch'in-Han ti fang-shih yü ju-sheng* 秦漢的方士與儒生 [The Occultists and Confucianists of the Ch'in and Han dynasties]. Shanghai.
———. 1970. *Wu-teh chung-shih hsia ti cheng-chih ho li-shih* 五德終始下的政治和歷史 [Politics and history under the doctrine of five elements]. Hong Kong.
Lai, Whalen W. 1982. "K'ang Yu-wei from 1879 to 1893: From Enlightenment to Utopian Sagehood." Unpublished paper, March.
Langer, Suzanne K. 1951. *Philosophy in a New Key*. A Mentor Book, New York.
Lei Hai-tsung 雷海宗. 1968. *Chung-kuo wen-hua yü chung-kuo ti ping* 中國文化與中國的兵 [The Chinese culture and the Chinese soldier]. Hong Kong.
Levenson, Joseph R. 1958. *Confucian China and Its Modern Fate*. Berkeley.
Li Jui 李銳. 1979. "Ch'ing-nien Mao Tse-tung ti ssu-hsiang fang-hsiang" 青年毛澤東的思想方向 [The direction of young Mao Tse-tung's intellectual development]. In *Lishi yanjiu* 歷史研究, vol. 1.
Li San Pao 李三寶. 1975. "*K'ang-tzu nei-wai p'ien* ch'u-pu fen-hsi—K'ang Nan-hai hsien-ts'un tsui-tsao tso-p'in" 康子內外篇初步分析—康南海現存最早

作品 [A preliminary analysis of K'ang Yu-wei's earliest extant essay, *K'ang-Tzu nei-wai p'ien*]. In *Ch'ing-Hua hsüeh-pao* 清華學報 [Tsing Hua Journal of Chinese Studies], n.s. 11, nos. 1, 2 (Dec.): 213–47.

Li Tse-hou 李澤厚. 1958. *K'ang Yu-wei T'an Ssu-t'ung ssu-hsiang yen-chiu* 康有爲譚嗣同思想研究 [A study of the thought of K'ang Yu-wei and T'an Ssu-t'ung]. Shanghai.

Liang Ch'i-ch'ao 梁啓超. 1896. *Hsi-hsüeh shu-mu-piao* 西學書目表 [A bibliography of Western learning]. In *Chih-hsüeh ts'ung-shu ch'u-chi* 質學叢書初集 [Works of substantial learning], 1st ser. ts'e 9–10.

―――. 1936. *Yin-ping-shih ho-chi, chuan-chi* 飲冰室合集、專集 [Collected works and essays from the Ice-drinker's Studio: Collected works] and *Yin-ping-shih ho-chi, wen-chi* 飲冰室合集、文集 [Collected works and essays from the Ice-drinker's Studio: Collected essays]. Shanghai.

―――. 1956. *Chung-kuo chin san-pai-nien hsüeh-shu shih* 中國近三百年學術史 [An intellectual history of China during the past three hundred years]. Taipei.

―――. 1963. *Ch'ing-tai hsüeh-shu kai-lun* 清代學術概論 [Intellectual trends in the Ch'ing dynasty]. Hong Kong.

Liang Shu-ming 梁漱溟. 1963. *Chung-kuo wen-hua yao-i* 中國文化要義 [The essence of Chinese culture]. Hong Kong.

Lin Kuo-p'ing 林國平. 1965. "Shih t'an Wang Fu-chih ti fa-chan kuan" 試探王夫之的發展觀 [An exploratory study of Wang Fu-chih's view of developmental change]. In *Wang Ch'uan-shan hsüeh-shu t'ao-lun chi*.

Lin Ta-chuang 林大椿, ed. 1976. *Tsung-t'ung Chiang-kung hsüeh-shu ssu-hsiang t'an-yüan* 總統蔣公學術思想探源 [An inquiry into the origin of President Chiang's scholarship and thought]. Taipei.

Liu Shao-ch'i. 1969. "How To Be a Good Communist." In *Collected Works of Liu Shao Ch'i, Before 1944*. Hong Kong.

Lo Jung-pang, ed. 1967. *K'ang Yu-wei: A Biography and a Symposium*. Tucson.

Lu Hsün 魯迅. 1961. "Kuan-yü T'ai-yen hsien-sheng erh-san shih" 關於太炎先生二三事 [Concerning a few events in Chang Ping-lin's life]. In *Lu Hsün ch'üan chi* 魯迅全集 [A complete collection of Lu Hsün's writings], vol. 6. Peking.

Lu Pao-ch'ien 陸寶千. 1978. *Ch'ing-tai ssu-hsiang shih* 清代思想史 [An intellectual history of the Ch'ing dynasty]. Taipei.

McMorran, Ian. 1975. "Wang Fu-chih and the Neo-Confucian Tradition." In *The Unfolding of Neo-Confucianism*, ed. by de Bary and the Conference on Seventeenth-Century Chinese Thought. New York.

Metzger, Thomas A. 1977. *Escape From Predicament: Neo-Confucianism and China's Evolving Political Culture*. New York.

Mou Tsung-san 牟宗三. 1963. *Chung-kuo che-hsüeh ti t'eh-chih* 中國哲學的特質 [The characteristics of Chinese philosophy]. Hong Kong.

―――. 1968. *Hsin-t'i yü hsing-t'i* 心體與性體 [The substance of mind and the substance of nature]. Taipei.

Munro, Donald J. 1969. *The Concept of Man in Early China*. Stanford.

Nolte, Ernst. 1969. *Three Faces of Fascism*. New American Library.

Onogawa Hidemi 小野川秀美. 1960. *Shimmatsu seiji shisō kenkyū* 清末政治思想研究 [Studies in the political thought of the late Ch'ing]. Kyoto.

Parker, Gail Thain. 1973. *Mind Cure in New England*. Hanover, N. H.
Price, Don C. 1974. *Russia and the Roots of the Chinese Revolution*. Cambridge, Mass.
Rankin, Mary B. 1971. *Early Chinese Revolutionaries: Radical Intellectuals in Shanghai and Chekiang 1902–1911*. Cambridge, Mass.
Ronan, Colin A. 1978. *The Shorter Science and Civilization in China: An Abridgement of Joseph Needham's Original Text*. Cambridge, Mass.
Schneider, Laurence A. 1976. "National Essence and the New Intelligentsia." In *The Limits of Change: Essays on Conservative Alternatives in Republican China*, ed. by Charlotte Furth. Cambridge, Mass.
Schwartz, Benjamin, 1959. "Some Polarities in Confucian Thought." In *Confucianism in Action*, ed. by David S. Nivison and Arthur F. Wright. Stanford.
———. 1972. "The Limits of Tradition versus Modernity as Categories of Explanation: The Case of Chinese Intellectuals." *Daedalus*, Spring, pp. 71–88.
Shek, Richard H. 1976. "Some Western Influences of T'an Ssu-t'ung's Thought." In *Reform in Nineteenth-Century China*, ed. by Paul A. Cohen and John E. Schrecker. East Asian Research Center, Harvard University.
Su Yü 蘇輿. 1970. *I-chiao ts'ung-pien* 翼教叢編 [The collection of writings for promoting sacred teachings]. Taipei.
Su Yüan-lei 蘇淵雷. 1947. *Sung P'ing-tzu p'ing-chuan* 宋平子評傳 [A critical biography of Sung Shu]. Shanghai.
Sung Shu 宋恕. 1928. *Liu-chai pei-i* 六齋卑議 [The humble proposals of Sung Shu]. Yung-chia. In *Ching-hsiang-lou*, ser. 10.
Sung Yü-jen 宋育仁. 1897. *Ts'ai-feng chi* 采風記 [Notes on customs and mores].
T'an Shuang-ch'üan 譚雙泉. 1965. "Wang Ch'uan-shan lun chih yü hsing" 王船山論知與行 [Wang Fu-chih on knowledge and practice]. In *Wang Ch'uan-shan hsüeh-shu t'ao-lun chi*.
T'ang Chih-chün 湯志鈞. 1957. *Wu-hsü pien-fa shih lun-ts'ung* 戊戌變法史論叢 [A collection of essays on the reform movement of 1898]. Wuhan.
———. 1974a. "Hsin-hai ko-ming ch'ien Chang Ping-lin hsüeh-shu ssu-hsiang p'ing-chia" 辛亥革命前章炳麟學術思想評價 [An evaluation of Chang Ping-lin's scholarship and thought in the period prior to the Revolution of 1911]. In *Chung-kuo chin san-pai-nien hsüeh-shu ssu-hsiang lun-chi*, no. 5.
———. 1974b. "*Jen-hsüeh* pan-pen t'an-yüan" 仁學版本探源 [On the original texts of *Jen-hsüeh*]. In *Chung-kuo chin san-pai-nien hsüeh-shu ssu-hsiang lun-chi* 5, A.
———. 1975. "Ts'ung *Ch'iu shu* ti hsiu-ting k'an Chang T'ai-yen ti ssu-hsiang yen-pien" 從訄書的修訂看章太炎的思想演變 [The evolution of Chang Ping-lin's thought as reflected in the different editions of *Ch'iu shu*]. In *Wen Wu* 文物 [Cultural Relics], no. 345 (no. 11). Peking.
———. 1979. *Chang T'ai-yen nien-p'u ch'ang-pien* 章太炎年譜長編 [A chronological biography of Chang Ping-lin]. 2 vols. Peking.
———. 1985. *K'ang Yu-wei ti Chiao hsüeh t'ung-i shou-ch'ao-pen* 康有爲的教學通議手抄本 [The handwritten summary of K'ang Yu-wei's *Discourse on education and learning*].
T'ang Ming-pang 唐明邦. 1965. "*Chou-i wai-chuan* ti jo-kan pien-cheng-fa ssu-hsiang" 《周易外傳》的若干辯證法思想 [Some dialectical thoughts in *Chou-i wai-chuan*]. In *Wang Ch'uan-shan hsüeh-shu t'ao-lun chi*.

Taylor, Rodney Leon. 1978. *The Cultivation of Sagehood as a Religious Goal in Neo-Confucianism: A Study of Selected Writings of Kao P'an-lung*. American Academy of Religion and Scholars Press.

Tien Yee 天義 [The principles of nature]. 1966. In *Chung-kuo tzu-liao ts'ung-shu* 中國資料叢書 [Chinese materials series] 6, *Chung-kuo ch'u ch'i she-hui chu-i wen-hsien chi* 中國初期社會主義文獻集 [A collection of materials of the early stage of Chinese socialism]. Xerox copy, nos. 8–10. Tokyo.

Ting Wen-chiang 丁文江. 1959. *Liang Jen-kung hsien-sheng nien-p'u ch'ang-pien ch'u-kao* 梁任公先生年譜長編初稿 [The first draft of a chronological biography of Liang Ch'i-ch'ao]. Taipei.

Ts'ai Jen-hou 蔡仁厚. 1977. *Sung-Ming li-hsüeh, Pei-Sung p'ien* 宋明理學，北宋篇 [The Sung-Ming neo-Confucian philosophy, the Northern Sung part]. Taipei.

Tung Chung-shu 董仲舒. 1929–1936. *Ch'un-ch'iu fan-lu* 春秋繁露 [Luxuriant dew of the *Annals of Spring and Autumn*]. In *Ssu-pu ts'ung-k'an* 四部叢刊. 1st ser. Shanghai: Commercial Press.

Wakeman, Frederic, Jr. 1973. *History and Will: Philosophical Perspectives of Mao Tse-tung's Thought*. University of California Press.

Wang Ch'uan-shan hsüeh-shu t'ao-lun chi 王船山學術討論集 [A collection of essays on Wang Fu-chih's scholarship]. 1965. Peking.

Wang Fan-sen 王汎森. 1985. *Chang T'ai-yen ti ssu-hsiang (1868–1919)* 章太炎的思想 [Chang Ping-lin's thought]. Taipei.

Weber, Max. 1963. *The Sociology of Religion*. Boston.

Wei Yüan 魏源. 1964. *Ku-wei-t'ang nei-wai chi* 古微堂內外集 [A collection of Wei Yuan's scholarly writings]. Taipei.

Wheatley, Paul. 1971. *The Pivot of the Four Quarters*. Chicago.

Wu Tse 吳澤. 1971. "Wei Yüan ti pien-i ssu-hsiang ho li-shih chin-hua lun-tien" 魏源的變易思想和歷史進化論點 [Wei Yüan's thought on changes and his views on historical evolution]. In *Chung-kuo chin san-pai-nien hsüeh-shu ssu-hsiang lun-chi erh-pien* 中國近三百年學術思想論集二編 [A collection of essays on the Chinese scholarly thought in the past three hundred years], vol. 2. Taipei,

Wu Yü 吳虞. 1917a. "Tu *Hsün Tzu* shu hou" 讀荀子書後 [A postscript to the study of *Hsün Tzu*]. In *Hsin ch'ing-nien* 新青年 [New youth], vol. 3, no. 1.

———. 1917b. "Ju-chia chu-chang chieh-chi chih-tu chih hai" 儒家主張階級制度之害 [The evil of the Confucian conception of a hierarchical system]. In *Hsin ch'ing-nien* 新青年, vol. 3, no. 4.

———. 1917c. "Ju-chia ta-t'ung chih i pen yü Lao Tzu shuo" 儒家大同之義本於老子說 [On the origin of the Confucian ideal of great unity in Lao Tzu's thought]. In *Hsin ch'ing-nien* 新青年, vol. 3, no. 5.

Yang T'ien-shih 楊天石. 1974. "Lun hsin-hai ko-ming ch'ien ti kuo-ts'ui chu-i ssu-ch'ao" 論辛亥革命前的國粹主義思潮 [On the intellectual movement for the rejuvenation of the national quintessence in the years before the Revolution of 1911]. In *Chung-kuo chin san-pai-nien hsüeh-shu ssu-hsiang lun-chi* 5, A.

Yang T'ing-fu 楊廷福. 1957. *T'an Ssu-t'ung nien-p'u* 譚嗣同年譜 [A chronological biography of T'an Ssu-t'ung]. Peking.

Yang Wen-hui 楊文會. 1919. *Yang Jen-shan chü-shih i-chu* 楊仁山居士遺著 [The collected writings of the lay Buddhist Yang Jen-shan]. Nanking.

Yen Hsi-shan 閻錫山 and Chao Tai-wen 趙戴文. 1967. *Chih jen yung t'ao-lun chi*

智仁勇討論集 [Discussions on intelligence, benevolence, and courage]. Taipei.

Yü Chun-fang. 1981. *The Renewal of Buddhism in China: Chu-hung and the Late Ming Synthesis*. New York.

Yü Ying-shih 余英時. 1984. *Chung-kuo chin-tai ssu-hsiang-shih shang ti Hu Shih* 中國近代思想史上的胡適 [Hu Shih in the history of modern Chinese thought]. Taipei.

Index

Analects, 71. See also *Ssu-shu*
Anarchism, 138–139, 172–179, 181
Ancient Text School, 10, 22, 27, 28
Anti-Manchu sentiment, 104, 112–114, 116, 120, 148, 150, 170, 178–179
Autonomy, inner and outer, 159–161

Berkeley, George, 134
Bodhisattva, 54, 89, 142, 143
Book of Changes. See *I ching*
Book of Rites. See *Li chi*
Buber, Martin, 94
Buddha, 102
Buddhism, 12–14, 38, 144, 187; Chang Ping-lin and, 106, 108, 119–145; concept of mind-heart in, 78–79; convergence with Confucianism, 14–15, 30, 54, 57, 59, 84–85; K'ang Yu-wei and, 25, 31, 49, 56, 57; and Liu Shih-p'ei's poetry, 169; negative and affirmative components of, 142; revival of, among intellectuals, 12–15, 20, 120; T'an Ssu-t'ung and, 78, 84–85, 88. *See also* Hua-yen Buddhism; Pure Land sect; Zen Buddhism
Buddhist scholarship, in Europe and Japan, 12
Buddhist texts and sutras, 12–13, 14, 120

Canton. *See* Kwangtung Learning
Capitalism, 174, 175
Chang Chi, 173
Chang Chih-tung, 6, 68
Chang Ping-lin: anarcho-individualism of, 138–139; Buddhist world view of, 142–145, 182; compared with T'an Ssu-t'ung, 108, 141, 144, 182; convergence of revolutionary and Buddhist ideas, 142–145; conversion to Buddhism, 120; critique of traditional order, 118, 141, 143; early thought of, 107–112; education of, 104–106; exile in Japan, 112, 170; imprisonment of, 120; and nationalist movement, 112–113, 116–119, 144; political views of, 112–117, 139, 143; and reformist politics, 105–106; and revolutionism, 2, 112, 116–117, 138; views on human nature, 135–139; views on world religion, 130–131; Western influence on, 107, 116, 185
Chang Tsai, 72, 80, 81–82, 84–88, 93, 94, 97, 98, 101, 188
Ch'ang-hsing hsüeh-chi [An account of study at Ch'ang-hsing School] (K'ang Yu-wei), 35, 37, 41, 46
Chekiang literati, 104–105
Ch'en Chih, 6
Ch'en Ch'iu, 6, 19, 105, 105n.3
Ch'en Fu-ch'en, 105, 105n.3
Ch'en Hsien-chang, 39
Ch'en Li, 37
Cheng Kuan-ying, 6
Cheng Ssu-hsiao, 148
Cheng meng [Correct teaching for beginners] (Chang Tsai), 95
Ch'ien Hao, 46, 97
Ch'eng I, 96, 153
Ch'eng-Chu School, 41, 80–81, 82, 87, 96, 118, 154. *See also* Chu Hsi; Neo-Confucianism

218   Index

ch'i-based world view, 32-33, 35-36, 41-43, 73-74, 80-84, 87-88, 89, 151
Chiang Kai-shek, 190
Chiao Hsün, 154
Chiao-hsüeh t'ung-i [Discourse on education and learning] (K'ang Yu-wei), 26, 27, 28-29, 33, 35
Chien-ai. See Universal love
Ch'ien Mu, 11, 34
chih-shih (managing affairs), 16, 18
Ch'in, First Emperor of, 114
ching-shih (practical statesmanship), 15, 16, 18-19, 105
Ching-shih pao [Journal for practical statesmanship], 105, 105n.3
Ch'iu shu [Book of raillery] (Chang Ping-lin), 107, 109, 118
Chou, Duke of, 27, 28
Chou Tun-i, 39
Chou Yü-t'ung, 52n.139
Chou Yung, 120
Chou dynasty, 6
Chou Li. See *Rites of Chou*
Christianity, 6; Chang Ping-lin's critique of, 131-133; influence on K'ang Yu-wei, 31, 57; influence on T'an Ssu-tung, 77, 79, 84, 89n.99, 92, 103
Chu Hsi, 17, 18, 26n.23, 96, 152, 163; K'ang Yu-wei's views of, 28-29
Chu I-hsin, 48-49
Chu Tz'u-ch'i, 16, 22, 37
chu-tzu hsüeh (noncanonical philosophies), 10-12, 15, 20, 106, 109n.30, 118, 119
Chuang Tzu, 77, 88, 101, 119, 127-128, 169; Chang Ping-lin's commentaries on, 121-125
Ch'un-ch'iu [Annals of Spring and Autumn], 20, 28, 50, 51-52
Ch'un-ch'iu Tung-shih hsüeh [Tung Chung-shu's study of the Annals of Spring and Autumn] (K'ang Yu-wei), 48
ch'ün (grouping), debate over during 1890s, 6, 109-111, 112, 116
Chung-kuo min yüeh ching-i [The essential meaning of Chinese doctrines of social contract] (Liu Shih-p'ei), 164
Chung yung [Doctrine of the mean], 38, 45, 48, 49
Civil service examinations, 66, 146, 149
Communism, 175, 177, 189
Confucian China and Its Modern Fate (Levenson), 3
Confucian education, 17, 37-38
Confucian political ethics, 15, 16, 20, 114, 163-164
Confucian self-surveillance, 38-39
Confucian social ethics, 40, 49, 186; Chang Ping-lin on, 143; K'ang Yu-wei's concept of, 47-48, 49; Liu Shih-p'ei on, 150, 157, 162-163, 167; T'an Ssu-t'ung on, 99-100, 102
Confucian virtues, 29-30, 49, 89. See also *jen*; *Li*
Confucian world view. See Heaven and man
Continuity and discontinuity, 3
Copernican system, 74
Cosmological symbolism. See Kingship, cosmological symbolism of
Cultural identity, 8, 65, 118-119, 149
Cultural Revolution, 189

Democracy, 63, 114-115, 165, 166, 173, 174-175. See also Western liberal ideals
Desires, 90, 109; legitimacy of, 32, 83-84, 154-155
Despotism, 165, 167, 173
Doctrine of the Mean. See *Chung yung*

Electricity, 35, 87, 96
Empress Dowager, 67
Escape from Predicament (Metzger), 3, 184
Esperanto, 178
Ether, 35, 86-90, 109
Ethnic tensions, 104, 112-113. See also Anti-Manchu sentiment
Evidential scholarship. See Han learning
Evolution, 109, 136-137, 141; universal, 135. See also History, evolutionary view of

Fa-hsiang sect, 144
Fa-tsang, 128
Family, K'ang Yu-wei on, 61; Liu Shih-p'ei on, 178; in neo-Confucian philosophy, 95; T'an Ssu-t'ung on, 101
Fate, 111, 153-154
Feng Kuei-fen, 5, 5n.8, 15
Feudalism, 19, 115
Filial piety, 50, 61, 100-101, 163
Five relations. See Confucian social ethics; Filial piety
Four Books. See *Ssu-shu*
"Free associations," 176, 178
Fryer, John, 68, 77
fu-ch'iang. See Wealth and power

Geertz, Clifford, 75
Globe magazine, 52n.139
Great Learning. See *Ta-hsüeh*

Han Yü, 23
Han Learning, 10-11, 15, 18; Chang Ping-lin and, 105-106, 117; confluence of Sung Learning and, 18; evidential scholarship in, 105, 148; K'ang Yu-wei and, 28, 29;

in Kwangtung Learning, 22; Liu Shih-p'ei and, 147–148, 150. *See also* New Text School
Han-shan Teh-ch'ing, 13
Hangchou, 105, 107
Happiness: Chang Ping-lin on, 136; K'ang Yu-wei on, 56, 58
Heaven and man, 18, 36, 39, 45, 49–50, 55, 58, 73, 74, 80, 81, 83, 98, 172
Heraclitus, 139
History: Confucius' view of, 51; cyclical view of, 50–51, 69; devolutionary view of, 51, 69; as a dialectical process, 33; evolutionary view of, 52n.139, 53, 54, 157; Liu Shih-p'ei's view of, 173; three stages of, 51–52, 69–70, 103, 181
Ho Chen, 178
Hsi-ming [Western inscription] (Chang Tsai), 82, 94–95, 98, 101
Hsia Tseng-yu, 120
Hsiao Kung-chuan, 2, 53n.142
Hsin-min shuo [On the new citizen] (Liang Ch'i-ch'ao), 117, 156, 157
Hsiung Shih-li, 191
Hsü Chi-yü, 6
Hsü Hsing, 177
Hsüeh Fu-ch'eng, 5, 5n.8
Hsüeh-hai t'ang, 22
Hsün Tzu, 11, 12, 64, 107, 108, 109, 110, 116, 118, 133; on human nature, 12, 44, 107, 109; and fate, 111, 154
Hu Shih, 191
Hua-yen Buddhism, 57, 128, 144
Huang Chieh, 119
Huang I-chou, 105
Huang Tsung-hsi, 19, 164n.77
Humanity. *See jen*
Hume, David, 134
Hunanese literati, 72
Hundred Days Reform, 67

I ching [Book of changes], 33, 81, 82
Immortality, 57
Imperialist aggression, 2, 25–26, 67, 97, 102, 113, 143, 170, 178
Influence, as factor in intellectual milieu, 4, 8
Intellectual milieu, defined, 4
Intelligence, 29, 30
Internal dialogues, defined, 10
"Investigation of things" (*ko-wu*), 17, 38

Jang shu [The book of expulsion] (Liu Shih-p'ei), 149, 150, 164n.77
Japan, 67, 102, 115, 118, 120, 136, 144, 146, 170, 173, 175
Jehovah, 131–133

jen (humanity): and Heaven, 36, 47; historization of, 50–55, 56, 58; and *i* (righteousness), 30, 47; in the *K'ang-tzu nei-wai p'ien*, 29–30; and *kung* (public-mindedness), 163–164; as a moral ideal, 37–41, 188; neo-Confucian view of, 80, 82; radicalization of, 46–50, 58, 61; T'an Ssu-t'ung's idea of, 84n.80, 87, 89
Jen-hsüeh [A study of humanity] (T'an Ssu-t'ung), 79, 84–89, 97, 98, 103, 108, 145, 182
Jesus, 102
Journals, revolutionary, 105, 107, 107n.18, 108, 119, 146, 150, 173

K'ang Yu-wei: *ch'i*-only world view of, 32–33, 35–36, 41–42; on Chu Hsi, 26n.23, 28–29, 37–38; concept of human nature, 41–46; and Confucian moral cultivation, 25, 31, 37–41, 42, 46, 54; early education of, 21, 22; on education, 35, 37–38; influence of New Text teachings on, 33, 34n.58, 35, 50, 54; influence on T'an Ssu-t'ung, 84n.80; on *jen*, 30–31, 35–41, 47–50, 59, 84; as modernizer, 2, 3; moral-spiritual quest, 23, 24–26; political views of, 2n.3, 25–27, 34, 53, 63, 64–65; promotion of Confucianism by, 64–65; and reformism, 2, 27, 34, 53; religious dimensions in thought of, 64–65; self-image as sage-Bodhisattva, 24–25; and Tung Chung-shu's thought, 42–44, 45, 47–48; utopian society of, 53n.142, 56–65; view of industrial civilization, 59n.161; Western influence on, 24, 25, 32, 35n.66, 49, 52n.139
K'ang Yu-wei, reform movement of, 66, 67, 79, 104; opposition to, by Chang Ping-lin, 104, 108, 108n.21
K'ang Yu-wei, views on history: cosmological dynamism in, 50, 55; historization of *jen*, 50–55; Western influence on, 52, 54
K'ang Yu-wei, writings of: philosophical writings of 1885–1887, 25–34, 50, 53, 56; post-1890 writings, 50
K'ang-tzu nei-wai p'ien [The inner and outer books of the philosopher K'ang] (K'ang Yu-wei), 26, 29–31, 33
Kant, Immanuel, 125
Kao Hsüeh-ch'ih, 105
Kao P'an-lung, 24n.16
Kao Tzu, 41–43
Kiangsu Province, 146
Kingship, 5, 100, 114, 164, 166; cosmological symbolism of, 5n.11, 6–7, 99, 100, 165
Kropotkin, 176
Ku Yen-wu, 104, 106

Ku-ching ching-she, 105
Kung Tzu-chen, 51
Kuo Sung-t'ao, 16
kuo-ts'ui movement (rejuvenation of national quintessences), 118–119, 120
Kwangtung Learning, 22, 27; influence on K'ang Yu-wei, 28, 34n.58

Labor: K'ang Yu-wei on, 60; Liu Shih-p'ei on, 175, 177
Land ownership, 115, 170, 175
Langer, Suzanne, 182
Language, 125–126; linguistic categorization, 125–126, 127, 128, 129, 140
Legalism, 12, 19, 112, 114
Levenson, Joseph, 3, 8, 65
Li Ta-chao, 191
Li Yen-p'ing, 153
li (principles), 151–152, 154, 155, 156
Li (propriety), 29, 49, 96, 102; K'ang Yu-wei on, 48, 53; Tung Chung-shu on, 47, 48, 98–99
Li chi [Book of rites], 52; K'ang Yu-wei's commentaries on, 53
Liang Ch'i-ch'ao, 105; on civic virtues, 117, 156; on K'ang Yu-wei, 35, 37, 56n.150, 57, 59, 63, 65, 84; and Liu Shih-p'ei, 151; and T'an Ssu-t'ung, 66, 84
Liang Shu-ming, 191
Liao P'ing, 34, 108n.21
Lin T'ing-k'an, 11
Liu Hsin, 28
Liu Jen-hsi, 68–69n.14
Liu Shao-ch'i, 190
Liu Shih-p'ei: concept of mind, 158–159; critique of Confucianism, 150–167; critique of sociopolitical order, 150, 156, 166–167, 172, 174–179; early life, 146–149; on education, 176–178; family background, 147, 148, 149; on human nature, 152, 156, 158, 176; poetry of, 148n.14, 149n.23, 167–170, 172; and revolutionism, 2; social vision of, 176–179; Western influence on, 150, 151, 158, 160–162
Liu Tsung-chou, 38
Liu Wen-ch'i, 148, 149
Liu Yü-sung, 149
Lu Hsün, 118
Lu, state of, 51
Lu-Wang School, 37–38, 80–81, 82, 87, 160
Lü K'un, 166
Lun-li hsüeh chiao-k'o shu [A standard text on ethics] (Liu Shih-p'ei), 156–164

Ma I-fu, 191
Mahayana Buddhism. *See* Buddhism
Manchus, 2, 91, 104; protest against government of, 109n.30, 113, 114, 150, 179. *See also* Anti-Manchu sentiment; Ming loyalists
Mao Tse-tung, 190, 191
Marriage, K'ang Yu-wei on, 61; T'an Ssu-t'ung on, 101
Materialism, 86–87, 109, 133, 134
May Fourth generation, 91, 102, 118, 178, 186, 190
McKinley, William, President, 113
Meiji reforms, 27, 34, 136
Meiji Restoration, 144
Mencius, 12, 28, 38, 39, 41, 44, 54, 64, 71, 82, 95, 99, 108, 154, 159, 161, 177; Chang Ping-lin's views on, 107n.18, 109; T'an Ssu-t'ung and Mencian self-cultivation, 71
Mencius, K'ang Yu-wei's commentaries on, 45–46, 48, 49, 52
Metzger, Thomas, 2, 3, 184–185
Millenarianism, 191
Min pao [The people], 112, 113, 116, 170, 171, 179
Ming literati, 143–144
Ming loyalists, 104, 144, 148
Missionaries, 31, 52n.139, 89, 91, 98, 158
Modernization, concept of, 2–3
Mohism, 9, 71, 89; ideal of savior, 49; late Ch'ing revival of, 8, 11; universal love in, 30–31, 87, 95–96, 163
Monarchy. *See* Kingship
Mongols, 91
Moral voluntarism, 54–55, 154, 160, 161
Munro, Donald, 164

Nanking, 149
National quintessence. *See kuo-ts'ui*
Nationalism, 2, 35, 116–119, 144, 156, 184, 189; ethnic, 2, 112, 113, 116, 117, 148–149, 150, 170, 179; reactive, 2
Needham, Joseph, 55n.149
Neo-Confucianism, 10, 18, 55, 73, 78; concept of mind-heart in, 80, 152; instinctual repression in, 83, 154–155, 162; metaphysical dualism in, 31, 32, 41, 84–85, 151, 155
Neo-Confucianism, Sung-Ming, 28, 39, 46, 95–96, 147, 150, 152, 153. *See also* Ch'eng-Chu School; Lu-Wang School
New Text School, 10, 20, 22, 27, 32, 51, 108; view of history, 54; view of Six Canons, 28. *See also* K'ang Yu-wei
Nihilism, 131, 133, 138, 139, 141
Nolte, Ernst, 186
Noncanonical philosophies. *See chu-tzu hsüeh*
Northern and Southern dynasties, 149

Orientational order, 8, 121, 156, 185. *See also* Orientational symbolism; Traditional institutional order
Orientational symbolism, 151, 182; defined, 6
Ou-yang Chung-ku, 67n.7

pa (politics of expediency and force), 26, 27
Pai-hu t'ung [Comprehensive discussions of White Tiger Hall], 44, 48
Pantheism, 131
Pao Ching-yen 172, 187
Pao Shih-ch'en, 15
Parliament, 5, 6, 115, 174–175
Peasants, 170, 175, 177
Pei Yüan-cheng, 67n.7
P'eng Shao-sheng, 13, 14–15
Populism, and Confucianism, 164–165, 166, 167
Practical learning. See *shih-hsüeh*
Practical statesmanship. See *ching-shih*
Practicality, 15, 16–17, 19, 20, 72–73
Price, Don, 2
Private property: Chang Ping-lin on, 115; K'ang Yu-wei on, 60, 61, 63; Liu Shih-p'ei on, 175, 176, 177, 178
Pure Land sect, 13, 14, 130. *See also* Buddhism

Quiescence, 39, 93, 153

Rationalization (Weber), 3
Reform, 5; Chang Ping-lin on, 105–106; K'ang Yu-wei on, 2, 27, 34, 53; T'an Ssu-t'ung on, 2, 66, 67, 103. *See also* Journals, revolutionary
Reform movement, 104, 105, 112
Reformism and revolution, 118; dichotomy between, 1–2. *See also* Revolution
Reincarnation, 108, 123–124, 143
Revolution, 2, 112, 116–117, 138, 143, 170–171, 175; family, 178; morality and, 116–117, 171; social, 179. *See also* Reformism and revolution
Rites of Chou, 27, 28
Rousseau, Jean Jacques, 165, 166, 173, 176

Sagehood, 160, 190; K'ang Yu-wei and, 25, 29, 41–42, 54; T'an Ssu-t'ung and, 89
Sage-king, 20, 27, 29, 56, 64, 165
Sage-statesmanship, 17
Schopenhauer, Arthur, 139
Schwartz, Benjamin, 93
Self-cultivation, 15, 17–18
Self-determination, 31, 55, 98
Self-Strengthening Study Society, 52n.139, 105

Senses, 133–134; Buddhist, 124–126, 127, 130, 140
Sexual morality, 90–91. *See also* Desires
Shang Yang, 114
Shanghai, 107, 108, 120–121, 146, 149
Sheng-ch'ao hsün-yang lu [The record of martyrdom at Yangchou] (Liu Pao-nan), 148
Shih K'o-fa, 148
shih-hsüeh (practical learning), 16, 72
Shih-li kung-fa [Principles of truth and universal laws] (K'ang Yu-wei), 26, 31
Shih-wu pao [Chinese progress], 105
Sino-French War (1884), 25
"Situation": defined, 4; existential, 4, 8; historical, 4, 8
Social Darwinism, 110–111, 143; and race, 62, 110
Social inequality: Chang Ping-lin on, 115, 136; K'ang Yu-wei on, 60–61; Liu Shih-p'ei on, 170–171, 173–175, 177
Socialism, and K'ang Yu-wei's thought, 63; and Liu Shih-p'ei's thought, 173, 175
Sociopolitical order. *See* Traditional institutional order
Son of Heaven: individual as, 36, 49–50, 98, 101; mystique surrounding, 5, 165
Southern Sung Utilitarian School, 19
Ssu-shu, 17, 18, 71; K'ang Yu-wei's commentaries on, 42, 45, 46, 48, 49, 50, 54
Statecraft, 16, 17, 26; school, 15, 16. *See also ching-shih*
Stirner, Max, 173, 174
Suffering, 142; Chang Ping-lin, on, 136; K'ang Yu-wei on, 56–59
Suicide, 139–140
Sun Ch'iang-ming, 19
Sun I-jang, 11, 105n.3, 106, 107n.14
Sun I-yen, 19
Sung Shu, 19, 105, 105n.3, 120
Sung Yu-jen, 6
Sung Learning, 17, 18, 148; in Kwangtung Learning, 22
Symbolism. *See* Kingship, cosmological symbolism of; Orientational symbolism
Syncretism: of Buddhism, Taoism, and Confucianism, 14–15; of Han and Sung learning, 18; in K'ang Yu-wei's thought, 64

Ta-hsüeh [The great learning], 17, 18, 29, 38, 70, 152, 156, 157, 162
ta-t'ung (age of grand unity), 52, 56n.150, 58, 179
Ta-t'ung shu [A discourse on the grand unity] (K'ang Yu-wei), 56, 57n.158, 59n.161

Tai Chen, 23, 43, 147, 150–152, 155–156, 158n.56
Tai-hsü (Buddhist monk), 12n.32
T'ai-chou School, 160
T'an Hsien, 105
T'an Ssu-t'ung: and Buddhist teachings, 78, 84; childhood of, 75; and concept of *chung*, 70, 99; concept of *jen*, 79–80, 84–89, 93–94, 97, 98–99, 102, 103, 145; Confucian and Buddhist influences on, 84–85; and Confucian world view, 69–70, 71, 74, 108; critique of traditional moral order, 90–91, 93, 99–103, 141; death and martyrdom of, 67, 103; devolutionary view of history of, 69; image of China in the world, 69–70; lack of sympathy for nationalism, 67, 97; official career of, 66; poetry of, 68, 75–76, 84n.81, 193–195; preoccupation with death, 76–77, 89; and reformism, 2, 66, 67, 103; travels of, 68, 78; view of the West, 90–91, 92–94; Western influence on, 68, 71–72
T'ang Chih-chün, 34, 52n.139
Taoism, 38, 57, 71, 77, 78, 85, 88, 93, 101, 119, 121–123, 172, 187; and Liu Shih-p'ei's poetry, 169–170; synthesis with Buddhism, 14–15, 123–124, 128
Teng Shih, 119
Three bonds. *See* Confucian social ethics
Three Principles of the People, 189
Three teachings, unity of, 14
Tien Yee [The principles of nature], 173, 175, 176, 178, 179
t'ien-hsia, 16
T'ien-t'ai Buddhism, 141
Time: in Chang Ping-lin's thought, 126; in K'ang Yu-wei's thought, 54, 58; in Liu Shih-p'ei's poetry, 168
Ting Wen-chiang, 191
Tokyo, 108, 120–121, 170
Traditional institutional order: late nineteenth-century crisis of, 1, 5–7; legitimacy of, 5, 6, 165, 166
Transcendence, 122–123, 169, 172, 182
Tseng Kuo-fan, 16–17, 37
Tung Chung-shu, 30, 33, 35–36, 42, 43–44, 45, 47–49, 171
T'ung-chih Restoration, 5
Tzu Ssu, 38
Tzu Yu, 64

United States, 115
Universal love, 30, 87, 163
Universalism, and nationalism, 2
Utilitarianism, 171

Utopianism, 56, 103, 145, 179, 185, 190. *See also* K'ang Yu-wei, utopian society of; Liu Shih-p'ei, social vision of; *ta-t'ung*

Wang An-shih, 121
Wang Chin, 13
Wang Chung, 147; and Mohism, 11
Wang Fu-chih, 43, 72, 80, 82–88, 89, 93, 94, 104, 148, 164n.77, 167; cosmological dynamism of, 82–83, 92
Wang Ken, 24n.16, 148; Liu Shih-p'ei's biography of, 160
Wang Nien-sun, 11
Wang Yang-ming, 24n.16, 38, 39, 144, 148, 159, 160, 161, 171, 188
Wang Yin-chih, 11
wang (politics of principle and compassion), 26
Wealth and power, 18–19, 27, 67, 99, 114, 115, 138, 171
Weber, Max, 3, 8
Wei Yüan, 6, 16, 51
Western culture, 118–119, 136, 149, 185, 186
Western influence, 8–9, 185, 186, 189
Western learning, 3, 6, 8, 20, 24, 25, 52n.139, 61, 72, 107, 112
Western liberal thought, 49–50, 59, 100, 160, 160n.61, 161–162, 165, 167, 174
Western religion. *See* Christianity
Western science, 6; Chang Ping-lin and, 109, 133; and classical Mohism, 8; K'ang Yu-wei and, 32, 35; Liu Shih-p'ei and, 151; T'an Ssu-t'ung and, 72, 73–74, 77, 79n.67, 86
Western technology, 92–93
Williamson, Alexander, 31, 98
Women, 178; K'ang Yu-wei's views on, 60–61; liberation of, 178; T'an Ssu-t'ung's views on, 91, 101
Wood, Henry, 77, 79, 84
Wu Yü, 118
Wu-neng Tzu, 187

Yang Ch'ang-chi, 191
Yang Wen-hui, 12–15, 78, 79, 169
Yangchou, 146, 148; school, 18, 147, 149, 150–151, 154, 158
Yang-chou shih-jih chi [Ten days at Yang-chou] (Wang Hsiu-ch'u), 148
Yang-min ch'üeh-lu lu [A record of repulsions of barbarians by the Yangchou people] (Liu Shih-p'ei), 148
Yen Fu, 52n.139, 109, 110, 171
Yen Hsi-shan, 190

Yen Yüan, 19
yin and *yang*, 32, 33, 36, 44, 47, 74, 151
Yogacara school, 14, 85, 87, 120–141
Yü Ying-shih, 10
Yü Yüeh, 11–12, 105, 106, 107

Yuan Chi, 187
Yün-ch'i Chu-hung, 13

Zen Buddhism, 13, 14. *See also* Buddhism; Pure-Land sect

Designer:	Jim Mennick
Compositor:	Asco Trade Typesetting, Ltd.
Text:	10/12 Baskerville
Display:	Baskerville
Printer:	Braun-Brumfield, Inc.
Binder:	Braun-Brumfield, Inc.